The Reform of Life

Germany's Early Reform Movements and Their Influences

Stephen E. Flowers, PhD

© Stephen E. Flowers 2023

All rights reserved. No part of this book, either in part or in whole, may be reproduced, transmitted or utilized in any form or by any means electronic, photographic or mechanical, including photo-copying, recording, or by any information storage and retrieval system, without the permission in writing from the Publisher, except for brief quotations embodied in literary articles and reviews.

For permissions, or for the serialization, condensation, or for adaptation write the Publisher at the address below.

Printed in the USA

Lodestar
tilruna72@gmail.com
www.seekthemysteries.com

ISBN 978-1-885972-84-2

Second printing

Book Design by Donna Cunningham
http://www.donnalc.com

The Reform of Life
Germany's Early Reform Movements and Their Influences

Stephen E. Flowers, PhD

Contents

Preface 9
0. Intro. 10
1.0. Historical Context 17
   1.1. The Nineteenth Century... 17
   1.2. The Wilhelmine Era 20
   1.3. Weimar 22
   1.4. The Post-War Period 24
2.0. Das *Deutschenbild* 26
3.0. Overview of the Reform Ideology 34
   3.1. The Romantic Foundation 35
   3.2. Overview 38
   3.3. The Wandervogel Movement 44
   3.4. Some Leading Personalities of
        the Reform Movements 47
4.0. Fields of Reform 56
   4.1. Culture: The Radical Reformers 56
   4.2. Religion 57
       4.2.1. Reforms of Orthodox Religions 58
       4.2.2. Imported Religions 62
       4.2.3. New Religions 65
           4.2.3.1. Theosophy 65
           4.2.3.2. Anthroposophy 68
           4.2.3.3. Armanentum and Ariosophy 72
           4.2.3.4. Mazdaznan 74
           4.2.3.5. Other Religious Alternatives 77
   4.3. Politics 81
   4.4. Education 85
       4.4.1. Reform Pedagogy 89
       4.4.2. Waldorf-Pedagogy 92

- 4.4.3. *Volkshochschulen* 96
- 4.5. Health and Nutrition 98
  - 4.5.1. Early Practitioners 99
  - 4.5.2. Diet Reform and Vegetarianism 104
  - 4.5.3. Anti-Alcohol 109
  - 4.5.4. The Physical Body 111
    - 4.5.4.1. Physical Form and the Body in Motion 112
    - 4.5.4.2. Dance or Body Culture in Motion 113
    - 4.5.4.3. Runic Gymnastics 117
    - 4.5.4.4. Nudism and *Freikörperkultur* 120
  - 4.5.6. Sexuality and Reform 127
  - 4.5.7. Fashion and Clothing 134
- 4.6. Community and Society (Habitation) 137
  - 4.6.1. Living Spaces and Habitation 138
  - 4.6.2. Architecture and Urban Planning 142
- 4.7. Art and Literature 146
  - 4.7.1. The Homeland-Art Movement 148
  - 4.7.2. Literature and Philosophy 150
    - 4.7.2.1. Friedrich Nietzsche 153
    - 4.7.2.2. Hermann Hesse 156
  - 4.7.3. Fidus, the Artistic Face of the Reform Movement ... 159
- 4.8. Animal Rights and Anti-Vivisection 170
- 4.9. Economy 173
- 4.10. Environmentalism and Ecology 178
- 5.0. Detour: The Sexual Revolution 182
  - 5.1. Sigmund Freud and the Psychoanalysts 185
  - 5.2. The Beginnings of Sexology 187
  - 5.3. Magnus Hirschfeld: "The Einstein of Sex" 189
    - 5.3.1. The Scientific-Humanitarian Committee 190
    - 5.3.2. The Institute for Sexology 192

- 5.3.3. The Third Sex 193
- 5.3.4. Sexual Intermediacy 194
- 5.4. Other Sexologists 197
- 6.0. Sons of the Swastika 200
  - 6.1. A National Religion 203
  - 6.2. Politics and Economics 205
  - 6.3. Nazi Education 209
  - 6.4. Fashion and Clothing 211
  - 6.5. Health and Nutrition 212
  - 6.6. Anti-Alcohol Aspects 213
  - 6.7. The Naked Nazis 214
  - 6.8. Sexuality and Reform 215
  - 6.9. Urban Planning and Settlement Programs 216
  - 6.10. Art and Literature 219
  - 6.11. Animal Rights 222
  - 6.12. Environmentalism (Ecology) 225
  - 6.13. Conclusion 226
- 7.0. Children of the Sun: *Naturmenschen* and the Origin of the American Hippies 228
- 8.0. Influence on Contemporary American Society 242
  - 8.1. Nudism in America 248
  - 8.2. The Sexual Revolution in the Industrialized West 252
- 9.0. *Ausblick*: The Future of Reform Ideas 264
- Notes 274
- Bibliography 282

Acknowledgements

Michael Moynihan, Gordon Kennedy, Cort Williams, Zan McGreevey, and all of my professors and mentors in the Department of Germanic Languages and Literatures at the University of Texas at Austin 1973–1984.

Abbreviations

ALPC   American League for Physical Culture
FKK   *Freikörperkultur* "Free Body Culture" = nudism)
NSDAP   Nationalsozialistische Deutsche Arbeiterpartei (National Socialist German Workers' Party)

Preface

This is a book about the various aspects of the Reform of Life Movements that sprang up and grew in the German-speaking areas of Central Europe from between about 1880 to 1933. Of course, these ideas had deep roots and would continue to affect culture after this period, but it was during the targeted time that the influence of such movements were most intense.

For me an underlying motive for writing this book has been the perception of so many that Germany and the Germans remain somehow under the shadow of the image of the Third Reich. This image runs contrary to the general attitude toward the Germans as a people as discussed in section 2.0 of this book. A survey of the cultural features which gave rise to the Reform Movements in Germany 1880-1933 is a positive approach toward answering some of the sometimes-contradictory questions surrounding the "German image."

Certain readers will probably wonder as to why attention is focused on German-speaking culture at all. Ideas similar to what we will find in the Reform Movements of late nineteenth and early twentieth centuries Central Europe are also found in many other European cultures and their (often former) colonies. These ideas evolved over the centuries and were expressed through a variety of philosophical, social and political outlooks. The chief aspect that distinguishes the Reform Movement of the time period in question in the German-speaking territories is the degree of self-awareness and philosophical unity that these movements maintained—it had a special name: *Reformbewegungen*. A study similar to this one could also be gainfully undertaken with regard to the cultural and philosophical history of England and Scotland (Great Britain). A similar study of the reform movements in Anglo-American culture would be most welcome.

Stephen Edred Flowers
Woodharrow
The Yule Tide 2022

0. Introduction

The world has been quite astounded to learn that the prototype of the American Hippie of the 1960s was actually to be found almost a century earlier in the forests of Germany in the person of Karl Wilhelm Diefenbach (1851–1913). To be sure Diefenbach did not invent the ideas he expressed out of whole cloth. Rather his philosophy was part of a greater cultural wave beginning to swell up in Central Europe toward the end of the nineteenth century. Diefenbach exemplified a style of living and a set of ideas which he would teach to his disciples, including the artist known to the world as Fidus, who became the "illustrator" of the whole movement.

Those such as Diefenbach and Fidus were only one part of a vast array of movements to be found in German-speaking Central Europe in the late nineteenth and early twentieth century. There exists a whole spectrum of heterogeneous fields of interest which have been identified by similarity of ideology and familiarity of cultural milieu as making up what has come to be called the German *Lebesnreformbewegungen*—the Reform of Life Movements.

It is my hope that with this book the reader will obtain a deeper insight into these German Reform Movements and their general contexts than has generally been available up to now in the English language. However, it must be emphasized that there is no substitute for the ability to read and absorb the ideas directly from their voluminous sources in the German language. So, it is my hope that this book may also lead the reader to one more reason to learn that language.

Because many readers will use this book for reference-type reading, I hope I will be forgiven for often being repetitious with certain information, which needs to be brought to bear in several different places and if it were not repeated important context might be lost.

The natural questions arise: *What* was to be reformed by these Reform Movements? Why was this reform thought to be necessary or desirable? The new problems facing mankind, especially in countries such as Germany, Austria, France, England and the United States of America seemed to be artificial, or man-made, problems. This is what made them *new*, as opposed to being age-old or eternal problems of the human condition. These were largely caused by rapid industrialization and urbanization of the population. These trends moved individuals and communities away from their natural contexts into un-natural circumstances. This industrialization and urbanization was characterized by people leaving their ancestral rural settings to go to large, impersonal cities to take jobs in mechanized industry. People were forced together in crowded environments and in often unclean living conditions. A general sense of oppression and despair often weighed heavily on the people in these environments. This led to a desire for change, and people became increasingly open to the acceptance of some radical solutions. These "solutions" might include the mystical and occult (e.g. Spiritism and Theosophy) or Marxian revolution, and eventually National Socialism. But in this environment many new ideas and practices also flourished, often more quietly than the rest, all of which gave new meaning to troubled lives. These efforts at Reform have proven to have stood up the tests of time, and continue to provide meaning to many today.

Ultimately it can be seen that these new modernistic trends in the economic and cultural lives of people in the industrializing world quickly led to an intensification of feelings of personal alienation, the conditions were felt to be polluting of the land and air, and even to the very bodies of individuals, and with it all came an increasing sense of economic and political oppression. This sense of oppression was related both to the state and to the financial (e.g. banking) institutions. Increased industrialization caused a massive shift of the population from their ancestral rural homes into large cities where they felt alienated and exposed to toxic environments—physical and social. These were the ills against which the Reformers of all kinds set their sights.

For most Reformers, this situation led to a feeling of a loss of authenticity and tradition. Among many of them this also steered them toward (an often Romanticized) vision of their own Germanic antiquity, but this path was fraught with problems of confused sentiments and deficient information. This aspect of the history of the Reform Movements is to be a special focus of the third volume of my study *The Northern Dawn*.

Throughout the course of this work we will meet with individuals and ideas which seem to belong to the realm of the fanatic, eccentric and often to the realms of medical quackery. The contents of this book should not be taken as an endorsement of any of these particular ideas. However, the important thing to remember in all of it is that the problems just outlined and against which these efforts were consistently directed were and are *real* problems continually facing the human spirit in the Modern World. The Reformers are characterized by their boldness of thought and action in their efforts to make a difference in their lives individually and communally. It is also noteworthy that the impetus toward Reform was in no way unified or unanimous in its ideology or interests. Diversity of thought was a hallmark of the movement, and is the main reason why the phenomenon is typically referred to as the Reform Movements in the plural, rather than singular. This being said, these movements were bound together by the problems they identified and the general themes of their interests.

The whole question of "modernism" looms over the Reform Movements. On the one hand these movements were clearly directed toward a criticism of the Modern world as it had developed and was developing, but at the same time the Reformers were in their own way often hyper-modern in their aesthetics and in their aims and plans. Taken as a whole, the Reform Movements were extremely ambivalent as regards their attitudes toward *modernism* as such.

Throughout this book, the word "reform" will often be capitalized. When this capitalization occurs, it is meant to indicate that the word is intended to denote all or many of the connotations of the ideology of the movement.

It will be recognized by the students of cultural history that many of the problems against which the Reform Movements directed their energies were ones similar to the ones identified by Marxism and Socialist Revolutionaries. The capitalistic modernists believed humankind would and could prosper and educate itself out of its problems by the progressive application of science, industry and technology. The Marxist Revolutionaries, or Communists, argued that humankind's problems could only be remedied though the historical dialectic instituting the ownership of the means of production by the workers ("proletariat"), which would then lead to a Communistic Paradise with no need for laws. The problem with the latter solution, as the Reformers saw it, was that it either led off into a dingy and chaotic future or to a hellish world governed by dictatorship and violence. These choices were summed up in a Reform Age drawing by the Master Fidus:

A watch-word of the Reform Movement was: *Reform statt Revolution* (Reform instead of Revolution). By "Revolution," it was understood that it was Marxist (or Anarchistic) Revolution that was meant. Marxism did not generally appeal to the Reform-minded, as it did not satisfy the essentially Romantic yearnings and longings for tradition and cultural continuity found among many in the Reform Movements.

On some level, it was obviously understood that the organization of Reform ideas into a widespread political movement was not desirable. Such ideas had to enter the culture by way of individuals and smaller groups of people organized in organic communities. This is why there was an immediate gravitation toward what we came to call "communes." This answer to social and cultural questions was nothing new in the Germanic world generally, as such "intentional communities" had been organized by many rebellious and heretical groups in Germany and England for centuries.(1)

A key underlying concept, and one that would become a well-known and utilized idea in the USA during the 1960s and 1970s is that of *holism*. The holistic view of things is one that sees disparate and diverse aspects or parts of a greater whole working together in an organic manner in which optimal health and well-being is developed, encouraged and promoted. There is a world of difference between *holism* and *unity*. Systems which are holistic have parts that work together in a symbiotic and mutually beneficial manner, much as the parts of an organic body function together for the health and well-being of that being. This ideal has rarely, if ever, been realized in human history outside of extremely small groups. Usually when we encounter some sort of unity it comes in the form of hierarchized, coercive systems, such as we find in the modern nation-state. The Reformers looked beyond this reality, to dream of something better. The very idea of *reform* generally strikes a responsive and positive chord in the hearts of most people. Most people, probably from all times, have felt that there was "something wrong" with the world, or that it could in any case be *better*. Reform strikes a balance between conservatism and radical destruction (revolution, anarchy, etc.). As a concept it also harkens back to the past and to deep tradition in that it seems to suggest that things need to be formed once more, back into their original, healthy and pristine order.

Typically, Reformers looked back to the recent past and the ideas of the Romantics for a theoretical or ideological framework. The modern nation-state is an example of the power of civilization. But the Reformers are in many ways barbarians—that is they idealize the *Naturmenschen*—the "nature-folk," also sometimes called noble savages who are seen to be unspoiled by the excesses of civilization.(2) Many of the Reformers made reference to the ancient past of Germania as reported by the first century Roman historian Tacitus. The nudism (*Nacktkultur*) so dear to the Reformers is also an expression of the Romantic impulse toward direct contact between humans and nature. Essentially the Reform-impulse is neither a desire to revive the past nor a headlong thrust into the future, but rather a yearning to discover and manifest eternal truths.

1.0. Historical Context

In every case when one considers complex cultural developments and events, the historical context for those events and developments must be taken into careful consideration. One of the greatest current breakdowns in culture comes from a poor understanding of history. Once events and human beings are better understood in their historical positions, the happenings and the fateful things that befall ourselves and others take on a new and more vibrant life.

1.1. The Nineteenth Century

For cultural purposes, we have to consider the area in question for our exploration the entirety of the German-speaking parts of Central Europe. This includes what became the German Empire in 1871, the German-speaking parts of the Austro-Hungarian Empire and the German-speaking areas of Switzerland. This complex constitutes more or less a single cultural body because all members of it speak the same language which allows them to read the same books, speak freely to one another without translation and to experience other media in the same dialect. It is little remembered today that the German-speaking world was far more important to the northern half of Europe than it is even today. For example, the plays of Scandinavian dramatists such as Ibsen and Strindberg were often translated and performed in German before they ever debuted in their home countries.

There were certain ideas which dominated nineteenth century thought in the German-speaking world. These often cooperated with one another, but such ideas also just as often led to implacable conflicts. These were German idealism, biology, evolutionary theories, nationalism, romanticism, social Darwinism, Marxism and positivism. It is therefore little wonder that the most radical and impetuous children of that century would establish a variety of institutions and schools of thought which flowed from a heady brew concocted from these ideas.

Elite thinkers had held many radically divergent thoughts for a long time in Europe. Due to limitations in publishing, education and economic development this radicalism remained relatively contained. This began to change rapidly in the nineteenth century. Rational idealism practiced by Hegel and Kant was turned into a materialistic economic political philosophy by Karl Marx. There was also a widespread rationalistic attack on traditional Christian theology by the new biblical critics alongside of which there was a great influx of exciting and apparently effective ideas from the East. Ideas imported from Asia such as the Buddhistic and Brahmanic religions and philosophies, especially as embodied in the work of Arthur Schopenhauer, all led to a new way of thinking ready to wipe the old established philosophies and theologies away. One of the most important figures in popularizing the new revolutionary way of thinking was the artist Richard Wagner followed by his former acolyte, Friedrich Nietzsche. This package of ideas was a potent mix which planted a variety of seeds for cultural change.

Germany only became anything approaching a modern nation-state in 1871, whereas France and England (Britain) had been such since the Middle Ages. Despite this lack of political unity there was nevertheless always an awareness of what can be called *Deutschtum*, "German-ness." All central European native

German speakers shared a degree of common cultural identity These included many inhabitants of present-day Germany, Austria and the majority of the cantons of Switzerland.

Around the beginning of the nineteenth century all of Europe was embroiled in a cultural debate between Enlightenment thinking, now couched in Neo-Classical aesthetics, and the new approach to life proposed by the Romantics. Germany was no exception in this. The Enlightenment valued the rational mind above all else—questioned received traditions and extoled the virtues of simplicity, precision and clarity. Enlightenment aesthetics revolved around mechanistic models—the whole world was seen as a great machine or clock-work with the Creator as the great clock-maker. Politically the Enlightenment favored the development of international institutions and interconnections. In many ways it will be seen that the Reform Movements represented an active synthesis of the Enlightenment and Romanticism.

In the name of the Enlightenment Napoleon conquered much of Europe in wars lasting from 1803 to 1815. Romanticism criticized what was seen as the arrogant naiveté of the Enlightenment and insisted on the primacy of emotion for human happiness. Romantics turned to the wildness of nature, extoled the "noble savage," delved into the night-side of life, into dreams and myths. In the Romantic introversion, the individual body was revalorized as was the collective organic body known as the nation (or *Volk*). The unity between the body and the soul, language and history was given a new evaluation.

It should be noted that German Enlightenment thinkers tended to be conservative and optimistic. They accepted the political *status quo* of the fragmented state of the German people.

But the Romantics yearned for a political reality in which the *nation* (as a cultural concept) and the state (as a political organization) would be integrated into an organic whole.

A revolutionary fervor boiled over in a variety of states in Europe in the year 1848. (Coincidentally [?], this is the same year that Marx and Engels issued *The Communist Manifesto*.) These uprisings were generally suppressed by the conservative (*status quo*) forces of the royal state authorities. This moment in time also marked the end of those unified sweeping cultural movements in which politics, religion, art and literature could all be seen as exponents of one single philosophical position. After this time culture began to be fragmented into the compartmentalized aspects to be found in the now familiar modern world. At this point also artists, mystics, poets and writers tended to *go underground* to pursue their dreams.

In Germany, the great motivating factor in 1848 was the unification of Germans into a unified German state. This movement did finally bear fruit in the wake of the Prussian victories over Austria (in the Seven-Weeks War, 1866) and France in the Franco-Prussian War (1870-71). At the conclusion of the latter war, the Prussians under the "Iron Chancellor" Otto von Bismarck, forged the Second German Empire on 18 January 1871 in the Hall of Mirrors in the palace of Versailles.

1.2. The Wilhelmine Era

The era between the founding of the Second Empire and the end of WWI is called the Wilhelmine Era, because both principal Kaisers who ruled over the period were named Wilhelm. The last quarter of the nineteenth century witnessed the growth of the German Reich as a world power with the development of advanced technology, overseas colonies and a modern military. Additionally, Germany continued to pioneer policies of public welfare, e.g. health insurance, disability and old-age insurance. Moving toward the turn of the century Germany was the most technologically advanced, highly educated and industrialized country in the world. This did not mean that all Germans shared the unbridled optimism of the establishment state authorities.

The year 1880 is somewhat arbitrarily cited as the beginning of the actual manifestation of the Reform Movements. Events occurring both a short while before this date, and after it, lead to a general identification of this year with the dawn of a new cultural time period in cultural history in the German-speaking world. Among the events are the establishment of the German Empire in 1871, the events of the so-called *Kulturkampf* ("culture-war") which involved the struggle between modern secularism and medieval (and some newly invented) Catholic dogmas, in 1883 both Wagner and Marx died, in 1886 both Benz and Daimler invented the modern automobile, and in 1890 Bismarck was dismissed as Chancellor. The Reform Movements were essentially cultural, and not necessarily political phenomena. Such cultural trends are impossible to pin down in the same way political history might be. It takes decades, in some cases centuries, before a new way of looking at things goes from its embryonic state to a full-fledged ideology with numerous followers. One can see how an idea such as "socialism" can go from a rejected pariah in the 1950s in America to an "acceptable" or even popular idea by 2020. Radical cultural changes can be effected over half a century anywhere.

1.3. Weimar

The political events which led to what became called at the time the Great War, what we call World War I today, are among the most absurd in history, especially when we consider the damage it caused and the groundwork it laid for the continuation of the conflict known as World War II. Germany entered the war in 1914 full of optimism for victory, and when the war ended in military setbacks and domestic upheaval and internal revolution, with abdication of the Kaiser and utter chaos, the scene was set for the inception of, as the famous Chinese curse goes, "interesting times." In the aftermath of defeat, Germany reconstituted itself as what became known to history as the "Weimar Republic." The Reform ideology reached its peak of popularity and activity during these years. These were years of extremes. There was extreme economic deprivation, unemployment and inflation. These desperate times called for desperate measures, applied both within the human mind and spirit and in the body politic. Enormous innovations were achieved in a variety of creative fields. This creativity resulted in many productive outputs that are recorded in the history of ideas and the arts. One of the greatest products of Weimar for the rest of the world is measured in human resources. But eventually the nation was pushed into grasping for radical solutions to these profound, and seemingly insoluble problems and the ultimate disaster of the Hitler years was inaugurated in 1933. Although it is widely assumed in scholarly circles that the year 1933 brought a sudden close to Reform ideas, we will see in section 6.0 how in many ways the Nazi leaders were inevitably generational products of Reform ideology themselves. Powerful ideas are just that, *powerful*. They can be applied for the good or ill of mankind or the individual. The Nazi years immediately led to the widespread immigration of hundreds of thousands of those threatened by the new regime, mainly Jews or those of Jewish heritage, but also other "undesirables," most of whom became an enormous gift to the rest of the world. Ehrhard Bahr outlines a world he calls *Weimar on the Pacific* (University of California, 2007) about the life of some of these exiles in southern California alone.

The years of the Weimar Republic were ones in which Reform ideas flourished and ideas produced by their theoreticians flowed forth from a variety of presses throughout the German-speaking world. The Weimar Republic has been referred to by that designation by historians, although the official designation continued to be that of the German Reich. So, the questions might be: Why "Weimar"? The constitutional convention to restore a legitimate government to the country was held in the city of Weimar, which was chosen for historical, cultural and symbolic reasons. It was the city of Goethe and Schiller and a sort of cultural-literary capital. (To this reasoning might also be added that at the time Berlin was simply not a safe place for politicians of any stripe.) Historically, the Weimar period is divided into three phases: 1) crisis and turmoil [1918-1923], 2) a "golden age" of some sort of tranquility and optimism [1924-1929], and 3) the final crisis [1930-1933].

Haunting the whole history of the Weimar Republic were the ghosts of the chaotic conclusion to the Great War and the crippling terms of the Versailles Treaty imposed on the Germans. These cast shadows of impending doom over everything that happened and finally resulted in a catastrophic political and economic situation. These conditions led to a dynamic atmosphere that was especially acute in the subcultural corners of society.

A detailed discussion of the effect of Reform ideology on the Nazis and its effects on the actual policies of the Third Reich is presented in section 6.0 of this book.

1.4. The Post-War Period

After the Second World War the persistent charm of Reform ideology continued to make itself felt at the grassroots level of German culture and society. Its dominant popularity had given way to a quiet and permanent change in the attitudes of the average German and has formed the underlying cultural basis for a variety of "movements" in the German-speaking world today, including the German "Green" political party, formally: Alliance 90/The Greens (*Bündnis 90/Die Grünen*), often simply referred to as the Greens. The German movement was perhaps not the first to organize under this banner, but it has been the most successful, largely due to the long underlying history of the values they propose. To a greater degree than many might have wished, the Green movement has been generally moved into a Left-leaning stance and even theoretically coopted by Marxist principles. This often explains why writers and theoreticians in the Green movement are so vehemently opposed to the suggestion that the National Socialists had anything to do with "Green" ideology or that they were in any way "Socialists." It should be noted that after Mikhael Gorbachev abandoned leadership of the Soviet Union he established the Green Cross International, an "ecological activist" foundation.

But more profoundly than any of these political considerations the Reform ideology has made itself a part of everyday German culture and life. Every town of any size has a store called the Reformhaus where natural and homeopathic remedies and treatments are sold. Physicians regularly recommend these to their patients. One sees animal rights billboards with slogans such as *"Wir Machen sie krank, daraufin Machen sie uns krank"* (We make them sick, and so they make us sick) showing pictures of animals in abusive inhumane slaughter houses and the like. Many Germans, especially those who have to live in high-rise apartment buildings, have little huts in community gardens where they can raise their own vegetables.

Almost all aspects of the Reform Movements as discussed in the main sections of this book have left permanent marks on Central European culture of the present day. It seems as though these ideas came from deep roots as they rose up to public prominence in the late nineteenth century and so they found an enthusiastic reception in the years following and thus have made lasting impressions in the fabric of the current culture. These ideas cannot be categorized as "fads," as they might be elsewhere, but rather as atavisms of a deeper cultural reality.

2.0. *Das Deutschenbild*
The Image of the Germans

The Reform of Life Movement was and is a particularly *German* development. It often comes as a surprise to people who are not familiar with actual German culture and its history that such a movement developed in Germany at all. This sense of surprise hinges on the *image* Germany and the Germans have in people's minds. The realities of the Reform Movement and the image of the Germans just does not seem to fit in people's preconceived notions. The author Gordon Kennedy, when he first wrote his book *Children of the Sun*, which shows the German origins of the American Hippie Movement, could not get Hippie-oriented shops to stock his book at all. It was because the prevailing attitude of the store owners was: "Germans are a bunch of Nazis, man."

Germans are more interested in their image among other peoples than are most nations. The German government studies this, and scholars write books about it.

One can see why this question of image is so important culturally and economically to a country. It is something akin to a brand name or identity in the global scheme of things. Manfred Koch-Hillebrecht wrote a book in 1977 called *Das Deutschenbild* [The Image of the Germans] and surveys of the question are regularly undertaken from various perspectives and can be found on the Internet.

One of these is that of the BBC which conducts an international survey on the image of various nations among twenty-eight different countries. In recent years, Germany has consistently been the top-rated country in this poll, which rates countries as being "mostly positive" in their influence in the world and "mostly negative." Below is the result of the most recent such survey in percentage points:

	"mostly positive"	"mostly negative"
Germany	59	15
Canada	55	13
United Kingdom	55	18
Japan	51	27
France	49	21
USA	45	34
China	42	39
Russia	30	40
Iran	15	59

Curiously, in surveys of this kind, the Germans tend to view themselves much more harshly than do those outside Germany. Recently the counties which view Germany more negatively are not their former enemies in WWII, who tend to rank them very high, but those poorer countries in southern Europe (Spain and Greece) who resent German economic and financial power in Europe today.

Germany is seen as being honest, hard-working and advanced in matters of industry and science. Much of this harkens back to some perinneal aspects of their image.

Certainly, one of the important aims of this book concerns the German image. The aim is not to polemically change or alter the readers' views, but rather to complete the cultural picture relevant to the development of such an image of a whole nation. If this enormous part of German culture is allowed to remain generally unknown to most of the rest of the world, how can an accurate image of that nation be formed?

We are in a unique position to trace what is called the *Deutschenbild*—the "image of the Germans"—from a very ancient time forward. Because the Germanic peoples originally and for many centuries found themselves on the periphery of the power centers of literate European cultures (Greece and Rome) reports about them as a sort of an exotic object of attention began from an early date. Among the first, and certainly the most famous, of these is the book known as *The Germania* by Cornelius Tacitus (56-120 CE). This work was written about 98 CE and is an ethnography of the Germanic tribes, their institutions, beliefs and cultures. The Roman historian was a skilled observer and organizer of data in a logical manner. He did have his agenda which was not necessarily that of the presentation of history or ethnology in the scientific manner following the greatest ideals of the modern age. Of course, these ideals are rarely met even today, as most "history" remains mostly a *story* told by individuals with some sort of underlying motive. Tacitus paints a picture of the Germans as sincere and perhaps naïve people given to pious interactions with their gods via sacrificial rituals and acts of divination, freedom-loving people of honor and courage who brought up their sons to be courageous in battle and their daughters to be chaste and virtuous.

Tacitus therefore presents the Germans in a way that has been seen as a sort of proto-type of what in centuries later Enlightened men would call the "noble savage." The phrase "noble savage" often attributed to Rousseau, was actually first used in English by the poet John Dryden in his drama *The Conquest of Granada* (1672) wherein appear the lines:

> I am as free as nature first made man,
> Ere the base laws of servitude began,
> When wild in woods the noble savage ran.

What is well-known is that Tacitus had as his agenda the presentation of a people to the Romans who still retained all of the virtues that the historian and observer of his own Roman culture felt his people had lost due to decadence, treachery and loss of ethnic purity. Nevertheless, the text of *The Germania* does offer invaluable and unique insight into German culture 2000 years ago, if it is used with corroborating evidence of archeology, linguistics and comparative studies with later literary evidence.

The Middle Ages are marked by the Christianization process in Europe. This occurred in the Germanic regions over a period of several centuries stretching all the way from the fourth to the twelfth centuries. During this time, the heartland of the non-Romanized areas of Germanic Europe were in the central and northern parts of the region and were viewed by Christians, regardless of their ethnic heritages, as barbarians and heathens.

During the time of the Renaissance and Reformation states outside Germany had a number or reasons to be suspicious and hostile toward Germany, and as a result the image of the country was altered. The Italians reinvigorated the image of the Goths and Vandals of Roman times, those Germanic tribes who had overrun the Empire and defeated the Roman Empire itself. The reason for this was that the German mercenaries (usually under Italian command) were once more threatening order in Italy. There was another sack of Rome in 1527 by German mercenaries, but in public perception it was another invasion by Germanic barbarians! The vast regions of Europe which remained Catholic after the successful efforts of many Germanic states (many German ones, England, Denmark, Sweden, etc.) to fracture the Catholic hegemony over religion in Europe had practical reasons for despising these German religious rebels. What the pagan Roman Tacitus had seen as positive things, the Renaissance reevaluated as negative.

It was mainly as a result of the Enlightenment and a discovery and analysis of ancient texts, coupled with new agendas which were not based on Church dogmas that the Germanic world began getting a new evaluation. Among many Enlightenment thinkers in both England and especially France the Germanic world was seen as a land of freedom and individual liberty. This was important in the struggle against the Divine Right of Kings and tyranny.

With the rise of the Romanic Movement in the late eighteenth and early nineteenth centuries the Germanic world, and most especially the reputation of Germany (or Central Europe in general) gained great prestige. The world of dark forests, broken castles and mysterious occurrences that Germany evoked in the minds of many both within and especially without the country was part of the phenomenon that came to be called "Gothic." The Germans were mainly seen as a people given to eccentric ideas, intense—even obsessive—scholarly activity, dreamy poetry and philosophical speculation. After all, Germany remained as it had been in the time of Tacitus, a patchwork of hundreds of small and dozens of moderate-sized states, duchies, principalities and kingdoms.

Although the German-speaking core of the Austro-Hungarian Empire often considered itself part of a greater Germany, the political fact was that "Austria" was a vast, multi-ethnic empire (which included Hungarians, Czechs, Slovenes, Croatians, Romanians, Ukrainians and many others). But from a cultural perspective the German speakers of Austrian Empire were just as much *German* as any other.

At the time of the historical core of the *Reformbewegungen* in Germany (1880-1933), the image of Germany, as we have seen, had become largely transformed into an aggressive, militaristic one after the unification of many of the German states into the Second Empire under Prussian domination. However, it must be borne in mind that this is, after all, merely an *image*, not necessarily a reality. The Reform Movements can be seen as a reflection of the older, and apparently more perennial, images of the German as a freedom-loving mystic and dreamer coupled with that of the scientific explorer.

The most important single event or turning point in the image of the Germans was the Franco-Prussian War of 1870-71, followed by the declaration of the unified German state. This inaugurated an image of Prussian militarism which became generalized over the whole of the German people as seen first by the French then by the British. This was not just a matter of image in a vacuum, however. The main driving force behind the change in other major European states toward Germany was its new-found military strength, coupled with expanding industrialization and economic development that threatened to overtake the British, or was at least recognized as a significant competitor to the British Empire. This competition eventually spilled over into the events of the Great War (1914-1918), during which both the French and English ramped up their "anti-Hun" wartime propaganda to a fever pitch.

In the final analysis, it can be said that as long as Germany was an un-unified patch-work of tribal states and posed no military or economic threat to the major states of western Europe, the German image was free to be that of the dreamer and professor, but once unification occurred and serious competition commenced, the image of Germany changed into a militaristic and aggressive "Hun." Again, as we can see from what was actually occurring in German culture and society within its own border, this "image" had little to do with reality.

The events and circumstances connected to the era of National Socialism in Germany, of course, eventually cemented the image of Germany as a military menace, but in the early years of Hitler's leadership he and National Socialism were sometimes praised by some among the western allies of WWI. One notable example as the great British playwright George Bernard Shaw. The pro-German/Nazi sentiments were most often rooted in a combination of sympathy with the socialistic and eugenic aspects of the perceived program of the NSDAP and partially in the abject fear of renewed hostilities with Germany—no one, and especially the English, wanted to return to horrors of the trenches on the Western Front! The events of the actual world war, the most deadly and obscene orgy of human horrors ever visited upon the planet, could only deepen this anti-German, or perhaps more specifically, anti-Nazi, sentiment. Outright anti-German feeling was rather weak across a broad spectrum of the population in the US as to that point Germans made up the largest "minority" (i.e. non-Anglo-Saxon) population in the country. But anti-Nazi attitudes were strong, most often based on that feeling that they were unjustifiably arrogant, not due to their crimes which remained largely unknown at the time. The post-war manipulation of the image of Germans and Germany by the victorious Western Allies was ambivalent. On the one hand there was an intensive and determined Denazification program but on the other hand West Germany was seen as an important ally in the Cold War. "East Germans" inherited many of the negative stereotypes of the past.

Due to these factors, West Germany enjoyed a good reputation in the decades following the war, especially among Americans. This was enhanced by the large contingency of American military personnel stationed in Germany.

Among the nations of the world today, none is as aware of, and concerned with, its own image than the Germans. Reform ideology remains an aspect of German culture which remains vibrant in the country, yet it also remains an aspect of the culture about which most non-Germans seem to remain largely unaware. It is the aim of this book to bridge the gap between these two situations.

It is widely thought that the Germans have a negative reputation as a hangover from the Nazi Era. This is largely fueled by images, narratives and characterizations found in popular culture (films and television). The contents of the present book should provide a considerable counter-balance to this negative imagery by showing the history and ideology connected to the Reform of Life Movements, which, when understood often come as revelations about Germany and the Germans.

3.0. Overview of Reform Ideology and its Development

The Reform Movements under examination here are those found in Germany between about 1880 and 1933. To be sure the ideas represented by these movements often have roots that lie outside Germany, and ones that pre-date 1880 and also which have branches which reach in continuous fashion beyond the fateful year in German history in 1933. Britain and America offered many ideas to these movements, to which the Germans gave their own particular methods and expressions. One of the overriding aspects of German culture which provided the particular shape to the German Reform Movements was its middle-class, some would say bourgeois, character. The roots of such cultural and economic trends go all the way back to the time of the Northern Renaissance where we see ideas spawned in the philosophical think-tanks of the Italian Renaissance applied across a broad and practical socio-economic front. Perhaps due to the decentralized nature of German political culture, up until 1871 a complex patch-work of small states and principalities, various ideas spread more widely than one might find in the more centralized cultures of England and France. Many people working broadly over the whole German-speaking cultural sphere gave a specific character to these German movements.

What we in America or Britain identify as the "New Age" or Hippie movements, especially prevalent in the 1960s and early 1970s, represented ideas that had already become "mainstream" in the German-speaking world during the late 1800s and early 1900s. I remember visiting the famous *Externsteine* site in northern Germany in 1981, an attraction at the time known almost exclusively to the Germans themselves. There were people of all ages there. The young people either ignored the stones and their formations preferring to play Frisbee or might make a remark or two to one another about how "cool" the stones looked. But the elderly Germans, in their 70s or 80s, pointed to the stones with their hiking sticks and waxed poetic about the wonders of the rising spring time sun, or the ancient rites that must have taken place there among their ancestors. Many Americans might have had the image of the typical German as an "uptight" rightwing sort, but as we are learning, nothing could have actually been further from the truth. What we learn in the contents of this book is that German culture of the decades before and after 1900 was a complex of new ideas and these ideas were often implemented, both subjectively and objectively—not always with good outcomes.

The whole idea of *Reform* became what we call today a "brand." There is a major chain of stores in Germany today which have their origin around 1900 called *"Reformhaus."* The first of these with that name actually opened in the year 1900. The formulaic concept *Reform* clearly implies that there has been a "de-formation," or degeneration of things that are important and that there is a need for restoration or radical improvement across a wide spectrum of human life: body, mind and culture.

3.1. The Romantic Foundation

One could delve back into deep antiquity to search for the roots of the Reform Movements in pre-Christian pagan traditions making their spirit felt in the modern world, but the most direct connection with the past for the Reform Movements proper is most clearly German Romanticism.

Romanticism in general was an international movement in the arts, philosophy and religion which rebelled against the Neo-Classical or Enlightenment attitude that the world was a great machine and that it was governed entirely by mechanical processes in a logical and rational (if as yet undiscovered) set of laws. This kind of thinking dominated most of the elite of Europe between the middle of the 1600s into the early 1800s. But a new generation began to express itself in the late eighteenth century which saw that man's problems were not that he was not logical or rational enough (not just that) but that he lacked natural authenticity and wisdom drawn from the night-side of nature. Romanticism struck roots in France (with Jean-Jacques Rousseau and in England with Edmund Burke), but nowhere did it strike deeper and more productive roots than it did in the German-speaking states of Central Europe.

The period of cultural Romanticism would endure from about 1770 to 1848—measured by the year of Goethe's death. The Romantics encouraged a turning away from the values of Classicism—that is away from external rules and logic and more toward internal feelings and intuition. Romantics were marked by a new set of interests, some might say obsessions. These were:

1. Nature

2. Psychology (study of the human soul)

3. Love (new role of women as spiritual advisors)

4. Religion (subjective approach)

5. Nationalism (culture)

By *nature*, the Romantic understood the direct and sensual perception of nature itself and the emotions that experience of nature can provide, as well as the philosophical idea of nature being the standard by which truth is measured in the human spirit. With the idea of *psychology*, this human spirit, mind or soul was understood as the perceptive and feeling part of the individual human being. This self or individual soul was the "place" where the world was perceived and understood. When most people think of the word "romantic" (especially in the English-speaking world) the idea of *love* immediately presents itself. This may seem shallow, but it is not. The idea that another human being or other human beings and the individual's feelings of love toward them is an essential part of the human experience and one fundamental to happiness. This connection with others is essential to the Romantic impulse. Romantic men of the age valued their relationships with women very highly. Sexuality was important, but women were also seen as "priestesses" and as important advisors and muses for creativity. Women too began to take a more prominent place in art and the creative life. The Romantic was often obsessed with religious ideas. These were not always concepts at home in orthodox confessional religions, and could span from "atheism" to occultism. The mystical direct experience of the spiritual was paramount. Finally, especially in Germany, Romanticism was connected with nationalism. Romantics were most often devoted to the idea of the political union of all German-speaking people into a single political state. Germany remained a collection of many smaller states until most of western Germany was united in 1871. When we review this list of special Romantic interests, we will note that they form a coherent and integrated whole, between two bookends based on the Latin stem *natio*: "to be born, generated." This gives rise to the words for both *nature* and *nation*. This list of ideas forms a map for the Romantic path and shapes the foundation of what would become the Reform Movements.

The Romantic period, its philosophers or thinkers and activists (such as Fichte, Herder, the Grimms [Jacob and Wilhelm] and Friedrich Ludwig Jahn) and literary figures, poets or scholars (such as the early Goethe, the Schlegels [August Wilhelm and Friedrich], and E. T. A. Hoffmann) formed the underlying theoretical basis for the Reform Movements, while the actual Reform activists and creative people put these theories into action on one level or another.

Although historians of ideas often declare the Romantic period to have ended around 1850, in point of fact the ideologies of both Romanticism and its predecessor, Classicism project themselves right down to our present-day lives. These mindsets have never disappeared, probably because they are rooted in things far older than the labels we use to understand and discuss them.

3.2. Overview

When we look over the whole of the Reform Movements in Germany we see certain themes and basic tenets which animate most of them. The main one stems from the Romantic focus on the philosophical idea of *nature*, and life and health defined by a natural approach. This idea then extends itself into every aspect and avenue of life and living: how people live, the social dimension, living-space and structures, the diet and the production and preparation of food and the spiritual or intellectual conclusions drawn from this natural attitude toward life. Especially in Germany, this natural approach gave rise to a certain kind of nationalism. This stems directly from the Romantic Movement in Germany, where mid-nineteenth century Romantics were almost all proponents of the unification of the German-speaking states into one nation-state. This form of nationalism was characterized as solidly a *liberal* idea as the conservative attitude was simply to conserve the status quo whereby the various kings, princes and electors would continue to rule their small states. To the Romantic activists this was not natural because it seemed indeed more natural for all German-speaking people to belong to one state called *Germany*. This natural "state" already existed—had not the Roman historian Tacitus, writing in the first century of the Common Era, even titled his book *Germania* (Germany)?

The Reform Movements as such were not particularly political because they tended to be focused on particular issues or interests, as described in this book. But the Reform ideology did have a certain political attitude as a "third way" between and *contrary* to both Communism and Capitalism. Because the Reform Movements are rooted in a spiritual attitude, the world of human spirituality was greatly influenced by the underlying interests of the Reformers. In this same vein, Reform ideology greatly shaped certain schools of art and literature and these expressions are among the most powerful vehicles by which the Reform Movements projected their image and message into the present-day.

From the deep roots of the earlier nineteenth century ideas began to branch out into the ever increasingly well-read and well-educated middle class in the German-speaking world. The contemplation of the great questions of life and the human spirit were no longer left to an elite of thinkers, philosophers and scientists. A broad spectrum of the average bourgeoisie, especially those living and working in highly urbanized and industrialized cities, were becoming increasingly critical of the drift of their culture. But instead of merely thinking and talking about these things, an increasing number were also willing to take action and make changes in their personal lives as acts of individual Reform and to organize and collaborate with others for the sake of broader social, political and religious Reforms.

In many ways, the Reform of Life Movements, in their aggregate within the culture of German-speaking world, constituted a new religious form expressed in diverse ways but with certain underlying principles. By analogy we can see a similar phenomenon which took place in the Anglo-American world in the 1960s and 1970s with the so-called "New Age" movement which shared many of the same roots as the German Reform Movements.

The effects of Reform ideas on religion were profound. These extended into the orthodox confessing faiths such as Catholicism and Protestantism but also into the Jewish religion. Additionally, the Reform Age welcomed an influx of exotic religions and religious ideas from sources such as Buddhism, Hinduism, Taoism and Zoroastrianism. Besides all this, however, the Reform Movements spawned a host of what we today call "new religions."(3) Many of these were in one way or another rooted in the revolution in religious ideas inspired by the Theosophical Society. These included Anthroposophy and so-called Ariosophy.

Because the expression of political ideologies are usually reflections of deeper mindsets and motivations in human culture, the ideas of the Reform Movements were inevitably demonstrated in political action. But this did not mean that the effects of Reform ideology were in any way uniform or monolithic in their actual effects. Reformers could be politically liberal or conservative, Marxists or monarchists and were well represented among the National Socialists. It appears that a general lack of awareness of the applications of Reform ideas in the political sphere often led to often unintended and certainly undesirable consequences. In Russia, ideas akin to the Reformers (the Cosmists, for example) were coopted by the Bolsheviks and some might see a similar fate shared by the New Agers in America. As we will see in §4.3 politics were affected by Reform ideas, but the Reform Movements themselves clearly steered clear of partisan politics and ideologies following the general sentiment expressed by the image created by Fidus and shown in the Introduction.

Education and higher learning in both the *Natur-* and *Gesisteswissenbschaften*, i.e. in the natural sciences and humanities, had reached a high level in the German-speaking world by the mid-nineteenth century, but Reform-minded thinkers both inside and outside formal academia saw the need for a more student-centered mode of teaching. Reform-Pedagogy was a movement felt within established educational institutions as well as in new alternative modalities such as the *Volkshochschulen* ("folk-high-schools") and the Waldorf Schools, for example.

The whole broad field of what might be called health and nutrition was one in which the Reform Movement were perhaps most conspicuous and certainly best received. General health included alternative therapies and treatments in medicine and new approaches to diet. New therapies included homeopathy and the use of water for curative powers, and so on. Much of the Reform-based diet focused on the practice of vegetarianism and the abstinence from alcohol. A multi-faceted rationale for the banning of vivisectionism, i.e. the use of animals for scientific or medical experiments, was also intimately connected to the general belief in the health of all creatures.

Another highly visible aspect of the Reform Movements was interest in physical exercise and focus on the health (and *beauty*) of the human body. This found expression in elaborations on the long-standing interest in Central Europe in gymnastics. This also found strong representation in the practice of nudism, or what came to be called *Freikörper Kultur* (FKK).

Linked to the practice of nudism was also the idea of clothing reform in general. The relationship of the individual human body to its immediate physical environment was seriously contemplated. Matters of style, comfort and the materials used to clothe the body (or not) became subjects of philosophical consideration. This was especially true when it came to women's clothing, a topic which raised the greatest controversies, as it continued to do after this time.

Of fundamental importance in the whole Reform Movements was the concept of sexuality, which made itself felt in a variety of the fields of reform. Some of this was subtle and built into other endeavors, such as nudism, clothing reform, women's emancipation and suffrage movements as well as youth-movements, but also there was the overt development of what became knowns as sexology, or the scientific study of human sexuality.

One of the greatest forms of alienation which the Reformers strove to alleviate was that of humans living in social and spatial environments. Therefore efforts were made to improve the philosophies of the idea of community and living circumstances. Architecture, planning of cityscapes, parks, greenbelts and so on were envisioned and in many cases actualized.

These aspects of life dealt with the physical environment, but also the relationships of individuals' minds one to the other is seen as important. These concerns are largely addressed in new attitudes and levels of creativity in art—graphic arts, music, theater and most especially literature. Through literature, for example, an artist such as Hermann Hesse could convey a whole new attitude toward life to the masses. Several forms of graphic arts such as Art Nouveau and the Sezessionist style were influenced by Reform concepts, and later we will discuss the artist who became the maker of the most impressive lasting images of the aesthetics of the time: Fidus.

By the late nineteenth century, with the effects of the industrialization and urbanization that most Reformers so decried, the individual had, by necessity become what could be called a *homo œconomicus*—a member of an economic species. Therefore, in order to address the woes of the circumstance some Reformers turned to new political and economic theories for theoretical solutions.

One of the main ideas most closely associated with the Reform Movements—along with the health and nutrition of the individual human body—is that of environmentalism or the study of ecology. *Ecology* itself as a word and concept was first formulated in a systematic and scientific way in the contemporary world by the German zoologist Ernst Haeckel in his work entitled *Generelle Morphologie der Organismen* (General Morphology of Organisms), published in 1866. This was fundamental to the study of the environment in new ways which became the structural understanding of how organisms of all kinds are affected by the environment and the criteria necessary for a holistic understanding of biological health. It is here that we find the scientific basis for the Green Movement, already pioneered in the Reform Movements.

3.3. The Wandervogel Movement

Symbol of the *Wandervogel eingetragener Verein*

The new spirit of Reform rising up after 1880 inevitably caught the imaginations of the young people in German-speaking regions of Europe. This manifested itself as a new youth-movement(4) which both was the result of Reform ideas as well as a great accelerant to the breadth and depth of their spread. The main exponent of the youth-movement became known as the *Wandervogel*. This was especially strong in the Protestant areas. (Catholics were largely organized into Church-dominated youth activities.) The organized movement called the Wandervogel was founded in 1895 by Hermann Hoffmann in Steglitz near Berlin. They started out with just a handful of participants, but eventually grew to a movement with a membership of around 80,000. Their hikes and their general wandering lifestyle were themselves joyous acts of protest against industrialization and urbanization as they lived off of the land and out of their knapsacks as they hiked in nature through the woods while always singing various folksongs. Their expeditions sometimes covered hundreds of miles lasting three to four weeks. The Wandervogel was a movement influenced by medieval Romanticism (wandering scholars and musicians), the ideal of reviving old Germanic values, and so most of the members could be charactized as having nationalistic interests. The idea of individual wandering men was a long-standing one in German culture, but in this age the idea became organized into a mass-movement.

The word Wandervogel itself conveys a highly poetic and mystical meaning. It implies a free and weightless bird with virtually magical qualities. It can be translated as a "bird of passage"—and so does not mean exactly the same thing as a "migratory bird" (*Zugvogel*). This is why it is better left untranslated.

Historically, the Wandervogel developed into three main groups: The original became known as the *Alt-Wandervogel* (Old-Wandervogel), the *Steglitz-Wandervogel* were characterized by being alcohol-free and the *Jung-Wandervogel* (Young-Wandervogel), which was rather anarchistic, de-centralized, radical, and contrary to established norms. The Jung-Wandervogel freely mixed boys and girls and were not opposed to homosexuality. But all "organizations" of the Wandervogel generally strove to exist outside centralized control.

In 1889 Karl Fischer (1881–1941) succeeded Hoffmann as the leader of the main body of the movement. The basic characteristics of the movement had been established: an emphasis on the independence of the group, a frugal and simple lifestyle, self-responsibility, a spirit of adventure and freedom from traditional authority. There was an avoidance of marked paths and the comfort of youth hostels. Under Fischer the organization deepened its emphasis on Germanic roots and values and the greeting *"Heil!"* was introduced under influence from Austrian students.

Within the organization controversies included the question of the role of girls, the admission of Jews and the prohibition of alcohol. Also, the resistance of efforts by authorities and adults to exert control within the group was a key factor. The alcohol question was one that was part of the general Reform Movements, as we will see (4.5.3).

Although the Wandervogel was not a strictly hierarchical organization, as this was one of the things the youth wanted to get away from, there was a general division between newcomers, called *Scholaren* and more experienced members called *Bachante*. Each local group, or troop, had a high degree of autonomy. There was an overall sense of common belonging to the movement among all groups, held together by annual meetings and common reading of the journal *Wandervogel - Zeitschrift für deutsches Jugendwandern*.

It is important to realize that the Wandervogel was a cultural phenomenon, not a political or "revolutionary" one. Participants were between 12 and 18 years of age and were mostly from suburban or smaller-city, middle-class families. Most activities were found among northern German, Protestant youth. The soul of the movement was in German Romanticism. It acted as a place where like-minded youth could withdraw from the bourgeois world and be somehow transformed by their experiences before returning to their "normal" lives. In a way, the movement sought to have a transformative effect on the establishment lives of the countries involved. Members of the Wandervogel movement were most influenced by the writings of Friedrich Nietzsche, Paul de Lagarde, Julius Langbehn, and Houston Stewart Chamberlain, whose works often accompanied them on their hikes.

When the Nazis seized power in 1933, all youth organizations were eventually outlawed and assimilated into the Hitler-Youth (*Hitlerjugend*), which was in many ways inspired by the Wandervogel, but with political and paramilitary aims and purposes, and entirely within the control of the Nazi Party

The German youth-movement had an influence on Japan in the years before WWII and in order to promote healthy and vigorous activity among young people the *Shōkenkai Wandāfōgerubu* ("Health-Promotion Wandervogel Association") was formed by the Japanese Ministry of Education. Interestingly also the kibbutz movement in Israel and the Christian Bruderhof Communities both trace their origins to these German youth organizations. Of course, like so much else with its roots the Reform Movements, a watered-down version of the Wandervogel became what is known as *"Volksmarching,"* an organized non-competitive form of group hiking.

3.4 Some Leading Personalities of the Reform Movements

The widespread ideology of Reform found expression in a variety of human endeavors from philosophy to religion and from science to politics, but there were those few who radically embodied the concepts of *Lebensreform*—they attempted to live lives totally integrated into the concepts which were being espoused in the *Reform*-philosophy. The lives and ideas of these individuals will make their presence felt throughout the history of this movement, even if their names are sometimes almost forgotten today. These were the so-called *Naturmenschen* ("nature-men") of the movement and constituted its most radical sector.

These "spiritual leaders" of the Reform Movements are personalities whose influences were felt in several different fields of Reform, if not all of them. It is therefore advisable to preface the discussion of these various individual areas of Reform activity with some profiles of their histories and personalities.

Karl Wilhelm Diefenbach
per aspera ad astra

Karl Wilhelm Diefenbach in Front of His House on Capri

Karl Wilhelm Diefenbach (1851–1913) is often classified as a social-reformer and artist, but he was so much more. He was the grandfather of the whole phenomenon we came to characterize as the Reform Movements in the German-speaking realm. He pioneered nudism as a philosophy, was an advocate for peace and communal living. Most people who see images of Diefenbach today have to do a double-take because he looks the very image of the archetype of the American "hippie," which in fact he was.

He was the son of Leonard Diefenbach, an artist and teacher at the college preparatory school in Hadamar. Karl Wilhelm first learned from his father, but then went on to the Academy of Arts in Munich, where he was influenced by Arnold Böcklin and Franz von Stuck. His paintings found an immediate positive reception in the art world.

Diefenbach became severely ill due to typhoid fever and as a result had an operation which left one arm disabled. He turned to natural healing practices as treatment. Because he felt that his life had ultimately been saved due to the application of natural healing practices, he turned more to the ideas of natural medicine. The theories and writings of the early natural practitioners Arnold Rikli and Eduard Baltzer became guiding principles for him. Also, Around 1881, Diefenbach resigned from the church, and became an adherent of the *Freireligiöse Bewegung* (free-religious movement).

According to his own report, he experienced the "Ascension to the Sun" of his soul on the Hohenpeissengberg in the Alps on the morning of January 28, 1882. This signaled his transformation and his call to become a virtual prophet of the great movement toward Reform. He could be seen in Munich in his Jesus-like dress and preaching the virtues of the natural life. His basic ideas at this time included living in harmony with nature, rejection of monogamy, turning away from orthodox religion, vegetarianism, exercise in fresh air and the practice of nudism. He was widely met by ridicule in the city, so he sought greater freedom in the countryside.

In 1886, on the site of an old quarry at Höllriegelskreuth near Pullach in the Isar valley just south of Munich, Diefenbach established his first commune called the *Humanitas-Gemeinschaft* ("Humanitas Community"). This group sought to live according the principles of the natural dietician Eduard Baltzer. It was there that he met the young Hugo Höppener. Persecutions from the authorities did not end with his flight to his rural enclave. His acolyte Höppener was arrested for public nudity and served time in jail, but did not betray his master. Diefenbach memorialized Höppener's loyalty by giving him the moniker "Fidus" (loyal).

In conjunction with a large showing of his art in Vienna in 1892 he was swindled out of the ownership rights of many of his most outstanding works. After this disappointment, Diefenbach went to Egypt for period where he studied the ruins of ancient temples as examples of sacred architecture. With the help of a circle of friends, including the peace-activist Bertha von Sutter, Diefenbach was able to re-aquire the rights to his works in 1897. After this ended in success, a new artist commune called *Humanitas at the Himmelhof* in Ober Sankt Veit near Vienna. About twenty artists or disciples lived there at one time. This included another who would become an important spiritual leader of the Reform ideology, Gusto Gräser. Reports of life in this commune indicate that Diefenbach certainly had a tyrannical side to his personality: he demanded chastity while living with multiple female partners himself and he censored and controlled the mail that members sent and received, for example.

Diefenbach lived out his unconventional views on the nature of marriage. He had married earlier in life to Magdalena Atzinger, with whom he had one daughter, Stella. In 1898 he met a woman named Mina Vogler, whom he married, but in fact led a triadic marriage with Mina and her sister Marie, who became his favorite.

After this artists' commune failed, which would have seemed inevitable, Diefenbach made his way to the Greek island of Capri in1899. There he earned notoriety and had more great success, but back home he was eventually forgotten. However, the seeds he planted in the minds of many of his followers demonstrated a long-lasting influence throughout the Reform Movements in Central Europe.

Diefenbach died on the island of Capri in 1913 of an intestinal blockage.

His commune Humanitas at Himmelhof became a model for subsequent such communities, especially that founded by his follower Gusto Gräser called Monte Verità in Switzerland.

In the world of graphic arts Diefenbach is considered a Symbolist, but one independent of the social and political aspects of that movement internationally.

Diefenbach's works were mainly of the artistic kind, and in subsequent years they have been collected and preserved. His written output was small, as his main mode of working in the world was more direct and personal in the environment of the communes and communities in which he lived, taught and created.

Meister Fidus
[= Hugo Höppener (1868-1948)]

Fidus [ca. 1930]

Fidus was the rather magical moniker of a German artist and author born Hugo Reinhold Karl Johann Höppener. He was from the city of Lübeck and showed artistic brilliance from an early age. When he was only eighteen years old he met the artist and Reformer K. W. Diefenbach, already known by then as the "apostle of nature." Hugo was drawn into Diefenbach's world and because he actually served a brief time in prison for public nudity in Diefenbach's cause, without betraying his master, he was given the name Fidus "faithful" or "loyal") by Diefenbach. Fidus was closely associated with his Master between 1887 and 1899. At the age of twenty-two Fidus moved to a location near Berlin where he set up a commune and worked as a free-lance illustrator and on the Theosophical journal *Sphinx* as well as several other magazines such as *Jugend* ("Youth") and the gay journal called *Der Eigene* ("The Unique").

From an art-historical perspective the works of Fidus are usually classified as belonging to the Symbolist School and his general style belonged to what was generally called Art Nouveau, known in German as *Jugendstil*.

Ideologically Fidus was not only influenced by Diefenbach's Reform concepts, but also by Theosophical beliefs and doctrines as well as heroic Germanic myth and legend. His images of peasants, warriors and a myriad of naked figures in wondrously natural settings were inspirational to his generation and beyond.

After the end of WWI his artistic work was less and less in demand for illustrations in the publishing industry. Interestingly, Fidus was an early supporter of National Socialism, and became a member of the NSDAP in 1932, a year before the Nazis came to power. This connection did little for his career, as official National Socialist attitudes toward art and aesthetics ran counter to the style of Fidus. As a matter of fact, in 1937 his work was banned and confiscated, and its sale was forbidden. He fell into the category of idealists who were rejected by the Party. His case could be compared to that of the decadent writer, Hanns Heinz Ewers.

Not long after the War in 1948, Fidus died in obscurity in Woltersdorf in the Soviet Occupation Zone. His house, now called the Fidus-Haus is a sort of local museum and memorial to the artist's memory.

But Fidus was certainly rediscovered in the 1960s in America. His images became icons of the "Hippie Movement" and were used as models for various "psychedelic" concert posters, especially in and around San Francisco Bay Area in California, USA. Besides the Fidus-Haus in Woltersdorf, there are collections of his work in the Berlinische Galerie and a large archive in the Jack Daulton Collection in Los Altos Hills, California.

Gusto Gräser

Gustav "Gusto" Arthur Gräser (1879-1958) was a leading exponent of the communal mode of life as well as being a poet and artist. He collaborated with his brother, Karl, in these efforts. Gräser was born in Kronstadt (now Brașov) in Austria-Hungary. From his youth, he was influenced by the ideas and philosophy of Diefenbach. He lived in Diefenbach's community called Himmelhof near Vienna in 1897. Gräser became disaffected by what he felt was Diefenbach's authoritarian leadership style and left the community to form his own following the next year near Munich. But by 1900 he left that group and began to wander across the countryside, eventually participating with his brother and several other artists and writers including Hermann Hesse, Carl Jung, Stefan George, Paul Klee, Arnold Ehret, Mary Wigman, Rudolf von Laban, Ernst Toller, and occultists such as Theodor Reuss, Franz Hartmann and Rudolf Steiner in the establishment of the community of Mount Verità near Ascona, Switzerland. This had long been a favorite destination for the hikes of the Wandervogel. Gräser, who often took up residence in a nearby cave, served as a sort of "guru" for Hesse in this period and greatly influenced his ideas.

In 1911, Gräser moved with his family to the outskirts of Berlin where he became a local proponent of the Free German Youth Movement, but he met with official hostility and was expelled from there and from other places he tried to live. With the advent of the Great War in 1914 Gräser refused military service and was deported back to Austria in 1915. There he claimed to be a "conscientious objector" for which he was at first sentenced to death, but then he was ruled to be insane and committed to a mental institution. He was soon released, but his experience had not dissuaded him. He became an anti-war activist. Gräser led what was known as the "crusade of love" which inspired Hesse's story Journey to the East. Finally, Gräser lived in the commune known as Grunhurst. After the National Socialists came to power in Germany, the community at Grunhurst was eventually targeted for destruction in 1936. Many of the inhabitants were murdered (including some of Gräser's family) and others rounded up and sent to concentration camps. Gusto himself escaped and hid out in Munich living in the attics of supporters for the duration of the Nazi regime. After the war, he wandered the countryside again and died in Munich in 1958. His works were thankfully preserved in the Municipal Library of Munich.

The ideas, aesthetics and leading actions of the three individuals just introduced will find their way into the fabric of this study on various occasions throughout this book. I will give more details on their works at various times, but their leading roles have to be acknowledged from the beginning.

4.0. Fields of Reform

4.1. Culture of the Radical Reformers

Because the Reform Movements constitute a pluralistic reality, made up of a variety of different interests and personalities, often seeming to have nothing to do with one another, yet all bound by a common thread of principles, we can only meaningfully approach these movements individually. This is why we generally insist upon using the plural movements, and not the singular movement, when talking about the whole phenomenon. When we look out over the spiritual landscape of these movements we see a patchwork of fields of interest.

These fields appear in a broad panorama of features ranging from religion (philosophical values and approaches to the idea of spirituality of all kinds), politics (how people relate to one another in the power structure of society) and education as well as matters of health and nutrition. This latter category is itself extremely important among the Reform Movements and encompasses many sub-categories, e.g. health, diet, nudism, the concept of physical beauty, sexuality and even fashion. Beyond these also lie the modes of human habitation, living spaces and new views of economics. Underpinning and supporting the general ideas lying behind the spirit of Reform in ways similar to religion is the whole field of art and literature. It is here that the Reform ideas perhaps made their most lasting impressions on intellectual history. Finally, it must be recognized that perhaps more than anything else the Reform Movements became known as enthusiastic environmentalists and explorers of ecological sciences.

Every field making up the whole of the Reform Movements borders on and usually overlaps with other fields so that it can be said that no one field exists independent of the others and that to some degree or another each one depends on one or more of the others to complete itself. Many individual Reformers were active in several fields, while others tilled most of their crops with intensity within one or another of the fields. Because there was no one philosophy that governed all of the movements, such as one might find in Marxism with its dominant dogmas and structures, the ties that bind the various fields together are subtle and often ephemeral—but very palpable to those who felt and feel them. Some Refoemers were pagans, others Christians, some were materialists, others highly spiritual and mystical, some were ascetics and others libertines. One thing is certain: what bound them together was their common rebellion against a set of common foes: unbridled industrialization, heartless urbanization and violence done to nature in the animal, vegetable and mineral kingdoms.

4.2. Religion
(Religiosity and Spirituality)

In many respects the entirety of the Reform Movements can be characterized as a "religious" phenomenon. This is because these movements address central aspcts of human existence and provide alternative strategies for dealing with the ailings and shortcomings of the species. The questions posed by religions and the answers many provide are mirrored in the activities of the Reform Movements taken as an aggregate.

Certainly, the most radical aspect of religious Reform was the accelerated phenomenon we today refer to as New Religions during the period of the Reform Movements. Many of these grew in one way or another out of the Theosophical Society and its members, or was significantly inspired by that organization. These included Anthroposophy and what came to be called Ariosophy. Additionally, many ideas from the established world-religions such as Buddhism, Hinduism, Taoism and Zoroastrianism made significant inroads into the philosophies of Reform-minded individuals in Central Europe at the time. Often overlooked in all of this dramatic development is the degree to which Reform ideas had an effect on the mainstream religions at home in Germany at the times: Catholicism, Protestantism and Judaism. The changes made in the established religions were not as significant simply because these faiths had a long history going back to the Middle Ages of "reforming"—adapting and adopting—ideas in order to remain relevant within the culture.

Because in various ways the Reform Movements were oriented toward answering fundamental questions about the relationship of the individual human, or humankind in a social aggregate, to other parts of the environment—natural, social and spiritual—these movements only naturally made themselves felt in areas usually reserved to the concept of "religion."

4.2.1. Reforms of Orthodox Religions

When we look at the Reform Movements our attention is most usually drawn to the most radical and distinctive aspects of the phenomenon. When "religion" is considered, we most eagerly seek out the study of Theosophy or paganism, for example. However, it must be emphasized that the ideas of Reform were highly generalized and often subtle in their manifestations in the lives and minds of individuals as well as of already established groups. The same phenomenon can be witnessed and felt in the ways in which often radical, and to many at the time very 'strange," ideas incubated in the 1950s and 1960s in America have become entrenched and manifest cultural features of even "conservative" or "mainstream" American society, e.g. birth control, legalized cannabis, gay marriage. These, and many other, concepts can actually be traced back to the Reform Movements of over a hundred years ago. Reform ideas made themselves felt in subtle ways orthodox, or so-called confessional, religious organizations as well.

Catholicism

Of all religious sects, the one that resisted the modern world and the one that was least likely to be affected by the Reform ideologies was Roman Catholicism. The Catholic Church had in fact been reforming itself constantly since its own inception, but these reforms and counter-reforms had to be generated from within the church hierarchy itself, and when changes were made, the Papal Bulls usually insisted that what was actually happening was a reiteration of "what the church had always taught." The Roman Catholic Church remained a repository of medieval atavisms which were often drawn upon by later reformers and revolutionaries.

Several documents were produced by the Vatican in the nineteenth century which were intended to stem the wave of "modernism" in culture. One of the best known of these is called the *Syllabus of Errors* (Lat. *Syllabus Errorum*) issued by Pius IX in 1864. This cites some 80 errors, also called heresies, identified as aspects of the modern world. In principle, the Church was dedicated to the defense of its medieval intellectual structure, and this often involved resistance to change or *reform* of various kinds. This does not mean that rank and file Roman Catholics were opposed to Reform, but the Church as a corporation was. The Church was opposed to the atheistic, socialistic and materialistic (Marxist) trend in culture and politics, but also the pagan upwelling it saw in movement such as nudism and sexual libertinism.

The times called for youth organizations and organizations or activities such as those of the Wandervogel filled this demand. Notably, the Wandervogel was predominant in the Protestant areas of Germany whereas the Catholic Church tried to establish a youth organization to compete with this trend. The result was the *Katholische bündische Jugend* (Catholic Free Youth Movement) and other Catholic youth organizations—most of which looked very much like a prototype of the Hitler Youth with a sort of paramilitary look. Of course, such Catholic youth organizations were not the anarchistic affairs such as one might find in the Wandervogel movement. They, like the Hitler Youth, were instruments of a central authority. Catholic groups were officially banned by the Nazis in 1938.

Many of the early Nazis were raised as Roman Catholics (e.g. Hitler and Himmler) and Catholic areas of Germany (e.g. Bavaria) were the early hotbeds of National Socialism. This latter aspect stems from the fact that Roman Catholicism had historically been a bastion of Anti-Semitic thought and action. (5) It is likely that the linkage between "modernism" and the emancipation of the Jews was something generated by Catholic propaganda in the nineteenth century.

Protestantism

Germany, of course, had already had a considerable history with the word "reform" since the inception of the religious movement that became known as the Reformation, most notably led by the great reformer and protestant Martin Luther (1494-1546). The Middle Ages had been rife with alternate spiritualities and heretical sects, but each one, until the advent of larger cultural changes brought about around the year 1500 which ushered in what became known as the Modern Age, failed until the time of Luther.

On an official level the Evangelical Lutheran Church tried, as did the Roman Catholic Church, to take advantage of the general upwelling in Central European culture toward Reform concepts in order to redirect the dynamism of the times back into a conservative, *status quo*, direction. This redirection was known by the general designation of *"Erneuerung"* (renewal) of the church. In fact, of course, this was something that only had the appearance of reform.

As a demographic and cultural reality, it is found that the Protestant areas of Germany, i.e. the northern and eastern parts of the nation, were much more open to Reform ideologies and were far more likely to embrace Reform cultural features than were the Catholic regions. It is likely that this did not stem from a theological affinity between Reform and Protestantism, but rather more from the greater degree of latitude given to the individual in making moral or philosophical choices that was by nature part of the Protestant way. The Lutheran Church had to rely on argument rather than the wide array of centralized instruments that had always been available in the Roman Church.

Judaism

At first one might be tempted to think that the idea of "Reform Judaism" which actually has its roots in Germany dating back to the late eighteenth century, has something to do with the Reform Movements. However, it may be more accurate to call the movement in Judaism something known as the "Jewish Renaissance" (German: *Jüdische Renaissance*). This was a term coined by Martin Buber (1878-1965) in part to account for the influences of the new Reform ideology current around 1900. The main areas of interest for this Renaissance movement were art, music and literature as well as activities surrounding gymnastics, youth movements, settlements and efforts toward establishing a Jewish homeland (Zionism). Generally, the interests of individual Jews and organizations with a specifically Jewish identity were significantly different in their reception of Reform ideas than were non-Jews. However, many Jews, especially in Germany had become highly assimilated and "emancipated" over the years following the late 18th century. Many had converted to Lutheranism, especially in northern Germany. Individual Jews, such as Franz Oppenheimer, founder of the Obstbausiedlung Eden-Oranienburg (Orchard-Settlement Eden-Oranienburg) near Berlin which was a model for many successful communes of the time, or the great sexual Reformer Magnus Hirschfeld can be cited as persons of Jewish heritage who were important to the wider Reform Movements.

4.2.2. Imported Religions

Two major world religions from Asia were imported into German-speaking regions of Europe over the course of the nineteenth century. These were Hinduism and Buddhism. Both entered through academic circles, but by the age of Reform, they had penetrated in different ways into the popular culture.

The German-speaking world became increasingly open to exotic religious imports at a grassroots level after the middle of the nineteenth century. The philosopher Arthur Schopenhauer (1788-1860) was greatly influenced by Indian thought and Friedrich Nietzsche at least caused the name of Zarathustra to gain widespread popularity. German scholars investigated Buddhism, Hinduism, Taoism and Zoroastrianism and travelers visited the lands where these religions were practiced and encouraged their further study. It was more usual, however, for these religious concepts to be somewhat "Westernized" before they were accepted in a widespread way. This happened in some of the movement we will discuss here. Important among these will be the Theosophical Society and spinoffs from that such as Anthroposophy and so-called Ariosophy.

Principal among these was at first Hinduism and Hindu doctrines. For the most part philosophers there followed in the pioneering footsteps of the philosophers such as Hegel, the Schlegels, Herder Wilhelm von Humboldt and most especially Arthur Schopenhauer who ushered in knowledge of, and interest in, Hindu—based spirituality, Vedanta, etc. There was an Indian presence in Germany made up of businessmen, diplomats and chefs. On this basis, there developed the science of Indology, most prominently represented by Max Müller (1823-1900) and Paul Deussen (1845-1919). From the works of these men the religious doctrines of Hindu sects entered the popular culture of Central Europe (as well as elsewhere).

Besides Hinduism, Buddhism too found its way into Germany by the same channels. Because Buddhism is a universal method, not doctrinally tied to a specific population (as was Hinduism until recently) it found easier entre into the German-speaking world. Schopenhauer's main influence in this regard was the work of Isaac Jacob Schmidt (1779–1847), who was an expert in the study of the Kalmyks, an ethnically Mongolian and religiously predominantly Buddhist region in southern Russia.(6) After Schopenhauer's introduction a new generation of German authors and experts arose including Nyānatiloka Mahāthera (born Anton Gueth [1878–1957]) who became the first German-speaking monk of Buddhism, who completed many translations of Buddhist texts and the lama Anagarika Govinda (Ernst Lothar Hoffmann [1898–1985]) who wrote several Buddhist works in the Weimar period and became influential throughout the West. Other thinkers and artists such as Nietzsche and Wagner were also directly influenced by Schopenhauer and spread certain Buddhist ideas in German culture.

In conjunction with Theosophical efforts more instructional works on Buddhism were produced, and in 1906 the first Buddhist institution, the Buddhist Missionary Association for Germany, was founded by the Ideologist Karl Seidenstücker. This was followed by the establishment of other organizations in the 1920s, such as the Old Buddhist Community in 1921, the Community of Buddha in Berlin in 1922, there too the first European Buddhist monastery, the Buddhist House, was established in 1924. The whole movement was further bolstered by the publication in 1922 of Hermann Hesse's novel *Siddhartha*.

The exotic philosophy and method of human development described in Buddhism struck exceptionally deep roots in German culture and continues to have its effects today.

4.2.3. New Religions

Besides reforms of conventional religions and the import of religions from foreign lands, Europe, and especially Germany and Austria, became territories where what historians of religion now call "new religions" began to spring up. These were for the most part well-integrated into the whole Reform trend, and were largely esoteric schools of thought which functioned as expressions of middle-class explorations of the ultimate mysteries of the universe. As education had expanded in the nineteenth century, concerns usually left to the upper and lower ends of the socio-economic spectrum began to make marked inroads into the middle ground of the economic world.

4.2.3.1. Theosophy

The most important single event in the rise of alternative religions in the late nineteenth century globally and in Central Europe was the foundation of the Theosophical Society coupled with the works of its leading ideologue, Helena Petrovna Blavatsky (1831–1891). Blavatsky (née von Hahn) was descended from ethnic Germans on her father's side. She was precocious as a child but was married off to a man twenty-three years older than her named Nikfor Blavatsky, whom she soon abandoned to travel to Constantinople. She lived a Bohemian life for twenty-five years and emerged in 1871 to found a spiritualistic society in Cairo, Egypt called the Societé Spirite. She eventually emigrated to the USA and met the occultist and journalist Henry Steel Olcott and with him founded the Theosophical Society in 1875. Theosophy provided a modern, eclectic alternative myth with which to act as a substructure for the Reformation of mainstream culture and the directions it was taking. Its inherent eclecticism, combining elements from East and West, religious and magical, made it tailor made for its popularization among disaffected would-be Reformers.

In the early years of the Society, its doctrine differed little from other occult organizations, drawing most of its inspiration from supposed "Egyptian" and Middle Eastern imagery in conjunction with the practices of Spiritualism. But both Blavatsky and Olcott helped move the center of gravity of the organization more into the sphere of the spiritual world of the Indian Subcontinent and the Himalayans. This was in conjunction with the rising popularity of Buddhist doctrines in Germany discussed in section 4.2.2.

Theosophy appealed to the educated minds of the nineteenth century because it successfully incorporated the idea of evolution into a spiritual framework. Darwinism influenced many ideologies in one way or another and in Theosophy it found expression on all levels, cosmic and biological. Seen in the history of the development of humanity, Theosophy teaches an elaborate and metaphysical theory of "root races." According to this theory, we are presently at the end of the evolution of the Fifth Root-Race (the Aryans), but two further Root-Races will evolve which will be vastly superior to the sort of mankind which exists now.

Theosophy and the Theosophical Society as an organization had considerable success in Germany, but it was also the subject of various reforms itself. Certain of Blavatsky's ideas that were not very prominent were emphasized in the German-speaking world. For example, German Theosophy involved itself much more in the scientific, or pseudo-scientific, investigation of psychic phenomena than did the mainstream of the TS. Theosophy as such was introduced in Central Europe approximately ten years after their introduction in the English-speaking world. There was a fledgling Theosophical Society founded in 1884 and then new impulses of activity were led by Franz Hartmann, Friedrich Eckstein and Paul Zillmann. A translation program was systematically undertaken and *The Secret Doctrine* was translated in two volumes in 1897 and 1901. Thus, by 1902 it could be said that the Theosophical movement was well-established in Germany and Austria with ten major local groups and as many as 30 smaller ones. Eckstein founded a branch in Vienna in 1887, where a brilliant scholar and mystic named Rudolf Steiner was active. This group was artistic, subjective, sentimental, made up of cultured individuals devoted to "mystical Christianity" and "personal Gnosticism." (Goodrick-Clarke 1985: 30) After the beginning of the twentieth century this sector became increasingly anti-Catholic, nationalistic and was quite interested in native German mythology and folklore. This group influenced men such as Guido von List and Lanz von Liebenfels, and they in turn conditioned the local brand of Theosophy. From within the same Viennese assembly Rudolf Steiner pressed for a more mystical view of Christianity, uncomfortable with the anti-Christian and pro-Hindu and Buddhist tenor of the TS.

Many Reformers in a wide variety of fields of endeavor were influenced, directly and indirectly by Theosophical ideas.

4.2.3.2. Anthroposophy

Rudolf Steiner

Seen by historians as an offshoot of Theosophy is the philosophy and organization founded by the Austrian philosopher and esotericist Rudolf Steiner (1861-1925) called Anthroposophy. Steiner was already an accomplished literary critic and philosopher when he joined the efforts of the Theosophical Society in 1899. He had previously been an editor at the archive of Goethe's works in Weimar and received a doctorate in philosophy in 1891. He was named head of the TS in Germany and Austria in 1904, but broke with them in 1912 over several differences, but primarily over the Society's promotion of J. Krishnamurti as a "new messiah."

Anthroposophy would appear to be a play on the word "Theosophy," but in fact both are older coinages. Steiner's "human-wisdom" showed itself to be more practically oriented than Theosophy was and found many applications in a variety of human concerns. But nevertheless, Steiner was a dedicated esotericist and clairvoyant. He described Anthroposophy as "a scientific exploration of the spiritual world." Steiner's ideas have been implemented in methods of human spiritual development, education, agriculture, medicine, finance and the arts. Steiner can clearly be seen as one of the major figures in the Reform Movements, but one who had his own school of thought which encompassed all aspects. As the Reform generation strengthened after the dawn of the new century, the Anthroposophical Society moved more and more into practical and "real life" applications to effect Reform in human life. Steiner's system outlined and encouraged the spiritual development of individuals (with certain spiritual exercises) and the undertakings of developed individuals did further cultivate projects and ideas that can be classified as firmly belonging to the fields of Reform activity. A general view of Anthroposophy, Steiner and the place of his philosophy in the context of the Reform Movements is provided by Schwarte (1998: 595-609).

In essence, Anthroposophy represents an effort to expand the scope of the scientific method into the realm of what is normally thought of as religion or spiritual experience. This involved the development of objectivity with regard to inner experiences though imagination, inspiration and intuition. A key factor in his philosophy was that of individual freedom from external authority in the development of an authentic human being. Steiner's view of the individual human being, his anthropology, if you will, was largely drawn from Theosophy, which in turn was derived from Indian philosophy.(7) In this he embraced concepts of various parts of the soul, reincarnation and the doctrine of *karma*.(8)

The applications of Anthroposophy to practical fields include agriculture, medicine, education, architecture, economics and social organization and performing arts. One of the most enduring influences of Steiner's philosophy is found in the educational work of the Waldorf School. This will come under closer discussion in Section 4.4.3. Steiner introduced the idea of "biodynamic agriculture," which can be seen as the foundation of what became "organic farming." Many physicians were themselves drawn to Anthroposophy and made contributions in their fields of specialty inspired by Steiner's ideas. Steiner was himself a contributor to the field of architecture — most famously he designed two structures, each known as the Goetheanum, in Dornach, Switzerland. These were the headquarters of the movement. The first was burned down by an act of arson in 1922, an act thought to have been perpetrated by the Nazis. Steiner is thought to have designed around thirteen buildings in an expressionistic-organic style. Several architects from around the world have been influenced by Steiner's teachings. Steiner's wife, Marie Steiner-von Sivers originated a method of speech formation called Creative Speech, and the Chekhov Method was founded by Michael Chekhov. To this can also be added the esoteric doctrine of rhythmic bodily motion known as Eurythmy, which combined the performance of dance, music and speech.

It is this orientation toward applied utilization of esoteric ideas for the betterment of the individual and society that sets Anthroposophy radically apart from Theosophy. Theosophy took a more passive approach to its theories, often condemning practical application as "black magic." Anthroposophical ideas have been applied to the world of finance, banking and business development. Much of this was rooted in Steiner's philosophy concerning social reforms. These ideas were given expression in a number of works written between 1915 and 1921 on the idea of *Dreigliederung* ("three-folding") of society. These were collected as *Aufsätze über die Dreigliederung des sozialen Organismus und zur Zeitlage 1915–1921*. This tripartite division of the social order was characterized by freedom in the cultural sphere of life, equality of rights under the law and economic fraternity. In this regard, Steiner must be seen as a principal exponent of Reform ideas.

In the area of personal Reform, Steiner also provided a system of guidance to the individual in the form of spiritual exercises and a practical philosophy toward individual development. Once again Steiner can be seen to be a paradigmatic exponent of the spirit of the Reform Movements. His approach was based on certain older traditions but the application of a pedagogical methodology marks his thought as belonging to the twentieth century.

Steiner's philosophy is more of an outgrowth of the ideas of Goethe than it is of Theosophy, and the level of support his ideas have received over the years reflects a high level of intellectual and artistic prestige. Supporters have included artists such as Saul Bellow, Selma Lagerlöf, Andrei Bely, Joseph Beuys, Andrei Tarkovsky and Wassily Kandinsky. Albert Schweitzer was a friend and supporter as well.

Remarkably, in the early twenty-first century it could be said that there were branches of the Anthroposophical Society in fifty countries and that there were as many as 10,000 institutions of various kinds around the world based on Anthroposophical principles. This makes the philosophy of

Steiner one of the most successful to have originated in the era of the Reform Movements.

4.2.3.3. Armanentum and Ariosophy

There is a long and continuous history of the attempts by individuals and organizations to reawaken the unique Germanic spirit, its myths and values, and the Reform period was a hotbed of this. The reason for the elevated interest in the revival of ancient indigenous patterns should be fairly obvious. The desire to go "back to nature" is clearly mirrored by the urge to discover national roots and a more organic, holistic, understanding of the meaning of the individual and the autochthonous communities of nationality, language and culture. Such trends are found to be common over the whole globe, but this movement in the German-speaking world has historically come under special scrutiny due to the role it played in the rise of National Socialism in Germany (1920-1945). The whole history of the reawakening of indigenous Germanic culture is traced in my series of works under the collective title *The Northern Dawn*. (9) The role this played in National Socialism is frequently discussed in my book *The Occult in National Socialism* (Inner Traditions, 2022).

The main driving force behind this movement in the German-speaking world in a mystical sense was the Austrian poet and writer Guido von List (1848-1919).(10) In popular culture the way had been prepared for List both by Wagner's Ring and the previously discussed Theosophy. List wrote novels, dramas and short stories rooted in the supposed Germanic past of his native Austria but he also did folkloristic and mytho-magical investigations of the landscape and legends of his homeland. A sizable collection of these was published in 1891 under the title *Deutsch-mythologische Landschaftsbilder*. He came under the pervasive spell of Theosophy by the early 1890s and developed his own mystical system of language and myth he called *Armanentum*.(11) List was generally an exponent of the alternative Reform ideology prevalent in Vienna in his day.

In 1904 List inaugurated a series of works which began with his exposition of the runes called *The Secret of the Runes* (*Das Geheimnis der Runen*). Although List's works were firmly in the sphere of the occult or mythic, they had their function in the political or social struggles of the Austro-Hungarian Empire of his day, promoting the primacy of ethnic Germans and the German language in the multi-ethnic and multi-lingual empire.

The foundations List laid with his work would affect a segment of German-language occultism and runic mysticism for generations to come. The Guido-von-List-Society would last into the period of the Third Reich, but went underground and became moribund until it would be revived in the late 1960s in Germany.

Ariosophy—"Aryan-wisdom"—coined by an ex-Cistercian monk named Jörg Lanz von Liebenfels (Adolf Lanz) was also heavily influenced by Theosophy and members of the order founded by Lanz, the Ordo Novi Templi (Order of the New Templars) were often also members of List's group—including Lanz himself. But the ONT hardly represented much in the way of Reform ideas.(12)

4.2.3.4. Mazdaznan

Otoman Zar-Adusht Ha'nish

At first glance this system might appear to be a neo-Zoroastrian religion. But in fact it has few essential philosophical points of contact with historical forms of orthodox Zoroastrianism. Mazdaznan [pron. MASS-dass-nan] is an eclectic synthesis of Zoroastrian ideas with Manichean, Christian and Hindu/tantric ideas. It was first created by a German immigrant to America named Otto Hanisch (1844 or 1856-1936) who used the religious moniker Otoman Zar-Adusht Ha'nish. Hanisch clearly owed far more to Reform ideas of diet, health and spiritual exercise than to Zoroastrianism. Hanisch, whose actual legal name was Erich Otto Haenisch himself claimed to have been born in Tehran in 1844, but he was actually born in Posen in 1856 to a Protestant family.

The system of Mazdaznan was synthesized from dietary theories, breathing exercises, meditation, physical exercises which included yoga-like postures. Mazdaznan also offered an alternative vision of the history of mankind and that of religion. as well as a whole alternative view of history and religion.

The curious name of the system is explained as *ma*, "good," *zda*, "thought" and *znan*, from *jasnan* meaning "masterful." Following this eccentric analysis, the whole word is supposed to mean "master of divine thought."

Few facts are known about the life of Hanisch. He himself created a variety of myths about himself. He first appeared on the public scene in Chicago sometime around 1890. He had contacts with his native Germany, and the system quickly spread to Europe. Around 1900 Hanisch organized a church called the Mazdaznan Temple Association of Associates of God in Chicago. In Germany this organization was led by a married couple named Frieda and David Ammann. They founded the lodges of the *Mazdaznan-Tempel-Vereinigung für Deutschland und die deutschsprechenden Länder* (Mazdaznan-Temple-Union for Germany and the German-speaking Countries) in a number of German cities. These later came to be called the Zarathustra-Bund. Hanisch himself visited Germany regularly up to 1932.

Many of the teachings of Mazdaznan were part and parcel of the ideology of the Reform Movements, with an emphasis on diet (e.g. what foods can or should be eaten with others), methods of cleansing the gastrointestinal tract, breathing exercises and the use of certain physical exercises for the purpose of gaining health and spiritual insight. These were called the "Egyptian postures." Mazdaznan appears to have been designed to be popular for the times with a combination of an exotic "eastern" pedigree, but one that did not stray too far from the conventional forms of religion with a focus on the body and its functional health, but with a promise of mastery over that body and the material universe through the powers of the mind.

Mazdaznan was frequently mentioned in journals dedicated to FKK. Many important members of the Reform Movements at one time or another declared their adherence to Mazdaznan. These included Adolf Just, Dr. Karl Strückmann, the illustrator Fidus and the gymnast and dancer Suzanne Perrottet (Wedemeyer-Kolwe 2004: 153). Johannes Itten, who was a proponent of the philosophy was also an important designer and teacher in the Bauhaus movement. A Swiss Anthroposophist, who was also connected to the Guido-von-List-Society named Karl Heiser became an active leader in Mazdaznan around 1900 and even ran a commune called Aryana near Zürich. It is also known that the ONT brother Detlef Schmude was also an associate of the group. In the German-speaking realm Mazdaznan expressed itself in a friendly manner toward National Socialism and its racial policies at the time. Despite this, however, the organization was banned by the Nazis in 1935, their literature eventually was also forbidden and in the end totally closed down in 1941. It remained banned in East Germany, but was revived in the West in 1959. Mazdaznan has had a lasting impact on the German sub-culture and continues to be active today in Germany, although it had largely been forgotten in America. Then as now it can count several thousand followers in Germany.

Advertisement for Mazdaznan

4.2.3.5. Other Religious Alternatives

Another view of the human mind or spirit, or lack of same, is embodied in the movement that is generally referred to as "free thought" or atheism and which gained new impetus in Europe at about the same time as Reform ideas were coming in vogue. The idea that there is no "personal god," i.e. a god (or gods) which exemplify or portray quasi-human characteristics has been on record since very ancient times. Ancient Indian philosophies such as Buddhism and Vedanta take this stance, although they continue to use the terms and psychologies of traditional thought.

The modern form of atheism was given its greatest impulse by French thinkers of the pre-Revolutionary period (e.g. Voltaire) and formed in the secular and anti-clerical ideology of the Revolution itself. In Germany, this heritage of positivistic free thought was exemplified by Ludwig Feuerbach, Paul de Lagarde and others who were critical of established theologies and to some degree identified with the school of "free thought" (*Freidenken*) and enshrined in the atheistic Communist philosophy of Karl Marx (1818-1883). The philosopher Ludwig Feuerbach (1804-1872) laid a foundation for much of this philosophy as it influenced the Reform Movements. He envisioned a "religion of humanity" and wrote a highly influential critique of Christianity in 1841 entitled *The Essence of Christianity*. This work affected other thinkers as diverse as Darwin, Marx, Engels, Freud, Wagner and Nietzsche. He was a student of Hegel in Berlin, and is seen by some to be the link between Hegel and Marx. Feuerbach was an advocate of atheism and materialism, but did so in an imaginative manner which ascribed a significant role to human creativity and to the power of the human mind.

Almost all of the ideas of the Reformers could be justified or explained within the framework of a logical, positivistic framework, but for the most part they were not. There seemed to be a persistent antagonism between Reformers and ideologues of both the "right" and "left." But at the same time, the dedication to the idea of the liberty of the individual human soul to determine for itself the best course of action clearly appears to owe a significant debt to the revolutionary impetus toward "free thought."

Already in the middle of the nineteenth century there developed in the German-speaking world a movement called the *Freireligiöse Bewegung* ("free-religious movement"). Humanists who wished to pursue a spiritual existence, but who were highly skeptical of previously organized confessional churches began to form independent communities from among (former) Catholics and Lutherans alike. Their focus ran from the mystical to the rationalistic. They might be pantheistic or even atheistic. By the time in which the Reform Movements were established in Germany these organizations were already well-developed themselves. By the twentieth century these groups generally supported such Reform ideas as the secularization of the state and the separation of the churches from the educational system. Members of the free-religious communities often crossed over into other organizations that ran the gamut from the Monist League to the Communist Party. In the time of the Weimar Republic several of these smaller groups attempted to form a "cartel." Because of their general emphasis on individual liberty as regards conscience, and so on, they were targeted for suppression by the National Socialists. Most were eventually dissolved, but some with "*völkisch*" leanings persisted.

As far as their teachings are concerned, free-religious groups tend to share certain characteristics: First, the idea of absolute individual freedom with regard to faith, without the imposition of external authority or dogmas. Also, there is a devotion to the idea of using reason as a deciding factor in all concerns. Finally, there is a dedication to the principle of tolerance with regard to the religious differences between individuals or groups. There is a freedom of religion and a freedom from religion as dictated by the conscience of the individual. Obviously, there is no fixed or established view of the nature of divinity.

Certainly one of the most important thinkers of the late nineteenth century, and one whose ideas burst forth in a popularized manner at the dawn of the twentieth century was the German philosopher Friedrich Nietzsche (1844-1900). His pronouncements of "God is dead!" and concepts such as the "over-man" (*G. Übermensch*), the eternal return (*ewige Wiederkehr*) and the Will to power (*Wille zur Macht*) shook the contemporary world and continued to do so for generations to come. Although he proclaimed a way of thinking "beyond good and evil," he nevertheless clearly had strong ideas about what was "good" and "bad." His was a revolution against the prevailing order in the name of a higher awareness—something that places him in the realm of a "world-savior."

Perhaps the most prominent figure in the history of German biological sciences in the late nineteenth century is the Jena professor Ernst Haeckel (1834-1919). Haeckel introduced the ideas of Darwin to German science, although his version of evolution was not an orthodox Darwinian one. He popularized his ideas through the Monist League (Ger. Monistenbund), which he founded in 1906. He also wrote books with a broad-based appeal, e.g. *Natürliche Schöpfungsgeschichte* [Natural History of Creation] (1868), *Anthropogenie* [Origin of Man] (1874) and culminating in his most important book *Welträtsel* [Riddle of the World] (1899).

Haeckel's ideas made significant contributions to the field of biology, zoology and the life-sciences generally. He is credited with coining the terms anthropogeny, ecology, phylum, phylogeny, and stem cell. In his own time he was thought of as a leading scientist, but subsequently many of his ideas have been frequently rejected (sometimes for "political" reasons, and for scientific ones as well). Haeckel's interest in the philosophical and political implications of his scientific work and the theory of evolution has relegated him to a grey zone between mainstream science and the occult realm of rejected knowledge.

Haeckel brought together three key concepts: 1) Romanticism, as a nationalistic *Naturphilosophie* with its developmental (proto-evolutionary) idea of both interconnectedness and of the existence of distinct natural kinds, 2) Materialism as a positivistic, empirical science opposed to idealism, and 3) Darwinism, wherein the idea of struggle is seen as the basis for the laws of human society. Far from being a pure scientist, Haeckel was also an activist.

Philosophically, Haeckel's Monism was allied with atheistic "free-thinking" (*Freidenken*) in Germany, and as such was not ideologically that distant from certain concepts of the Bolsheviks. The main distinguishing feature was that the Monists focused on biology while Marxists were obsessed with matters of economics and social class.

In the final analysis, the role of what is commonly called "religion" is both extremely important in the world of Reform in German-speaking cultures and one that runs the gamut between orthodox frameworks to pure secular humanism. Additionally, "religion" is both something that provides shape and direction to Reform and one that is more often the of radical Reform itself.

4.3. Politics

Modern European political parties and ideologies are very much akin to traditional churches in that they have definite ideologies and principles of organization and policies which they promote and attempt to enforce upon all members of that party.(13) As such secular politics and political ideologies are something foreign to the spirit of the Reform Movements. Reformers tend to be free-thinking individuals, and organizations of individuals who are bound together in the interests of specific aims or causes particular to Reform agendas. However, it can be seen that each of the fields of Reform touches on some aspect of what might be called "politics."

To a great extent, the Reformers were deeply apolitical. For them politics began to be left behind with the general failure of the revolutionary movements of 1848 in Germany. These political uprisings were largely aimed at the unification of the German-speaking states into one nation. The disillusionment caused by the failure of this would-be revolution sent many into various underground and often highly artistic and even mystical directions. These events can be seen as occurring at a time when, globally speaking, a sense of culture-wide artistic and cultural movements came to a final end. The grand epochal procession in the history of cultural ideas from the Renaissance and Reformation, to the Baroque Age, to the Enlightenment with the German interlude of *Sturm und Drang* in Germany, to the Neo-Classical Age to the Age of Romanticism came crashing down. What emerged is what we have now: A fragmented culture made up of an ever-increasing patchwork of specialized tastes and values. This process, begun in 1848, continues and has not yet run its course. The direct effects on and by politics upon the large culture cannot go unheeded.

It might be remarked that the general feeling of conservatism in society, represented by both those who called themselves "conservatives" as well as monarchists, might tend to be the very elements of society and culture which the Reformers targeted for "change." Conservatives tend to be complacent and self-satisfied sorts, determined to go along with the crowd. This trend can cut all sorts of ways and even the most radical fashions can quickly be overcome by conservative tendencies. The Reformers saw problems in society and wanted to fix them, but usually did not take "political" pathways to these solutions. When we examine the conservative philosophy, we are reminded that the conservative philosopher Arthur Moeller van den Bruck expressed it through the formula: "Conservatism is making things that are worth keeping." Conservatism literally means holding on to, *conserving*, things—ideas, institutions, ways of life.

The apex of conservatism in Germany could be identified with the monarchy and the monarchists who supported it. After the Kaiser abdicated at the end of WWI in 1918, a third of the people still longed for a return of the monarchy. Certainly, some of them supported Reform ideas.

We can mark the beginnings of organized political socialism in Germany with the publication of the *Communist Manifesto* in 1848. The General German Worker's Association was founded in 1863, and shortly thereafter the political party called the Social Democratic Workers' party came into being in 1869. These two groups merged in 1875 as the Socialist Workers' Party of Germany (*Sozialistische Arbeiterpartei Deutschlands*)—the SPD. Socialist parties in general were officially banned in Germany between 1878 and 1890. When the ban was lifted in 1890 the SPD became the largest Marxist political party in Europe and generally gained the greatest number of votes in general elections over the years.

The SPD remained radical in theory, but in practice more moderate. In general the SPD embraced the concept of reform, striving to transform the German society by means of incremental democratic and economic reforms. During WWI the SPD supported the war effort, while a more radical wing of the party was anti-war and split off forming the USPD (Independent Social Democratic Party of Germany). This wing soon evolved into the Communist Party of Germany (KPD).

Marxist Communism, and its tactically lighter form "socialism," attempted to address the ills of society in terms often similar to those that moved the Reformers. Their targets were often the same: industrial exploitation and conservative cultural devotion to the status quo, etc. But when we compare the "political" aims and most especially the underlying understanding of the world exemplified by the Marxists and the Reformers a great and insurmountable gulf at once appears. Marxists were adherents to an entirely materialistic philosophy and saw the solutions to human problems entirely within the parameters of a political and socio-economic model. For Reformers, many of whom might have tended somewhat toward the Left in mundane partisan politics, the Marxist/Socialist solutions to problems were too superficial and far too hostile to individual liberty to be very attractive to the most often idiosyncratic and eccentric tastes of the average Reformer.

As an adjunct to Socialism in Germany the Anarchistic movement began in earnest after about 1870 and continued to grow through the years. Anarchism in Germany was not as violent as those movements in eastern Europe. The anarchistic answer to political questions was one similar to that the free-religious philosophy had toward religion, the power was to be made diffuse, and not held in the hands of one or restricted to a few. The principle of individual liberty reigned supreme, in theory at least. The kinder, gentler approach to Anarchy in Germany is reflected by the bumper sticker slogan widely seen in the 1980s: *Anarchie ist machbar, Herr Nachbar!*—"Anarchy is feasible, Neighbor." These were usually seen in close proximity to ones that read: *Atomkraft, Nein, Danke*—"Atomic Power, no thanks."

Finally, as regards the realm of politics, we have the National

Socialists. The stance of this organization in relation to the complexities of the Reform Movements is outlined in greater detail in section 6, "Sons of the Swastika." From a political perspective, however, it should be noted that the Nazis designed their system to appeal to some degree or another with all phases of German culture and society as a method of gaining power and consolidating that power in the hands of the Party elite. Clearly, the Nazis brought an end to much of the Reform Movement, but as section 6 shows, much of it was also incorporated into the program of the Party. This is mostly attributable to generational aspects—that the Party leaders were themselves products of the times so influenced on so many levels by Reform ideology.

In most ways the world of partisan politics and governmental power structures represented worlds that Reform-minded individuals wished to distance themselves from. Such political and socio-economic structures were seen as the sources of cultural corruption and the Reform Movements tended to try to offer alternatives to them, rather than engage them or try to gain influence within them. Much of this attitude had its origins in the mid-nineteenth century. Partisan socio-economic answers to profound cultural issues were simply seen as too superficial to be effective in the long run.

4.4. Education

One of the most important foundations of the whole Reform impulse in Central Europe in the late nineteenth century can be seen to have been the groundwork laid by earlier reforms in education undertaken in Germany from the late eighteenth century forward. New ideas about the methods used to educate people, or pedagogy, were progressively implemented on a broad scale and quickly had their ramifications throughout society.

The modern, industrialized and urbanized society of late nineteenth and early twentieth century in Central Europe required an ever more educated populace in order for the economy to work properly and the citizens to be able to be gainfully and happily employed. This necessitated a new and more comprehensive system and philosophy of education. A general overview of the topic is given by Diethart Kerbs (1998: 315-317).

Pedagogical reform took place slowly in Germany, as the educational system was, as might be expected, firmly ensconced in conservative traditions which had served the culture well. In pre-WWI Germany, the Gymnasium (university preparatory school) required nine years of Latin (Greek and French were also required), some lectures were still delivered *in Latin* at the university! Then, as now, the educational system did not take a "one size fits all" approach and the practical education in the trades was incorporated into apprenticeship programs.

Generally, the concept of Reform-Pedagogy is connected to the concept of viewing the educational process from the standpoint of the child or pupil. Rather than seeing education as an "indoctrination" or programming of the student from above, the pupil's motivations, aims and desires are taken into account. In many ways, the movement seems to have been an advanced step toward separating education from an entirely church-based perspective. Several thinkers had given some consideration to these ideas in various countries over the years, among them the Moravian Johann Amos Comenius (1592-1670), the French writer Jean-Jacques Rousseau (1712-1778) and the German-speaking Swiss Johann Heinrich Pestalozzi

(1746-1827). Pestalozzi is widely considered as the father of modern educational science. Theories for new ways of teaching were being widely developed in the nineteenth century, but began to be put into broader practice in the time-period of the Reform-Movements in Germany. But it must be said that Rousseau's 1762 work *Émile, ou de l'education* (Emile, or On Education) remained the perinnial touchstone for the reform impulse in education.

Other important German teachers who paved the way for widespread Reform included Johan Bernhard Basedow (1724-1790), Christian Gotthilf Salzmann (1744-1811) and Fridrich Fröbel (1782-1852). Basedow opened his Philanthropinum in Dessau in 1774 dedicated to his new ideas on education of the children of noblemen. On the other hand, Salzmann founded his Schnepfental school directly based on the ideas of Rousseau. His work *Elements of Morality, for the Use of Children* was translated into English by Mary Wollstonecraft. Fröbel, whom I will discuss below in regard to the institution known as the Kindergarten, firmly believed that the individual student should not be indoctrinated, but rather encouraged through play and self-expression to develop intellectually and morally.

Another figure of considerable importance in the development of new forms of education in Germany was Johann Friedrich Herbart, who was a true post-Kantian philosopher in his own right who lectured first at Göttingen and thereupon inherited the chair of Kant himself in Königsberg. His methods and philosophy of education were linked to his larger philosophical system. These methods can be summed up in five steps: "Using this structure a teacher prepared a topic of interest to the children, presented that topic, and questioned them inductively, so that they reached new knowledge based on what they had already known, looked back, and deductively summed up the lesson's achievements, then related them to moral precepts for daily living."(Miller 2003, 114)

Practices generally associated with school-life such as rote drills, memorization of facts coupled with vigorous practice of corporal punishment for misconduct and poor performance were all called into serious question and rejected by most reformers.

Etymologically the word "education" is a borrowing from Latin *educare* (*ex-ducare*) from which the German *erziehen* and *Erziehung* are loan-translations. These words literally refer to a drawing or conducting outward of something that is already latent within the student and seems to refer to an almost Platonic idea about knowledge itself. The question then becomes one of for whose sake or in whose service is this educational process undertaken? Plato might have seen it in the service of the individual soul so that it might come to know its own individual truth and reality, but in the Middle Ages the Christian Church turned its purpose to the interests of the Church itself and the "spread of the Gospel." The purpose of education went from an individual one to a corporate or collective one. The Romantics and early Reformers seem to have had in mind to return education to its original purpose, but as history has shown there seems to be a tendency to pull it back into service of corporate interests—of industry, church, political parties, etc.—rather than individual development. Here, as everywhere, Reform concerns have to be guarded with knowledge of history and philosophical outlook.

The field of education continued to be an ideological battleground, which it had been since the Middle Ages.

Religious forces, capitalistic business interests and Marxist ideologues all openly vied for dominance. However, the ideas of Reform were largely oriented in directions different from these modern interest groups. Because Reform was a generally fluid and flexible concept, it could only thrive in institutions of its own creation, e.g. the Waldorf Schools, whereas government-controlled education in general drifted in a more Marxian direction over the years.

4.4.1. Reform-Pedagogy

Although reforms had been undertaken in education, and many philosophical new approaches developed for many decades in Germany, the actual term *Reformpädagogik* was not used until 1818 by Ernst Krieck and then more fully developed by Herman Nohl in his book entitled *Die pädagogische Bewegung in Deutschland und ihre Theorie* (The Pedagogical Movement in Germany and its Theory [1933]).

Reform Pedagogy understood in the most specific sense opposed not only the overly rigid methods of the so-called classical curriculum focused on drills and recitations but also the system begun by Herbart, which was seen as too elitist and unstructured. After WWII Reform Pedagogy has generally been called Alternative Pedagogy (in English these theores have become known as Progressive Education and in France *Éducation Nouvelle*).

Obviously, one of the most lasting pieces of legacy from the German educational reform movement is the institution known even today by the German term Kindergarten. The term and much of the concept was the product of the German reformer Friedrich Fröbel (1782–1852). The idea of communal care and rudimentary education for children of the age of two and above for families in which both parents worked in industry was first instituted in Bavaria and elsewhere in the late 18th century. But in 1837 Fröbel opened the first such formal institution with pedagogical aims and coined the term "Kindergarten" because he believed that children should be nurtured and cultivated "like plants in a garden." Typically, children were engaged in a variety of learning activities: play, singing, music, socialization with other children. By the Reform Era the Kindergarten movement was widespread throughout Germany.

Systems of reform pedagogy generally share a number of common features or ideas. These include emphasis on collaborative learning projects, practical or experiential projects, focus on problem solving activities, segmenting work in thematic units and goals and were often set in the form of understanding and activity rather than factual or rote knowledge. A major goal of the teachers was to be the instilling of a motivation toward a sense of lifelong learning. Beyond these aims, however, the Reformers usually also had a certain social or even "political" dimension to their ideas. These could vary from school to school, but included the development of certain social skills through group-work and teaching of social responsibility. In Germany before 1918 there continued to be the social and political distinction between the nobility and the common citizens, and this was implicitly criticized by Reform-Pedagogy.

In England Cecil Reddie (1858-1932) founded the Abbotsholm School in Derebyshire in 1889 largely inspired by what he had learned about educational reform in Göttingen in his doctoral studies (1882-1883). Reddie's school then participated in cultural cross-fertilization as teachers from other countries, especially Germany, trained at his school and then returned to their homelands to establish similar ones. Reddie's ideas were influential in Japan as the Taisho-era Free Education Movement.

Educational reforms came into a harmonious relationship with the greater and more widespread ideology of Reform after about 1890. In conjunction with the Youth Movement and Reform ideas, mankind's problems were seen as ones stemming from the damage caused by "civilization." One of the key events that causes us to focus on the year 1890 is the publication of the book *Rembrandt als Erzieher* (Rembrandt as Educator) by Julius Langbehn. The values of beauty, naturalness and outer veracity came to the forefront in a whole subculture. There were certain organized efforts to institute Reform ideas into the educational system, e.g. the *Bund für Schulreform* (School-Reform Group) founded in 1908 which later unified with the *Allgemeiner deutscher Verband für Erziehungs- und Unterrichtswesen* (The General German Alliance for Matters of Education and Instruction). In 1915 a number of related groups unified under the name *Deutscher Aussschuss für Erziehung und Unterricht* (German Board for Education and Instruction). These groups were generally made up of educators and instructors at various levels seeking to improve education. But it should be seen that such efforts were often an uphill battle against the entrenched state-controlled and church-dominated systems which were the official mode of educational organization at the time.

Also as a part of the general Reform and Youth Movements, women began to be able to enroll in universities. These reforms took place between 1900 (in Baden) and 1909 (in Mecklenburg). By 1909 the universities were at least officially co-educational.

Major ideas for reform of education included schools for professional development in the trades on a wider scale, establishment of schools in rural settings, the teaching of tolerance and communal education and the inclusion of more art in the curriculum.

With the fall of the old regime after the end of WWI and the inception of the Weimar Republic Germany entered a period of dynamic flux and Reform ideas of all sorts, including those in education, gained a wider field of activity. There was room for experimentation but also for political jockeying. An important official direction was formulated in the constitution of the Weimar Republic which basically stated that the talent and disposition of students and not their social heritage should be decisive as regards their opportunities for education.

Reform Pedagogy was something which could be an exponent of all kinds of political orientations. These ran the gamut from socialist to liberal to the nationalist direction (here elements of Anti-Semitism and eugenics were present). However, in its best forms the movement was relatively free of political influences.

4.4.2. Waldorf-Pedagogy

In section 4.2.3.2 we encountered the esoteric teachings of Rudolf Steiner and his Anthroposophical Society. Steiner's ideas, as radical as they might have been, had ramifications well beyond the usual sphere of such occult thinking. Among the lasting legacies of this movement has been a reform of how humans are educated in the form of what became the Waldorf Schools. These schools aim for a holistic approach to education in which the intellect, creativity and practical aspects are integrated. For a general overview of the Waldorf Schools in the Reform Movement see Heiner's article (1998: 411-424).

The first actual Waldorf School was established in Stuttgart in 1919. It was funded by the Waldorf-Astoria Cigarette Company, hence the name of the whole system of Steiner education. It was first set up as an alternative mode of educating the children of the employees of this company. The school served the educational needs of others outside the factory as a coeducational school for pupils from all social classes. Waldorf schools are affected by Steiner's Anthroposophy in that things such as reincarnation, karma and eurhythmy are usually incorporated. In general, the role of Anthroposophical ideology in day-to-day instruction is not mandated and is a matter of the individual teacher's judgment.

The Steiner system recognizes and utilizes three stages of development in the student: early childhood (pre-school), elementary level (between 7 and 14) and secondary level. It is noteworthy that based on original principles, the use of electronic media is generally discouraged as far as the educational process is concerned. This is due to the idea that such media encourage a certain *passivity* in the student.

Essential to Steiner's theory of education is his conception of the nature and make-up of the pupil—or all human beings. The human is essentially a tripartite entity consisting of an intellectual-cognitive, artistic-creative and crafting-practical parts, or thinking, feeling and volitive functions. Steiner wished to integrate all of these aspects into a holistic model of education.

Formal education begins a bit later than in many systems, at around seven years of age and emphasizes the pupil's development of imagination and emotional experience. Academic material is presented in the context of visual arts, story-telling, drama, music and crafts. The Waldorf system tries to avoid the use of standardized "text books."

There are certain aspects of the way in which instruction is carried out that borders on a ritualistic method by which introductory activities such as singing, music and poetic recitations precede the presentation of the core lesson in academic subjects. These main lessons last about two hours.

One of the main tasks of an educator at the elementary level is to model a love of learning and nurturing curiosity, imagination and creativity in the children. Underlying it all is the intended purpose of instilling in the children the idea that the world is a beautiful place.

A pedagogical aim of the Waldorf system is to allow for the individualization of the pace of learning in the belief that children will first understand and then activate skills and concepts when they are ready to do so.

An interesting social aspect of early schooling in the Waldorf system is that a group of children is kept together throughout the early years as a cohesive unit so that they develop deep relationships with one another, which can last a lifetime. Also, this class of pupils generally has only one core teacher for all subjects, and this teacher follows the group of pupils for a period of a number of years. Originally this was for the whole eight years of elementary education. Specialized teachers were often brought in for certain subjects, such as music or foreign languages. Typically, two modern foreign languages were taught, typically English and French.

Usually at about fourteen years of age the pupil enters the secondary level of education with more focused academic subjects taught by specialized teachers. By the completion of this the pupils were well-prepared for entry into the life of the university. With all of this, however, activities such as art, music and crafts are not left behind. Emphasis is placed on the development of critical intellectual thinking coupled with independent judgment and moral awareness.

A major emphasis of the purpose of secondary education is to teach a sense that the world is in fact a *true* place, a real place in which we live. This particular aspect was probably originally in place as a counter to the growing influence of "Eastern" religions (Hinduism and Buddhism) which taught that the world was "illusionary." Here we see a feature that is part of the distinction in Steiner's mind between his Anthroposophy and Theosophy, with its more Eastern beliefs.

Because of Steiner's philosophy involving the spiritual nature of the individual and of education being seen as the unfolding of the individual spiritual identity of the student, the Waldorf approach has been held in contempt by rabid secularists and materialists. The stability of the underlying traditions of Steiner education also make it resistant to those passing fads and "latest trends" so often promoted by state-sponsored educators which are aimed at "transforming" students according to certain ideological, political and socio-economic theories.

With the National Socialist assumption of political power in Germany following 1933 the Waldorf schools were generally suppressed. They mostly reopened after the end of WWII, but remained closed in East Germany, for obvious reasons, and for the same reasons that they were shut down by the National

Socialists. Steiner's philosophy is an anathema to collectivist and authoritarian regimes. The purpose of a Waldorf education is to produce individual pupils with independent and creative thoughts.

Presently the Waldorf Schools represent the largest independent system of schools in the world. They are found in at least 75 countries and constitute 1200 schools and 2000 kindergartens. Additionally, there are some 500 centers devoted to special education. The Waldorf approach is also frequently applied in the curricula of homeschooling.

It should be noted that although the theories behind the Waldorf schools and their methods are rooted in the esoteric concepts of Rudolf Steiner these ideas are not explicitly taught there and students typically have no awareness of this background.

4.4.3. *Volkshochschulen*

Another alternative form of education that has become extremely important and widespread in Germany is one that actually originated in Denmark under the leadership of N. F. S. Grundtvig (1783–1872), who was a writer, poet, philosopher and Lutheran pastor by profession. The first *Folkehøjskole* inspired by his work was opened in Denmark in 1844. The way was prepared in Germany by the extension programs of German universities whereby professors gave public lectures as well as the educational programs of the *Arbeiter- und Handwerker-Bildungsvereine* (Educational Associations of Workers and Craftsmen). A German prototype of the folk universities was provided by the Humboldt-Academy in Berlin (1879).

The Volkshochschule-Movement in Germany really only came into full development immediately after the end of World War I. The tremendous amount of well-educated teachers and academics in Germany certainly made for a significant supply of instructors for the folk universities. These were intended as instruments for both individual personal growth and education and for practical instruction in vocationally oriented classes. Each locality of the folk universities was rather autonomous in how it was run and what the variety of classes would be. Courses were often oriented toward providing formal presentations of the kind of information that one would otherwise only have available through the regular universities. Courses in culture, history, languages as well as practical and work-oriented curricula were well-represented. There were typically no "entrance exams," or end of term exams or grades given. Information and knowledge were pursued based on the interests of the students.

The impact of Reform-Pedagogy in Germany had widespread influence on every aspect of German culture. This formed a network of international stimulus felt in all industrialized nations from Germany to Scandinavia, Britain and America. These educational reforms were especially powerful as they were supported by various organized and established institutions such as private and government schools and the underlying philosophy behind Reform-Pedagogy has certainly been felt historically. The technical teaching methods inspired by this movement have proven effective, but also volatile because they can easily be perverted from serving the interests of the individual student and put back in the service of corporate (state, church, party) interests.

4.5. Health and Nutrition

The part of the Reform Movements that perhaps touches more people than any other is the one devoted to the health and diet of individual human beings. Dietary concerns can be understood in isolation, but for most of the Reformers questions of diet reached out into a much wider scope of understanding. They touched on matters of health, animal rights, abstinence from alcohol, economic questions, matters of land reforms (regarding farms where the crops were produced) and even religion (e.g. in Mazdaznan). The practice of a diet inspired by Reform ideas is the first line of contact between these ideas and the actual lives of most people. It is also the part of the movement that was most rapidly exported to other countries (see §7). However, dietary concerns were really an extension of the even more basic philosophical question of health: the maintenance of good health and the desire to be liberated from disorders, disease and sickness. The natural healing movement is reviewed by Wolfgang Krabbe (1998: 77-86).

It is said that the basis of the early movement toward natural healing methods was first and most directly laid out by the French philosopher Jean-Jacques Rousseau in his work *Émile ou De l'education* wherein he writes "Everything is good as it comes from the hands of the Maker of the world, but degenerates once it gets into the hands of man." Of course, the roots of natural healing practices go back much further than that, having their origins in indigenous folk-medicine which remained a perinnial interest among Reform-minded healers.

An important root of alternative concepts of what constitutes a healthy human body was offered by the Scottish physician

John Brown (1736-1768) who put forward a theory of vitalism that was influential on the Natural Philosophers of Germany during the Romantic Movement. His theories are referred to as *Brownianismus* in German, but have been virtually forgotten in the English-speaking world. This posited that the human physiology is ideally a balance between two polar extremes of excitability (*Erregbarkeit*), one low and the other high. Either extreme causes illness.

Because in one way or another the Reform movements proposed holistic methods to address problems, the whole issue of health of the human body is tied into many other fields of practice, from food, to medicine, to activity—everything the body took into itself and all of its activity in its environment were parts of the puzzle of health.

4.5.1. Early Practitioners

In the German-speaking realm of Europe there were a number of practitioners who tried to forge new pathways in human health and well-being. These earlier health practitioners established the basis for the more widespread popularity of such ideas in the years of the Reform Movements in general. Most of them were enthusiasts for hydrotherapies, naturopathy and advocated for the most part a vegetarian diet. Among the earliest of these was Theodor Hahn (1824-1883). He had been influenced by practices of his cousin J. H. Rausse. Hahn was perhaps the first to use the German term *Naturheilkunde* ("natural therapy") for what it was he was trying to do. He, like many other such practitioners typically worked out of spas or health resorts, many of which had long traditions of using "healing waters." Ancient writers on health, including Hippocrates himself (ca. 400 BCE), wrote about the healing properties of water. Hahn operated out of facilities in Switzerland near Zürich and St. Gall. In the 1850s he expanded his practice from the water cure to dietary regulation (macrobiotics, vegetarianism, whole grain breads, etc.). He rejected the consumption of alcohol, coffee, meat and spices. Hahn's form of vegetarianism influenced the artist, Richard Wagner. Hahn wrote several influential books including *Die naturgemässe Diät* (The Natural Diet) in 1859 and *Das Paradies der Gesundheit, das verlorene und das wiedergefundene* (The Paradise of Health, the Lost One, and the One Regained) in 1865.

Another early naturopath was Louis Kuhne (1835-1901) who combined strict vegetarianism (with abstinence from salt and sugar) and a peculiar method of hydrotherapy known as the "friction sitz-bath." This latter method consisted of having the patient sit in a pan of cold water accompanied by vigorous rubbing of the lower abdomen, buttocks and genitals with a rough linen cloth. This "nerve stimulation" was supposed to release toxins from the body. The true function of this treatment remains unclear. Kuhne also used techniques to avoid constipation. The theoretical explanation for these treatments was that the body was being attacked by various toxins leading to the degeneration of the internal organs of the individual, so these toxins had to be eliminated. In this way, a wide variety of apparent diseases could be treated.

Beliefs and practices surrounding Reform concepts of health care were organized in the late nineteenth century. The *Deutsche Verein für Naturheilkunde und für volksverständliche Gesundheitspflege* (German Association for Natural Healing and for Commonly Intelligible Hygiene) was founded in 1883 and in 1900 renamed the *Deutscher Bund der Vereine für naturgemäße Lebens- und Heilweise* (German League of Associations for Natural Ways of Living and Healing) . This was an umbrella organization that unified many different local organizations with similar ideas. By the eve of the First World War there were some 885 local organizations comprising about 150,000 members. They published a journal called *Der Naturartzt*. ("The Natural Physician").

Adolf Just

Adolf Just (1859-1936) was a very influential naturopath during the zenith of the Reform Movements. He is perhaps most famous for his motto "Return to Nature," which both summed up the spirit of Reform and was a philosophy of health on all levels. He founded the health resort or sanatorium called *Jungborn* ("Fountain of Youth") in 1895. The next year he published the work for which he is best known: *Kehrt zur Natur zurück!* ("Turn back to Nature"). This was translated into English by fellow naturopath Benedict Lust in 1903 with the title: *Return to Nature!*

This philosophy was exercised by consuming natural foods, drinking clean water, breathing fresh air and, most peculiarly, the use of certain earthen clays. An active life style in a natural environment was the key to the philosophy of "back to nature."

Just tried to meld some sort of Christianized concepts into his ideology, considering that humanity can regain salvation by recovering the original natural relationship with the Creator and by living in harmony with the original creation. He felt that by studying and observing the lives of animals, creatures which had not been affected by the Fall of Man, a way could be found back to primordial salvation or purity. Being in harmony with nature was for him tantamount to restoring Man to the Adamite condition of being in harmony with God.

As is the case with many naturopaths, Just rejected the use of pharmaceutical drugs, but he also extended this attitude toward homeopathy and even the practice of artificial physical exercise, such as gymnastics, all of which he regarded as unnatural. In principle, he rejected everything he saw as not in harmony with nature, such as automobiles, modern houses, the use of chemicals in agriculture. As with many other Reformers, he opposed the use of animals in research (vivisection) and the use of vaccines, which he saw as a mode of poisoning the population.

Just's ideas were popularized though his many written works. Besides *Return to Nature!*, he wrote extensively on the use of earthen clays in healing and many of these works were also translated into English. The company Just founded to market the healing earth products, *Heilerde-Gesellschaft Luvos Just* ("The Healing Earth Society Luvos Just), is still a thriving one. The product is used both internally (in capsule and powder forms) and externally as compresses, packs and baths. This substance is purified loess which is principally made up of montmorillonite. (14)

As a business, Luvos was founded in 1918 in Blankenburg Luvos was established by alternative medicine practitioner Adolf Just in Blankenburg in 1918. Previously, in 1895, Just had founded the *Jungborn*. This was his center for alternative healing in the Harz Mountains. His most famous patient at Jungborn was the great writer Franz Kafka. Because the Jungborn was located in an area that became part of East Germany after

WWII, all of Just's establishments were moved to Friedrichsdorf in the Taunus region. Luvos clay products are unique in being recognized by the pharmaceutical establishment in Germany as having therapeutic legitimacy in the treatment of diarrhea, heartburn and stomach pain related to acidic reflux.(15)

Arnold Ehret

Another highly influential practitioner of Reform health concepts was Arnold Ehret (1866-1922). His name is associated with ideas that have come to be called Ehretism. His philosophy of diet and health was popular in his lifetime, and continues to exert significant influence in the alternative health movement.

Ehret arrived at his theories as a result of his struggles with his own health condition. He was released from military service in 1887 due to a diagnosis of a chronic cardiac condition. A number of specialists working on his case came to the conclusion that his problem was rooted in an inflammation of the kidneys. Through experimentation on himself Ehret concluded that health and vitality could be restored through a combination of fasting, elimination of mucilage and a diet based mainly on fresh fruit and fruit juices. In 1899, he became formally introduced to the ideology of the Reform Movement at Oranienburg and allied himself with the "vitalists." Ehret began publishing his ideas in 1909 and became widely famed for his ability to fast for long periods, supposedly going 49 days without eating solid foods.

Before the First World War had started Ehret had traveled to California and made connections with the botanist and horticulturalist Luther Burbank and another German Reformer, Benedict Lust. Circumstances surrounding the war made it difficult for Ehret to return to Germany, so he settled down in the vicinity of Los Angeles.

At its most basic level Ehret's philosophy saw the human body as an oxygenation machine, that really needed only oxygen to function optimally. In order to arrive at this state, one needed to avoid all intake of mucus-creating foods (e.g. meat, milk, potatoes, rice). The diet ideally consisted of fruits, fruit juices (glucose), nuts and vegetables as free as possible of starch. After 1911 Ehret began to publish works in German, which were translated into English.

Eventually Ehret became more influential and better known in the USA than he was in Germany. His teachings became especially popular in California and became part of the complex of ideas and practices which gave rise to the New Age and Hippie movements in America.

Ehret's ideas bordered on what became known as "Breatharianism"—the belief that a person can live from air and sunlight alone. This concept is rooted most often in Indian beliefs surrounding the power of *prana*.

Ehret died in the USA in Los Angeles when he fell outside a hotel where he had just given a lecture on "Health Thru Fasting." The fall resulted in a fractured skull and he died as a result.

In more recent times, a notable enthusiast for Ehretism was Apple co-founder Steve Jobs, who for years lived on nothing but fruit and juices.

4.5.2. Diet Reform and Vegetarianism

One area of life in which Reform ideas have become well-known throughout the Western world is in the field of diet and nutrition. Typically, Reform-minded individuals and thinkers promoted vegetarianism (to some extent based on the animal rights aspect of the movement) and the consumption of raw or "unprocessed" foods. In America, this all became known as a "health food" movement. It went from small stores in modest sized buildings to mega corporations. In Austin, Texas I could still (at least for the moment before it is torn down to make way for more condos to house Californicators) show you the building that first housed a Hippie grocery store called "Whole Foods."

Dietary Reform

From the standpoint of general health, the prevention of health problems is far more preferable to the necessity of healing the body once it is sick. The Reformers were great enthusiasts for all things which fostered what they considered to be good healthy life-habits. One of the main elements in this regard was the reform of the diet of the typical modern person. Dietary reforms were to a great extent inspired by the importation of new ideas from the East, which were seen in section 4.2 with the introduction of ideas from Hinduism and Buddhism.

A part of the reasoning behind the embrace of natural foods and vegetarianism was connected with a general skepticism and distaste toward the industrialization of food processing and the increasing role of capitalistic interests in manufacturing processed foods. This often involved increased use of sugar, preservatives and artificial ingredients. Very often the Reformers of diet were physicians who saw these changes as being connected to the increase in certain disease processes, e.g. cancer.

The German pharmacist and naturopath Theodor Hahn (1824–1883) was an early proponent of these ideas and his many books, among them *Die naturgemäße Diät* [The Natural Diet] (1857) and *Praktische Handbuch der naturgemäßen Heilweise* [Practical Handbook of Natural Healing Methods] (1866), became very influential. He was a proponent of what had come to be called "macrobiotics."(16) He emphasized whole grain products, diary, raw vegetables and raw fruit. Over the years, the product commonly referred to as *Vollkornbrot* ("whole-grain-bread"), a black bread containing minimally ground grains, became a staple of the movement.

The Swiss physician and dietician Maximilian Bircher-Benner was a highly influential practitioner in the Reform movement. He is best known today as the inventor of the cereal known as *müsli*. His thought was quite radical, as he developed a theory of nutrition characterized as *Sonnenlichtnahrung*—sunlight nutrition whereby foods were evaluated according to their "light-value." This is highly reminiscent of the esoteric theories of the ancient founder of Manicheanism—Mani (216-276). In my book *The Mazdan Way* (2017: 44) I wrote:

> Basically, Mani taught that the spiritual light was trapped in matter and that for the Manicheans the purpose of human life was "to strive actively to liberate particles of light through their rituals and practices." (Foltz 2004: 107) One of the main ways imprisoned light was liberated in the world was by the consumption of raw, uncooked food in a ritual setting with the subsequent singing of hymns designed to send the light liberated from their veggies soaring heavenward on the wings of song.

I point this out to demonstrate first how ancient such ideas are, and just how connected to ancient esoteric ideas Reform concepts often were.

Vegetarianism

Vegetarianism in the modern world was perhaps first pioneered in the Anglo-American cultural spheres as early as the 18th century. At first this usually came in conjunction with ascetic Christian sects that saw the eating of meat as "unnatural." Vegetarian societies were formed in England as early as 1801. Most were ovo-lacto vegetarians, as the milk and eggs were given freely by the animals. Famous English proponents of vegetarianism were Percy Shelley and George Bernard Shaw.

In Germany, vegetarianism began to grow at the beginning of the nineteenth century under the influence of the vitalist physician and student of Franz Mesmer's ideas named Christoph Wilhelm Hufeland (1762-1836). His 1805 book *Makrobiotik* ("Macrobiotics") was highly influential. In the 1860s vegetarianism began to be organized in central Europe. In 1867 Eduard Baltzer founded the *Verein für naturgemäße Lebensweise* and Gustav Struve's 1869 book *Pflanzenkost. Die Grundlage einer neuen Weltanschauung* ("Plant-based Food: The Basis of a New Philosophy") became a seminal text. In 1850 Theodor Hahn read Rousseau's (1762) book *Émile ou De l'education* where the Greek philosopher Plutarch is quoted as saying that meat-eating is unnatural and the cause of sickness. In this regard, Plutarch was referring to the supposed teachings of Pythagoras. It was from this point forward that vegetarianism became a basic part of the practice of natural healing practices in Germany. Books on the subject proliferated in Germany throughout the latter half of the nineteenth century. By the time of the inception of the major phase of the Reform Movements in Central Europe, the population had long since been prepared to accept the idea of vegetarianism as a method of improving human health and well-being. Additionally, the practice of avoiding the slaughter of animals was seen as a part of the new increasingly animal-friendly philosophy so important to many.

In 1892, various vegetarian organizations unified into the German Vegetarian League in Leipzig. The next year the Eden community was founded near Berlin, discussed in section 4.6. Various Reform-oriented groups and communities heavily supported the practice and concept of vegetarianism. There were three theoretical branches of the vegetarian movement which worked in a symbiotic way. One was primarily motivated by the avoidance of meat from the standpoint of human health. Another approached the practice from a social/economic critique of civilization. These were often utopians or socialists. Finally, a great number of people were mainly motivated by the avoidance of cruelty to animals on an ethical basis and this was seen as a pathway to the ennobling of humanity.

Richard Wagner for a long time had supported and promoted the idea of turning away from the eating of meat, as well as from using animals in scientific and medical research and experimentation. But it was only in the last few years of his life that he became a practicing vegetarian. This general attitude often found a great number of supporters in Anti-Semitic and Nationalistic circles. However, even more often the cause of vegetarianism found adherents among Left-oriented persons politically. In the USA, this was sometimes seen in conjunction with the cause of the abolition of slavery, feminism and women's suffrage.

In the early twentieth century the vegetarian movement became stronger and more widespread. However, there was a marked decline in interest during the time of the Weimar Republic, as most people were suffering from food-insecurities. The whole world of organized vegetarianism in Germany collapsed in 1935 under the Nazis in the face of a planned absorption of the movement by the National Socialist Party.

4.5.3. Anti-Alcohol

Some find it rather odd that the German Reform Movements would generally be characterized as being opposed to the ingestion of mind-altering substances, and especially alcohol, when the movement in the West that in many ways followed in the footsteps of the Reformers in the 1960s seemed so devoted to these substances. The answer to the apparent contradiction is certainly cultural and historical.

A general overview of the topic of the anti-alcohol aspects of the Reform Movements is provided by Judith Baumgartner (1998: 141-154).

The brewing and distilling of alcohol for purposes of altering human consciousness had been around since the Stone Age. Up until the beginning of the eighteenth century no one seemed to object to these practices.(17) The origin of opposition to the ingestion of alcohol stems from "temperance" movements among the practitioners of various Protestant sects and was primarily energized by women. The anti-alcohol movement was especially pronounced in the USA, but also in Scandinavian counties. Its first widespread expression is found in a book called *An inquiry into the effects of spirituous liquors* (1782) by the Quaker Benjamin Rush. By 1810 the Temperance cause —abstinence from alcohol— had become a mass movement. This was essentially a women's movement in the USA. In 1874, the Women's Christian Temperance Union was founded in America.

Although the "puritanical," religious impetus for anti-alcohol sentiments were present in Germany, mainly as an influence from the USA, the movement did not become significant until the early nineteenth century in the German-speaking world. When this idea did become one with some traction in the culture, it gained this interest not so much on "religious" grounds as on a basis of health and cultural or intellectual well-being.

In Germany, the misuse of alcohol, or of overindulgence in it, was closely linked with matters related to industrialization and urbanization of the population. The often-deplorable living and working conditions led to widespread unhappiness and dissatisfaction, which in turn led to the "self-medication" that alcohol provided. Industrialization played another role in this problem as well: technological advances made the mass production of alcoholic beverages to be more efficient and in greater supply than ever before was possible. Alcoholic drink became ever bigger business. The patenting of refrigeration technology in 1871 greatly expanded the possibilities of mass-producing beer. This aspect of the big-business, or capitalistic, dimension of the misuse of alcohol became a motivating factor in the anti-alcohol movement in Germany during the late nineteenth and early twentieth centuries.

Below is an editorial cartoon, with words translated from the original German, promoting the ideas of the anti-alcohol movement by Georg Wilke. This appeared in the journal *Junge Menschen* [Young People] in 1927.

Die Waffen (The Weapons)

der Reaktion   des Fortschritts
(of Reaction)   (of Progress)

Anti-Alcolhol Propaganda

Alcohol was viewed as a blight on the urbanized citizenry of the working classes. It was seen as an exploitive influence which drew people's minds away from productive and creative activities down into a dark hole of delusion and mental illness. Many writers and intellectuals joined with the effort to encourage, for example, people to spend their money on buying books instead of wasting it on drink!

4.5.4. The Physical Body

The special role of the living, physical human body and its movements in the cultural life of Germany has a long history. Already in the 18th century. Enlightenment thinkers emphasized the unity of body and spirit, and thus physical exercises were seen as exercises of the spirit also. The father of German gymnastics (*Turnen*), Friedrich Ludwig Jahn, known as "Vater Jahn," founded organized gymnastics in 1807. *Turnen* took on a political and cultural meaning beyond the education of the individual body and mind in response to the occupation of a number of German states by the French under Napoleon (1793-1814). Organized gymnastics assumed a role in the Romantic struggle toward German nationhood as a unified state. In the early nineteenth century the activity was often banned by the smaller German states, as it was seen as a threat to the political status quo. But in the latter half of the century gymnastics organizations, especially those attached to the fraternities at the universities, became part of the established order.

A common saying or slogan often heard in the German language is *"Bewegung ist Leben!"* (movement is life). This is a formula with its immediate origin in the writings of Leonardo da Vinci, taken from the Greek philosopher Aristotle. But its popular use in German speech is a testimony to the spirit of the Reform movement.

The physical action of the human body became a fundamental part of many aspects of culture in German-speaking Central Europe. The three main facets of this can be summarized as exercise, art and magic. Exercise, such as gymnastics, and the philosophies and ideologies that supported this activity were principally seen as a way of promoting health (and beauty) of the individual body. Such activity found expression in various art-forms, most especially *dance* which took on enormous meaning in the time period.(18) The role of the body and its movement, or lack of movement, also assumed a great role in the spiritual or magical teachings of many schools of thought during this time. These ranged from the magical theories of the "Philosopher King of Weimar" Ernst Schertel (19) to the runic gymnastics of rune-magicians such as Friedrich Bernard Marby and Siegfried Adolf Kummer, to the Eurythmy of the Anthroposophists, as well as the increasing popularity of the discipline of yoga as imported from India.(20)

4.5.4.1. Physical Form and the Body in Motion

Throughout Europe and America in the late nineteenth and early twentieth century practices, art-forms and even spiritual exercises involving the position of the physical body and its motions came to a very high level of attention. The art of expressive dance assumed an important position in culture at this time. An important book on the subject was written by Karl Toepfer called *The Empire of Ecstasy* (California, 1997). Dancers rose to the level of famous artists in Central Europe and elsewhere. In addition to the primarily artistic approach to the human body in motion attention should be given to the trend toward the spiritual or psychological practices connected to this idea. We are here reminded of Steiner's Eurhythmics, of Gurdjieff's "Movements," the "Egyptian Postures" found in Mazdaznan and the many dance performances taking place in the avant garde world of the day which proposed to be transformative on the audience as well as artist. The figure that was most powerful with regard to combining the concept of art and magic in connection with motions of the human body is the so-called Philosopher King of Weimar, Dr. Ernst Schertel (1884-1958). Schertel melded art and magic, nudism and psychology—he often put his dancers into hypnotic trances and had them dance in a cloud of hashish fumes. I have devoted a special study to Schertel in my book *Dancing with the Demon* (Arcana Europa).

4.5.4.2. Dance or Body Culture in Motion

In Germany, the art of dance made connections with various other aspects of contemporary culture such as spirituality or magic, socialism, nudism, feminism and eroticism. This was an area of the artistic and cultural world in which women were especially well-represented. Individual dance teachers also had their own studios and these were the workshops in which dance performances were created and performed in well-attended venues all over the country. Great women who excelled in this role were Mary Wigmann, Ida Herion, Bess Mensendick, Lotte Herrlich and many others. Each developed not only their own visions and styles of dance, but also such choreographers gave a tremendous amount of theoretical thought to their creations.

So, in Germany, as might be expected, the art of dance was not seen as mere entertainment, but rather it was equipped with theoretical underpinnings of considerable gravitas. One of the chief theoreticians was the genius musician, linguist and philosopher Wolfgang Graeser (1906-1928) who wrote a masterpiece, *Körpersinn* (Body-Sense) published in 1927,

one year before he took his own life at 22 years of age. He was a throwback character to the Age of Romanticism.
He synthesized ideas contained in politics, psychoanalysis, musicology and philosophy. He clearly saw the primeval forces expressed in both Bolshevism and Italian Fascism (the Nazis were not yet well developed by the time of his death).

It appears most likely that the "movements" introduced by G. I. Gurdjieff had as their origin the input of one of his followers Jeanne de Salzmann (1889-1990) who had earlier been an instructor in the Eurythmics method developed for Rudolf Steiner by Jaques Dalcroze. This supposition is further supported by the fact that the first recorded instance of instruction in these movements was to de Salzmann's class at the Dalcroze Institute at Hellerau. (Cusack: 2017: 96-122)

Perhaps the most important single figure in the world of dance in the early twentieth century was the Austro-Hungarian and German choreographer Rudolf (von) Laban (1879-1958). He is known as the "founding father of expressionist dance" and a general innovator in the field of modern dance. In an extensive discussion of Laban and his life-work Karl Toepfer (1997: 99-107 *et passim*) notes that: "His life teemed with so much activity and he left behind such a vast archive of documentation in several countries that no one… has been able to construct a coherent, comprehensive biography." One of his most significant accomplishments was the development of a method for the notation and documentation of the dance movements of the human body called Laban Movement Analysis. His theories of motion were based on the geometry found in crystalline formations. Laban's ideas were applied beyond dance in areas of architecture, education, industry and management. Laban lived an unsteady and bohemian lifestyle for many years, even going bankrupt once. In 1911, he rented a room in Munich's theater district and, still working as a commercial artist on the side, set up his first dance studio. Stresses of his lifestyle led to a general breakdown in his health and he entered the health institute Lahmann-Sanatorium Weisser Hirsch in 1912 and underwent a course in health restoration according to Life-Reform principles. Although he was married to Maja Ledere, he met and fell in love with a fellow patient, Suzanne Perrottet. The three seemed to have lived what would today be called a polyamorous lifestyle. Perrottet was herself an accomplished figure in the world of expressionist and dada movement and one of Laban's main collaborators. After this, he became even more a part of the Reform-Movement.

Laban become involved with the Reform community located at Monte Verità near Ascona. There he also met Theodor Reuss, the head of the *Ordo Templi Orientis* (OTO). Laban had already been involved with Freemasonry since 1913 and Reuss issued a charter for an OTO lodge called *Libertas et Fraternitas* to Laban in Zürich.(Dörr 2008) Monte Verità became an epicenter from which Laban tremendously influenced the dance community. He conducted a series of dance courses there between 1913 and 1919 met many students and fellow masters of the craft and it led to his establishment of his own self-sufficient community near Zürich. He also established his own *Schule für Bewegungskunst* (School for Motion-Art). Laban taught and collaborated with Mary Wigman and Katja Wulff.

Dance students at Laban's Choreographic Institute in Berlin (1929
(Note the typical Jugendstil Design)

Much of Laban's professional life was conducted in Germany. When the Nazis came to power he cooperated with them actively on a professional level and had (as was required in terms of political correctness) to say positive things about National Socialism. He designed a piece of choreography for the 1936 Berlin Olympics—which found disfavor with Joseph Goebbels because it insufficiently illustrated National Socialist ideology. The next year he left Germany and immigrated to England. In London he established the Laban Art of Movement Guild and the Trinity Laban Conservatoire of Music and Dance in Manchester which continued until the time of his death.

Another of the most fascinating of all the dance impresarios was Dr. Ernst Schertel who together with Ida Herion led the *Traumbühne Schertel* (The Schertel Dream Stage) based in Stuttgart from 1925 to 1927. Schertel had been a proponent of dance for many years and wrote about his theories in the pages of *Die Schönheit* (Special Edition 1913) in an article entitled *"Tanz und Jugendkultur."* At the time, he was a teacher at the prestigious college preparatory school at Wickersdorf.

In a dissertation on Schertel Anna Börner (2014: 34) notes that he considered dance to be a *ur*-phenomenon of culture which had been profaned as it left its mystical and cultic roots. It was Schertel's intention to return dance to its sacred status by which the dancer will be sacralized by the action and the observer will be likewise elevated by observing the art. Schertel treated his activities with dance in a highly *magical* way. His "performances" were held as private affairs in rented theaters. Dance was envisioned as the interplay between "seen and seeing bodies." These theoretical ideas seem to some extent based on Wagnereian attitudes toward art.

Dance, performing it and observing it, has a direct effect on the mind of the individual and society. The popularity of dance performances in Germany in the early twentieth century helped fuel enthusiasm for the Reform Movements. Bodies in motion, especially choreographed and coordinated movements, have a cultic effect. It is an often-overlooked aspect of the magic employed by the Nazis that it was just this kind of coordinated mass movement that was so much a part of their rituals and ceremonies which helped bring them to power. Toepfer (1997) discusses this aspect in some detail.

4.5.4.3. Runic Gymnastics

Nowhere is the intersection between the form of the human body and discreet symbolic concepts clearer than in the practice variously known as *Runengymnastik* (runic gymnastics) or **Runen-Yoga* (rune yoga). The former term was used by Friedrich Berhard Marby (1882-1966) while the latter one was favored by Siegfried Adolf Kummer (1899-1977). The basic concept in both cases was the use of bodily postures which were imitative of rune-shapes. Typically, while the posture was engaged, a sound-formula (*mantra*) would be spoken or sung to complete the connection between the body, sound and meaning of the rune in question.

It would appear that the idea was first articulated by Marby, but Kummer had his own innovative approach. Both seem to have been greatly influenced by the growing popularity of the practice of Eastern yoga, but the culture of the day was awash with practices designed to harmonize body, soul and sound.

Serious scholarly attention has been given to the phenomenon of runic gymnastics by Bernd Wedemeyer-Kolwe.(21)

What makes runic gymnastics so conspicuous is the degree to which the postures and movements can be linked up to definite shapes, sounds and meanings. It is usually the case when it comes to "dance" or expressive choreographed performances that the meaning is rather nebulous and left to the imagination of both the performer and observer of the action. With runic gymnastics, such ambiguity is eliminated.

Runic Exercises Described by S. A. Kummer in his
Heilige Runenmacht (Uranus, 1932: 30)

The theories of those promoting the idea of runic gymnastics was that through the striking of these symbolic poses, in conjunction with the chanting of certain sounds, a sort of engagement in the energies and power currents of the earth could be achieved and these forces even directed under the will of the practitioner.(22)

The close connection between the ideas behind runic gymnastics and the Reform philosophy is demonstrated by the fact that the exercises, or rituals, are predicated on the idea of a holistic model in which physical form (body), sound and definite symbolic meanings are unified. Often these elements are also linked to other factors such as color and motion, whereby the performance in the flesh acts as a springboard into a transcendent realm of meaning. Beyond informational meaning, the exercises, or rituals, are *experienced* as actual transformative occurrences wherein some therapeutic or environment-altering event is seen to be effected.

Due to the fact that the symbolic values of the runes were often used by the National Socialists for purposes of propaganda or "branding" of their cause, the whole concept of runic gymnastics or rune-yoga became tainted with suspicions of Nazism. After WWII certain occultists, such as Karl Spiesberger, successfully articulated these practices in ways totally apart from racist or Nazi ideologies. In point of fact, both Marby and Kummer were rejected by the Nazis and Marby even spent many years in concentration camps (where he is said to have led fellow prisoners in runic gymnastics!). After such ideas and practices were reintroduced on a more world-wide basis in the late 1980s the whole idea has found new acceptance and practitioners and teachers of the technique abound on the Internet in the wake of the new-found popularity of "yoga" in general.

4.5.4.4. Nudism and Freikörperkultur (FKK)

One of the fields of activity for which the Reform Movements is best known is the practice of *nudism*. In German this is known variously as *Freikörperkultur* (FKK)(23) or *Körperkultur* ("body-culture") or simply *Nacktheit* ("nudity"). An overview of this aspect of the movement is provided by Koerber (1998: 103-114).

It was certainly Karl Wilhelm Diefenbach (see §3.3) who was among the very earliest proponents of nudity outside of any "therapeutic" purpose. By example, and though personal influence, he encouraged a number of successors such as Heinrich Pudor, Gustav Gräser, Guntram Erich Pohl, Richar Ungewitter and his personal student Hugo Höpperner (Fidus).

One ideological basis for this activity was put forward by Heinrich Pudor (1865–1943) in his 1891 book *Nackte Menschen—Jauchzende Zukunft* (Naked People—Rejoicing Future). The idea and the practice of nudity cut across many ideological divides, as there were right-wing and left-wing approaches to it. The most highly resistant segment of society were among the Catholic Christians—as they clearly saw it as a direct affront to biblical mythology. Nudity could be seen semiotically as a statement for a new and avant-garde culture or as a return to natural, indigenous culture (e.g. that of the ancient Germanic tribes). It remains such a prominent part of the study of this movement because it was so well-documented in an enormous amount of printed material. The pictographic nature of this documentation, whether in photographs or in the drawn and painted images of artists such as Fidus, make this dimension of the Reform Movement in Germany more international in its impact simply because it more easily transcends the language barrier.

To a great extent, the influence of the nudist philosophies is part of the spiritual or religious Reform ideology. The practice was a vector for the expression of a complex of ideas and an experience of something that went beyond mere physical sensation.

Nudity itself is an ancient Indo-European practice in different avenues of life, among several cultures. The Greeks practiced it to such an extent that in the process of higher education, for example in the Academy of the philosopher Plato, the students were *naked* in the outdoors among the trees. The Greek word for "naked," gymnos, gives us our Latin-derived word gymnasium, which literally means "a place where one goes naked." In Europe, the word gymnasium refers to a place of academic learning (e.g. German *Gymnasium*, "university preparatory school") having nothing to do with sports. Tacitus in his book *Germania* tells us that the Germanic peoples let their children go naked when they are young (chap. 20.1), and that they have entertainment involving naked youths doing acrobatic dances (chap. 23.1).

The whole idea of nudity as a reflection of a high moral state, being either natural or thoroughly modern, cannot be considered in the context of the history of Western culture without also paying attention to the direct rejection of the Myth of Eden expressed in its practice. In Judaic mythology, which came to dominate the West through Christianity, we find Genesis 3:7 which reads: "Then the eyes of both of them [Adam and his wife] were opened, and they realized they were naked; so they sewed fig leaves together and made coverings for themselves." This is the result of them having eaten of the forbidden fruit from the tree of knowledge of good and evil. This established, or reinforced, the attitude that nudity is connected with concepts of sin, immorality and shame and to sexuality in some fashion. The philosophy of the theoreticians of the *Nacktkultur* movement in Germany ran directly counter to this attitude. As such, *Nacktkultur* constituted an overt rebellion against the established religious order of the day.

The first FKK club was established in 1898 in Essen and by 1900 the activity had reached Berlin and the beaches of the North and Baltic Seas. It was along the beaches and in Berlin that FKK was most popular. Although nudism grew in popularity, it was opposed by conservative religious forces every step of the way as being immoral. From a theological or religious-historical perspective it should be recalled that in the Judeo-Christian tradition nudity (whether that of Adam and Eve or Noah) was closely connected with ideas of shame and sin with an immediate link between nudity and sexuality. By just practicing nudism itself, the Reformer was also expressing a profound from of *rebellion* against conventional religion. By 1913 there were around 50 organized *Nacktkultur* clubs. Membership grew out of the youth movement in general, e.g. the Wandervogel where the sexes were mixed and nudity was often found when they swam in lakes and rivers in the countryside.

During the late nineteenth century, a number of well-known champions of the practice of nudism in connection with a variety of other Reform ideas and "natural" lifestyles came to the forefront. Some of these, e.g. Diefenbach and Fidus were active in many other areas of Reform ideology.

There were many writers, organizers and philosophers of the nudist movement in the German-speaking world. Some of them were on the same *völkisch* wave-length as Pudor. These included Richard Ungewitter (1869-1958), who was an author, Anti-Semite and the first organizer of the FKK-movement and another author Hans Surén (1885-1972), who helped organize FKK activities in the Third Reich. See section 6.7 for more on these. Another important writer and publicist was Karl Vanselow (1877-1959) who published the important periodical *Die Schönheit* (Beauty). More oriented toward the Left was the Socialist Adolf Koch (1896–1970), and many others could be characterized as being apolitical, although such was a difficult stance in mid-Century Central Europe! One writer who was not aligned with any "political" stance seems to have been the magician Ernst Schertel.

It is noteworthy that the majority of the pioneers of the FKK movement had Protestant backgrounds. Nudism was usually a part of some larger view of life which might be connected with esoteric ideas. These were often connected with liberal or Left-leaning individuals, but more often it seems with the *völkisch* crowd. Some were connected with the Mazdaznan organization, the New Spirit movement as well as with the Ariosophist world. Names of the clubs show their ideological leanings: *Die neue Zeit* (The New Age) or *Bund freier Menschen* (League of Free Men). *Nacktkultur* was usually highly ideological, but its underlying ideology spanned the political spectrum. It found enthusiastic supporters on both the right and left. Among those with right-wing leanings there was a view that nudism was harkening back to the pagan Germanic past (as reported by the Roman historian Tacitus) while on the left nudity was touted as being a class-based equalizer, as the quality and expense of clothing was seen as a divisive cultural feature in this regard.

Between 1919 and 1945 Berlin was a center for FKK activities, sometimes called "Swedish bathing." This was especially true on the shores of the Motzener Lake a short distance from Berlin to the south which became a gathering place, especially for young people who enthusiastically embraced the alternative lifestyles represented by the Reform Movements. Many of these were drawn from the ranks of the Wandervogel. On the lake one particular place on the northeastern shore is known as the *Märchenwiese* ("fairy-tale meadow") and this became the epicenter of these activities.

During the so-called Golden Twenties in Germany (which appear to have been more theoretically, or spiritually "golden" than economically so!) FKK-culture developed in many areas especially in northern Germany. The first recognized "nude beach" was established on the Sylt peninsula in the Baltic in 1920 and by 1923 most FKK-clubs formed a sort of confederation called the *Arbeitsgemeinschaft der Bünde deutscher Lichtkämpfer* (Study Group of the Leagues of German Light-Warriors) which changed its name to the Reichsverband für Freikörperkultur in 1926. The friction between the Socialist and *völkisch* branches of the movement eventually resulted in the socialists reorganizing themselves under the name *"Freie Menschen: Bund für sozialistische Lebensgestaltung und Freikörperkultur"* (Free People: League for Socialistic Life-Formation and Free-Body-culture) in 1932. This league is reported to have had 70,000 members.

An essential basis of nudism was from the beginning a *therapeutic* one. A Swiss physician, Arnold Rikli promoted the practice of "sun-cures" as early as 1853. Patients took "light-baths" which he prescribed from his *Sonnenheilanstalt* (Institute for Solar Healing). In Germany, there were many places where people took naked "air-baths" for their health. Heinrich Pudor combined health programs with clothing reform, dietary regulations (vegetarianism), anti-modernism and even Anti-Semitism. He was followed by Richard Ungeeitter who founded the *Loge für aufsteigendes Leben* (Lodge for Ascending Life). Ungewitter utilized nudism as a part of a eugenic philosophy whereby potential male and female partners in the process of reproducing the next generation would be able to assess the health, strength and beauty of the bodies of potential partners from among other "racially pure" people.

As a rule, the representatives of the FKK movement tried to reject both any drift toward a pornographic or sexualized direction and at the same time they opposed any prudery. They claimed that clothing itself is what sexualizes the body, and wanted to emphasize the healthy and natural aspects of nudity. The body was to be controlled and disciplined, and through this avenue the whole philosophy eventually even found its way into National Socialism. (See §6.7) Nudists actually reversed the morality code such that being nude was the apex of virtue and being clothed was seen as an exercise in *immorality*!

An aspect of nudism as practiced in Central Europe during the early part of the twentieth century which often differentiates it from the form of nudism that became somewhat popular in America in the latter half of that century is the emphasis in Germany upon the concept of *beauty* and strength on the one hand and *eroticism* on the other. Typical images of "nudist magazines" in America were images of extremely ordinary bodies doing very un-erotic activities, such as playing volleyball or something similar. In Germany, the emphasis was often on physical beauty and strength in conjunction with nudity. One of the most influential journals of the day was *Die Schönheit* ("Beauty"). It is also interesting to note that one of the most important writers and thinkers in the cultural field of *Nacktkultur* was one Dr. Ernst Schertel (1884-1958). Most advocates of nudism emphasized the idea that humanity should lose our sense of shame at being naked, as reflected in the Hebrew mythology of the Garden of Eden and the Fall of Man. Indifference to nudity was a seen as a direct rejection of this common feeling. For Schertel, however, who emphasized the erotic aspects of everything as a psychological source of power, the feeling of "shame" could actually be exploited to increase the intensity of the experience.

Cover of *Körperbildung Nacktkultur* (Body-formation Nudism) Special Edition Number 4: Schämst du dich? (Are You Ashamed?) published by the Socialist Adolf Koch und Hans Graaz. Leipzig: Ernst Oldenburg 1930. Published under the auspices of the Freie Menschen (Free People).

By the time of the early 1930s the FKK movement was increasingly well-organized in Central Europe and the organizational zeal was beginning to spread onto the international stage. It is estimated that FKK club membership numbered around 100,000 in the early 1930s. In 1930, there was a general congress of nudist organizations from several European countries and they eventually formed the European Union for Free-body Culture. This international dimension was eliminated by the Nazi regime and all organized nudism was brought under the control of the NSDAP. (See §6.7.)

4.5.6. Sexuality and Reform

The sexual aspect of the nudist world is just one small feature of a much larger picture surrounding sexuality, the understanding of sexuality and sexual liberation which was emerging in Central Europe during the late nineteenth and early twentieth centuries. This time period reflected a strong obsession with sex which at first was mainly manifest in "bohemian" circles in major metropolitan areas, such as Berlin, Vienna, Paris and London, but which would become even more widespread after WWII throughout the free market nations of the West. The "sexual revolution" of the 1920s was a culmination of a decades-long development, which would be reiterated on a wider scale in the 1960s onto the 1980s—before reaching a new level of global penetration in the Age of the Internet.

I will return to the topic of sexual Reform, and more specifically the phenomenon characterized as the Sexual Revolution, as a special study in section 10 below.

A general overview of the role of sexuality in the Reform Movements is provided by Linse (1998: 211-226). Taken as a whole the subject of sexuality has branches that reach into a wide variety of topics from economics (the role of socio-economic changes brought about by industrialization and urbanization), health concerns with the spread of venereal diseases, social dimensions with the growth of sexually oriented entertainment and prostitution, as well as the importance of sexuality in the stability of marriages, gender roles and women's suffrage, and finally the new emphasis on sexuality in connection with the idea of eugenics and evolution after the popularization of the ideas of Darwin and Haeckel. After the middle of the twentieth century it is easy to see the universal focus on the idea of SEX, but it was in this age of Reform that these trends not only began but already found intense expression in certain social circles.

Certainly, one of the most important figures in this development of new attitudes toward sexuality was the Viennese physician Sigmund Freud (1856-1939). Freud's importance for sexual reform essentially lies in the serious attention given to the topic, and its connection with matters of human happiness and fulfillment beyond considerations of procreation. Freud opened a door though which many serious investigators could enter this field of thought with some respectability. Freud addressed issues surrounding the subconscious mind and the repression of desire as a major root of mental dysfunction.

The heart and soul of sexuality in the context of the Reform Movements revolved around the person of Dr. Magnus Hirschfeld (1868-1935) in Berlin. It can be said that Hirschfeld actually and figuratively founded the school of sexology (*G. Sexualwissenschaft*). Hirschfeld was more than a physician or scientist, he was also an activist and proponent of sexual liberation in various areas of life. As far as the organization of sexual reform was concerned, the most important institution was the World League for Sexual Reform which was mainly guided by the ideas of Hirschfeld. The organization held international congresses in the 1920s and into the early 1930s.

The most important features of the movement for sexual Reform included such things as the legalization of sexual activities between consenting adults (the general age of consent in Germany was and is between 14 and 15 years of age), considering sexual variations as medical rather than as "crimes" or "sins" and reforms to regulate prostitution to make it safer for all involved. From a legal standpoint, the movement focused on the repeal of Paragraph 175 which outlawed male homosexuality. Additionally, there was the promotion of the idea of general sex education for all, education in birth control and providing the means for this. On the legal front, there was a promotion of the economic and sexual equality of the sexes, the secularization of laws concerning marriage and divorce and programs to protect unwed mothers and their children (banning the concept of "illegitimacy"). Beyond these concerns, there was also the desire to develop an understanding of transsexual individuals and homosexuals. Finally, and something that was especially particular to the times, there was interest in the concepts of eugenics and selective births.

The books and records belonging to the World League for Sexual Reform were destroyed by the Nazis in a raid on the headquarters of the WLSR in May of 1933, and the institutions ceased to exist entirely in 1935.

Another important exponent of sexual Reform was the writer, publisher, photographer and philosopher Karl Vanselow (1877-1959). In the early years of the twentieth century Vanselow published a variety of Reform-minded periodicals. He became best known for editing his journal *Die Schönheit* ("Beauty") which was published continuously from 1903 to 1932. Another of his periodicals was *Geschlecht und Gesellschaft* ("Sex and Society") which was published between 1905 and 1914. In connection with this publication he was brought up on charges of indecency in 1907, but he was acquitted. He was brought up on similar charges in 1906 and 1909 in connection with photos that appeared in *Die Schönheit*. He was also acquitted of these due to the fact that the photos were seen as part of the greater nudism movement. Meister Fidus was a very prolific illustrator for *Die Schönheit*. A quote was attributed to Vanselow: "If we are not beautiful enough to be naked, well and good, so we want to be naked in order to become beautiful once more." This sentiment was a strong element present in the nudist movement in Germany at the time. Vanselow was a sometime writer of screen treatments for films produced at the UFA studios.

In general, Vanselow was a promoter of the same ideals as promulgated by Magnus Hirschfeld, but whereas Hirschfeld was more of an establishment and scientific figure, Vanselow was a master of the movement on the level of popular culture.

An unusual side-note on the life of Vanselow is that he became an enthusiast for the artificial, universal language called Esperanto, and even wrote poetry in that language as well as a learning textbook.

Another intriguing and eccentric figure of the Reform world in Germany was Carl Buttenstedt (1845-1910), who was professionally a state official in the Prussian bureaucracy, but who made his name as a pioneer of flight technology on the one hand, but more famously as a sexual Reformer. As a theoretician of the possibilities of flight connected with airships and gliders he was in conflict with another Reformer, Otto Lilienthal. In general, Buttenstedt's theories were not influential in the field of flight technology. His mark was made with his intriguing theories and practices of erotic lactation. In 1903, he published an influential book: *Die Glücksehe—Die Offenbarung im Weibe, eine Naturstudie* (*The Happy Marriage—The Revelation in Woman: A Natural Study*). On the one hand this book could be classified as a work involving theories of health or medicine, in that his theories (which have ancient folkloristic roots) proposed a natural method of contraception, known medically as lactational amenorrhea, it was really in the more erotic aspect that his book was best received. His theory was known as the *"Buttenstedt'sche Empfindungsphilosohie"* (Buttenstedt's Philosophy of Sensation) or "Buttenstedt's Happy Marriage." This was quite well-known in the first third of the twentieth century. First, the practice he suggested would prevent pregnancy allowing for closer relations between man and wife, but the technique involved the husband sucking milk from his wife's breasts several times a day, although this was supposed to stop menstruation and ensure infertility, its main benefit, according to Buttenstedt, was the erotic pleasure both husband and wife enjoyed from the practice of what has come to be called erotic lactation. Buttenstedt noted that it was especially well-enjoyed by the wife. Some critics hailed the method, but at least one German critic warned that it would "pathologically increase sexual sensation of both partners." But obviously both seem to have agreed that it is erotically powerful. The book was ultimately banned by the Nazis in 1938 and the theory and Buttenstedt's connection to the practice largely forgotten.

The "Golden 1920s" in Germany (which were hardly "golden" in the conventional sense) was a world that would find many corollaries with the 1960s and 1970s in America. Recreational use of drugs and sexual experimentation came to the forefront in many urban areas. This culture is most interestingly portrayed in Mel Gordon's *The Voluptuous Panic* (Feral House, 2006). Barbara Ulrich also provides a graphic insight into the freedom women enjoyed in Weimar Berlin in her pictorial essay *The Hot Girls of Weimar Berlin* (Feral House, 2002). Almost every one of the sexual excesses of the twenty-first century was previewed in Berlin in the 1920s. Individuals experimented and social venues proliferated where people could meet one another. The so-called Kitze, the sex-trade or sexual underground, formed its own multilayered and multifaceted world in major cities, most especially in Berlin. During this time period, as never before, indulgences in sexual entertainment and the use of drugs (especially hashish and cocaine) all for recreational purposes was opened to the ever-growing economic middle class. What had been reserved to the elite, such as the circle around Lord Byron, was now becoming available to ordinary citizens with the imagination and curiosity to discover this previously hidden world. These experiences led to greater Reforms in society than almost any other feature in the culture of the time.

Interestingly this sexual obsession also entered into the spiritual or metaphysical dimensions of culture as well. As we saw in section 4.2.2 Eastern ideas found a receptive audience in Germany in the nineteenth century. One of the most shocking aspects of certain schools of Eastern philosophy or religion thoughtfully engaged concepts of sexuality and elevated them to a refined level of understanding. Chief among these are the concepts of tantrism in which sexual acts can be carried out with the force and understanding of religious or magical ritual. This entry of sexual symbolism and practices in conjunction with religion and magic was seen in several Western cultures.

These spiritual and magical dimensions of sexuality became part of the underground culture in the late nineteenth and early twentieth centuries. The German-based *Ordo Templi Orientis* (OTO) had come into being over a span of years between 1895 and 1906 organized by a group of pseudo-Masons, Theodor Reuss, Karl Kellner and Heinrich Klein. This organization was later influenced by the English mage and libertine, Aleister Crowley (1875-1947). In 1926, the OTO spawned an offshoot, the *Fraternitas Saturni*, which was headquartered in Berlin and led by the occultist and bookdealer Gregor A. Gregorius (= Eugen Grosche, 1888-1964). More a part of the Reform Movements than any of these, however, were the multifaceted works of the so-called Philosopher

King of Weimer, Ernst Schertel (1884-1958). Schertel is well-known for his contributions to the world of dance and dance-performance (Toepfer 1997: 56-69), but he was also devoted to the study and experience of sexuality in various alternative forms. He was active in the *Nacktkultur* movement, elements of which he re-endowed with an erotic component. Historically he was perhaps best known for his four-volume magnum opus *Der Flagellantismus als literarisches Motiv*.(24) More recently Schertel gained some dubious notariety in connection with his 1923 book entitled *Magie* ("Magic"). The notoriety in question came in connection with the fact that a copy of this book was found among Adolf Hitler's effects in the bunker in Berlin. The copy had numerous passages highlighted in the Führer's hand. A new careful translation of this work and a general introduction to Schertel's magical world in provided in my study *Dancing with the Demon* (Arcana Europa).

I will return in more detail to the idea of the Sexual Revolution in section 5 below.

4.5.7 Clothing and Fashion

One of the areas of life where Reform ideas made the greatest impact on the daily lives of individuals today is in the area of clothing reform. In the nineteenth century, as in times past, many humans, male and female, had to conform to fashions that were dictated by artificial and arbitrary ideas of "propriety" or attractiveness which resulted in people, especially women, having to wear restrictive and uncomfortable—not to mention downright unhealthy—kinds of clothing. The topic of Reform Movements' approach to clothing reform (*Kleidungreform*) is summarized by Ellwanger and Meyer-Renschhausen (1998: 87-102).

The whole idea of clothing reform stemmed from motivations similar to those which fueled interest in nudism (see 4.5.4. above). Clothing as such was theoretically considered unnecessary and in many regards was seen to be an unhealthy influence and hence it became the object of Reform. Although this extended to clothing for both men and women, it was most dramatic in the differences it could make in the lives and health of women. The motive of the Reformers was primarily in the direction of allowing more bodily freedom and comfort. Much attention, including that of physicians, centered on the wearing of restrictive (and even deforming) corsets. Notably one of the proponents of the elimination of the corset was Heinrich Pudor, who rejected the garment for symbolic reasons: because he saw it as a sign of prostitution, and therefore "impure." As a nudist he saw nakedness as pure and any sort of fetishistic clothing as signs of impurity.

As early as 1788, when the physician Samuel Thomas Sömmering wrote a paper entitled *"Über die Schädlichkeit der Schnürbrüste"* (On the Harmful Effects of Corsets) certain aspects of women's fashion were targeted as being detrimental to women's physical health. Both physicians and women's rights activists aimed at eliminating the corset from women's clothing. This restrictive garment was cited as cause for the deformation of internal organs, damage to the uterus and atrophy of the liver. Additionally, of course, corsets restricted breathing which often led to women passing out and in any event these garments greatly restricted normal bodily movement. Even Goethe had expressed the opinion that the corset was contrary to the interests of beauty and health.

Although clothing reform was enthusiastically embraced in the German Reform Movement after the mid-1890s, the original impetus for much of this came from America. In 1856, the National Dress Reform Association was founded in Seneca Falls, New York. This was followed in 1860 by the publication in England of Ann Caplin's book *Health and Beauty, or, Women and her Clothing*. Caplin's book pointed out the unhealthy aspects of tight corsets and she developed her own more comfortable and healthy form of this garment. Meanwhile in America toward the end of the 1860s Marie M. Jones briefly introduced her design for a "pants suit" for women. By the 1870s there were associations all over the country designed to promote "rational clothing" for women. In 1881, the Rational Dress Society was formed in England which was embroiled in the controversy between the development of a pants suit and the continuation of the dress, a compromise was reached with the design of culottes or bloomers. Such garments also became fashion-signals for women's rights activists from the 1850s forward. Most of these efforts initially met with steady cultural resistance.

In Germany, the International Berlin Congress of Women was held in 1896 where the topic of clothing for women was addressed. The next year the first exhibition of the *Verein zur Verbesserung der Frauenkleidung* (Organization for the Improvement of Women's Clothing) was held where new designs for women's clothing in line with Reform ideas were shown. Various organizations, journals and exhibits continued to develop over the next two decades.

During the late 1800s a good deal of attention was given to the reform of men's fashions. Different designers promoted different materials as being best for the health of the individual—wool, cotton or linen.

Just before 1900 special clothing suitable for women engaged in sporting activities (e.g. tennis, bike-riding and gymnastics) become quite widely acceptable to the general public. By 1910 high fashion designers had abandoned the corset, but still most women's clothing could hardly be considered actually comfortable. Those who held the Reform ideals would still have many decades of struggle to go.

Events connected to the First World War opened the door to increased reforms in various questions having to do with women and their lives, and this included the fashions they wore. The shortage of certain materials for clothing manufacture as well as the evolving image of womanhood all made the world more receptive to the ideas of the Reformers as regarded women's clothing.

Clothing Reform was in the focus of several other aspects of the Reform Movements. Animal rights activists in the 1920s began protesting the wearing of fur in fashion. Health advocates focused on the ill-effects of the corset and nudists were sympathetic to fashion reforms which allowed the body to be as free and unencumbered by material as possible.

4.6. Community and Society (Habitation)

One of the most fundamental ideas of the Reform ideology was that of getting "back to nature." In practical, experiential ways this was effected through wandering in the wide-open spaces and more especially in urban dwellers creating small agricultural spaces for themselves within the cities or nearby where they could in some sense return to the land. Often these city dwellers had themselves only recently left the countryside, or were just a generation removed from being farmers. They had a deep longing for a return to a more natural lifestyle. These garden plots provided this for many. As we will see, the Reformers sought to create living circumstances for modern populations that were more natural and congenial to a holistic approach to life. The most radical of these would create independent and self-sufficient communes.

4.6.1. Living Spaces and Habitation

The concepts of living spaces and habitation are two different, yet closely related ideas. The living spaces in which humans live involve the immediate environment right around where humans live (and sometimes work). This can also extend itself to the actual buildings in which people live and the characteristics of their material and architecture. The second concept, that of habitation, is directly related to the space in which people live and the ways in which it allows humans to interact with the environment in a healthy way.

Certainly, one of the most radical streams of thought with regard to the question of the spaces in which humans live was the urge to flee the large cities of Germany and create land-communes in the nearby countryside under the motto of "Back to Nature." This was generally fueled by the anti-urban and anti-industrial sentiments of the Reformers from the beginning. This solution was much more difficult to actualize in the old societies of Central Europe than it was, for example, in North America with all of its copious open and undeveloped land. At the same time Europeans could count on readily accessible resources, whereas the Utopian communities of America were often left to their own devices in a hostile environment, both natural and social/political.

We have already seen how the pioneers of the Reform Movements such as Karl Wilhelm Diefenbach, Gusto Gräser and Meister Fidus at one time or another and in various places, set up "intentional communities" or communes where they attempted to actualize their ideas of the Reform of Life.

Enclaves known as Schrebergärten ("allotment-gardens") or newly established Garden-Cities out in the countryside began to be developed at this time. The most radical kind of solutions were, of course, the experimental communes, such as those led by Diefenbach or Gräser, or the more agricultural operations such as the [Eden] Orchard Settlement.

[Logo for the Eden-Oranienburg Orchard Settlement]

The underlying philosophies that motivated similar lifestyles and activities ranged from that of social reform, nationalism, anarcho-religious and evangelical. In every case, there was a desire to experiment to find a "better way of living," and at the same time there was a high degree of what might be called "escapism" in the mix. In any case this widespread movement, which continues to this day, represents a revolt against the modern urban lifestyle, not in words or arguments, but in action and living. Garden communities can be seen all over Germany that generally consist of a small plot of garden land and a small hut where the inhabitants spend time regularly.

Most of those who used these properties were vegetarians, but as time went on carnivores were accepted, but generally the slaughter and sale of meat is forbidden.

These enclaves were economic units which produced fruit and vegitables which were often sold to the Reform-houses (stores which sold health food and products). This movement became very popular and widespread around 1900, was disrupted by the events of WWI, but returned to great success after the war.

The great model for this phenomenon was the orchard community of Eden, founded in 1893. The land was divided into numerous individual and independent "homesteads" with their individual living quarters and garden plot. Eden could not be characterized as a commune. It is a planned community. By 1930 Eden had around 850 inhabitants and with approximately 230 living quarter units. Because Eden had been friendly to the general *völkisch* spirit, the establishment was absorbed into the National Socialist system, and after 1945 it even continued under the Communist system in East Germany. The Eden community continues to thrive even today. There were many other such settlements or communities, largely based on the viable model provided by Eden, all around German-speaking Central European regions.

The *Artamanen Gesellschaft* (Artaman-League) was founded by Willibald Hentschel (1858-1947). He outlined his ideas in the seminal books *Varuna* (1901) and *Mittgart* (1904). In these books, he called for the colonization of territory through the spread of polygamous agrarian communities. The target area for this activity was seen to be the frontiers to the east of Germany. As he saw it, such farms would become the breeding grounds of a healthy and superior Nordic stock—a new humanity.

Hentschel was an interesting individual. After his time as a student (he studied under Ernst Haeckel) he married and began to buy farmland for his project in the east. After completing his studies, he began to acquire rural property in eastern provinces. He earned money from his writings as well as from patents in the chemical industry. It was his original plan to create a network of settlements which would have ten women for every man. This polygamous society would offer the greatest possibility for rapid growth of population for his system. Despite some initial success, the whole project originally suffered from the fact that not enough women could be persuaded to participate!

Around 1890 Hentschel became increasingly involved in political causes which were both *völkisch* and Anti-Semitic. He also became a leader in the *Deutschsozialen Partei* (German Social Party). He retired to his lands in Silesia, but events of WWI caused his lands to be given over to Poland. As a consequence, he lost his property and had to relocate his projects in northern Germany.

I delve somewhat deeper into the Artamanen movement in my book *The Occult in National Socialism* (Inner Traditions, 2022, 139-143). The most insightful over all study of the group was offered by Michael Kater (1971). We will return to the effects of the Artamanen movement in section 6.9.

Another development connected to the general movement toward people leaving the cities and developing their own communities based on special interests is the establishment of artists' colonies. Three prominent examples are Worpswede near Bremen, Höllriegelskreuth near Munich and Monte Verità in Switzerland. These became homes and retreats for artists of various kinds. In the earliest phases exponents of Art Nouveau, Impressionism and Expressionism were especialy prominent. But also writers and philosophers, as well as early psychologists were to be found among the inhabitants of these colonies. Monte Verità became an especially famous international enclave of occasional visitors from all over Europe and the center of activity for prominent figures of the Reform Movements, including Gusto Gräser, Carl Jung, and Hermann Hesse.

4.6.2. Architecture and Urban Planning

Reform ideology embraced the idea that the environment in which humans live should be harmonious with the health, well-being and balance of human existence, both physically and spiritually. This meant that attention was to be given to the buildings in which people lived and worked and the landscapes which surrounded them. In large measure this was a revolt against the unplanned, chaotic and unthinking manner in which urban dwellings (slums) and industries had defaced the beauty of natural and organic development.

Cover Art for *Die Geistige Monatsschrift*, by Fidus

The industrialized urban environments were frequently re-envisioned with large areas of park land or what we call greenbelts today. The metropolis of Berlin was completely surrounded with forested land, grass lands and lakes making a natural environment available to citizens from anywhere in the city by means of public transportation.

Reform architecture was characterized by new approaches to building design that made use of traditional building materials and style elements. The Reform attitude ran counter to the other innovative styles of the day, .e.g Bauhaus with its "form follows function" philosophy. In many ways Reform architecture was related to the Home-Land Art movement where locality and regional styles and designs were taken into account. The aesthetic of Art Nouveau (Ger. *Jugendstil*) made its presence felt in the movement for a time.

Garden Cities

As is the case with several other concepts in the Central European Reform Movements, the idea of the "garden city" was first developed in England. The pioneer was Ebenezer Howard who first demonstrated his ideas in 1898. He was reacting to the unplanned and wretched living conditions in many heavily industrialized English cities (e.g. Manchester and Birmingham). But Howard first began to express his ideas in the USA during a stay there in the 1870s. His American experiment failed. Howard's 1898 book *Tomorrow. A Peaceful Path to Real Reform* was a first try, then there was a new 1902 edition which was retitled *Garden Cities of Tomorrow*, which also appeared in German translation in 1907 *Gartenstädte in Sicht* (Garden Cities in View"). While Howard was in America he befriended Walt Whitman and Ralph Waldo Emerson and he associated with all sorts of free thinkers, anarchists and socialists all of whom influenced his ideas

Although Howard's ideas, and his book, gave great impetus and shape to the movement of creating garden cities, the idea of doing this was already being enacted in Germany even before Howard came upon the scene. The first great garden community in Germany was established in 1893. This was the already much discussed Eden Orchard-Settlement Oranienburg near Berlin. The earlier concept in Germany was known as *Villenkolonien* (villa-colonies) which began in the middle of the nineteenth century.

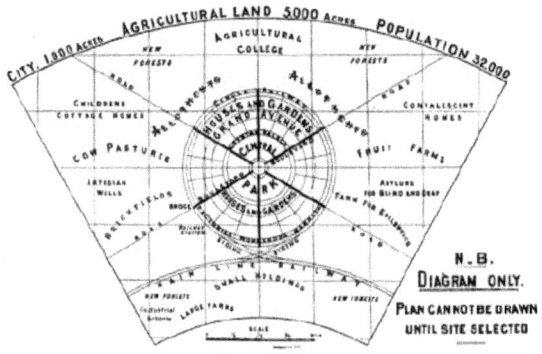

Diagram from Howard's Plans Reproduced in German in the 1909 Translation of the 1902 Edition of his Book

Between 1893 and 1939 over fifty planned garden cities or developments were established in Germany, and several in Austria and Switzerland as well. This progress was supported by an organization founded in 1902 and called the *Deutsche Gartenstadt-Gesellschaft* (German Garden-City Society) which was organized by a variety of leading thinkers of the day. People ranging from Fidus to Magnus Hirschfeld were involved. The society did not undertake the actual building of such cities, rather they advocated for the idea through presentations to city leaders and through a journal called *Gartenstadt* (Garden-City). This organization was obviously very successful.

The basic theory behind a completely planned new garden city was that it would be formed on land that had previously been used as farm-land, that it would be in fairly close proximity to larger cities and be served, both internally and in connection with the neighboring city by means of a rail-line. This would give the inhabitants a lifestyle free and independent of the urban blight, but would at the same time give its people ready access to the cultural features of a larger city.

Originally the German Garden-City Society promoted certain basic principles for the architectural and economic design of these communities. These included the idea that the land would be owned corporately by the community in order to prevent land speculation and deterioration of the design and purpose of the community. Over time, and as the movement grew, pragmatism and practical concerns made this idea less and less applicable.

The concept of the garden-city was actually weaponized by the Nazis in that they used the ideas inherent in it to design communities for the colonization of conquered territories in the east (Poland, Russia, etc.). The concept of a settlement bound in a collective *Gemeinschaft* (community) with rules and regulations for every aspect of a person's behavior is obviously just the kind of thing that a Nazi could appreciate—foreshadowing American "home-owners' associations," I suppose.

One cannot help but wonder why American visionaries (with all of the land available for such experiments) have not made use of this model. They are seemingly too busy trying to make previously existing cities conform to their "visions" with bike-lanes (when people have to commute to work over thirty miles in a hundred-degree heat) and other "brilliant" ideas. (The answer lies not in an actual "vision" but rather in an obvious effort to gain power and control over already prosperous cities.) This constitutes another chapter in the story of the deceptive misuse of good Reform ideas for selfish gain.

4.7. Art and Literature

The years in which the Reform Movements were prominent were times when the cultural and artistic values of society were rapidly shifting from being ones dominated by the nobility and extremely wealthy families (as well as religious institutions) and more and more toward the middle class which was made up of ever-increasing numbers of well-educated and ever more sophisticated individuals. Patronage of the arts shifted decisively from the upper class and church to the prosperous and educated bourgeoisie. This was a dynamic population, and one interested in many of the ideas of Reform on one level or another.

Reform ideology did not shape or condition all of art in the German-speaking parts of Europe during the time in question, of course. Reform ideas were just one part of the complex world of art and literature. This would become especially dynamic and volatile during the Weimar Period (1919-1933). Not only did Germany (and Austria) lose the war (under questionable and dubious circumstances) but the established, centuries-old, political institutions were upended and many societal norms called into question. The artistic community often responded to these questions in radically different ways. Some retreated into nationalistic symbols, while others embraced radical cosmopolitanism with a passion. Both branches bore remarkable fruits.

Aesthetically perhaps the heart of the Reform Movements was best expressed in the form of what is called in Germany *Jugendstil* (literally "youth-style") and what is internationally generally known as Art Nouveau ("new art"). This style of art was linked to the spirit of the Reform Movements more than any other, and was even called *Reformstil* (Reform-style) by some. The works of Fidus exemplify *Jugendstil*. Historically this style dominated for about twenty years between 1895 to just before the beginning of the First World War.

In relation to the history of German literature, the time period under examination here was dominated by the styles referred to as Realism, Naturalism and Expressionism. In the midst of these schools there was also a complex alternative trend referred to as "Countercurrents" to Naturalism. Realism (1850-1890) developed as a philosophical and artistic attitude toward the creative process in the middle of the nineteenth century. This was a movement away from Romanticism. Realism refocused artistic attention on the lives of ordinary people living conventional lives with a general rejection of the sentimentality of earlier times. Closely related to Realism is the school of Naturalism (1880-1900) which openly embraced the concept of modernism and was open to the philosophical influence of Marxism and other forms of socialism. The artist is seen as analogous to a *camera* recording events objectively. The advent of the technology of photography had a conceptual impact on the world of art at this time. Natural forces are seen as being determinative, whether a matter of heredity or environment. The world of the Naturalist was open to a more "Bohemian" lifestyle, one in which the outsider found a home. The interest in nature and the natural, as well as in a realistic and practical direction were all aspects that reflected the spirit of the Reform movements. The political dimension of Naturalism was suspect to many Reform-minded individuals. There were other trends that arose around 1880 inspired by the same factors that initiated the Reform Movements generally. These were those complex *Countercurrents* to Naturalism which swirled around between 1890 and 1920 and beyond. The visual style of the *Jugendstil* perhaps best exemplified the spirit of many of these countercurrents.

As with all such historical designations and discussions of the development of artistic or philosophical schools of thought the dates involved are usually only approximate guidelines, and it is always true that nothing ever disappears once it has entered the intellectual stream of a given culture. Older characteristics can always continue to influence and affect later developments.

4.7.1. The Homeland Art Movement

The *Heimatkunstbewegung* was a wide-ranging movement across the spectrum of the arts from literature to all other arts and crafts—from novels to cuckoo clocks. This movement in the artistic world grew out of a more general cultural trend known as the *Heimatbewegung* ("home-land movement") which emphasized the idea of a collective organic "folk-body" analogous to the physical body of an individual. The time period of the most intense expression of this artistic movement was between about 1890 to the early 1930s, but it had roots going back to aspects of the Romantic movement many decades earlier, and much of its spirit is still alive. In many ways, its literary expression was found in a style similar to that of Naturalism.

In conjunction with the publications of *Heimatliteratur* there often appeared illustrative works of art which can be thought of as "homeland art." The aesthetics of this art appeared to be "primitive" and natural, often making use of techniques (or the appearance of them) that hark back to older aesthetics and techniques, such as woodcuts.

Despite the "folksy" appearance of *Heimatkunst* it was intended to act as a means for cultural change, or reform, in the context of the so-called *völkisch* ideology. This methodology, as opposed to polemic argumentation, was carried out in the form of aesthetics rather than ideology. Nevertheless, there were a number of ideological manifestos and more philosophical works to bolster the effects of the aesthetic front. The *Heimatbewegung* was aimed directly against the *Modernistic* trends in culture. Theoretical keywords or concepts in this movement included such terms as tribe, folk-community (*Volksgemeinschaft*), folk and race. Here, as in so much else that was touched by these ideas, there was a split between those who were using these concepts as a modality to forge a greater national (Pan-Germanic) consciousness and those who were purely focused on localism and natural regional identities. Because members of the former group were allied with large systems (e.g. national governmental parties and corporations) the "debate" was a rather asymmetrical affair. Home-land Art was characterized as "healthy" and Modern Art as "sick" or "degenerate." The body-politic was seen as being sick and it could be healed with the infusion of healthy *art*.

The guiding publication of the Homeland Art Movement appears to have been a journal called *Der Kunstwart* (The Art-Guardian) which was published under that title from 1884 to 1937, when it was absorbed into a journal called *Das Innere Reich* (The Inner Reich or Empire). This absorption of the journal was part of the general National Socialist program called *Gleichschaltung*, whereby any and all expressions of thought were "coordinated" to be harmonized with official party-line ideology.

A troubling and fateful aspect of the Homeland Art faction was its dedication to the idea of Anti-Semitism. Although there was no clear reason for this stance, since Yiddish, a Germanic language, was the instrument of European (Ashkenazi) Jewish culture and they had their own localized cultural features, nevertheless this animosity was almost universal among those devoted to the Homeland Art Movement. The twin mythologies that the Jews were both the agents of unfettered banking and capitalism (mammonism) *and* the organizers of socialist, communist revolution, were designed to foment this sort of ethnic hatred. The Jews were simply envisioned as the agents of any and everything that the conservative detested— they were the all-purpose "Other."

The Homeland Art Movement was expressed through the works of a variety of authors, e.g. Julius Langbehn (1851-1907), Adolf Bartels (1862-1945), Hermann Löns (1866-1914) and Gustav Frenssen (1863-1945). Langbehn's seminal work *Rembrandt as Erzieher* (1890) was perhaps the most influential single work in this movement.

4.7.2. Literature and Philosophy

This survey of cultural history covers a great sweep of thought and ideas. It is often found in the consideration of cultural developments that the human mind is beset by what some call cognitive dissonance. Principles of thought are often thrown into conflict with one another and unexpected results ensue. For example, how did a general cultural movement devoted to highly localized and individual regional aesthetics and concepts be so easily diverted (in the creators' minds themselves) to the cause of absolute ideological conformity to a single standard of Nazi ideologues? The mysteries and mechanics as to how this takes place is ever-present throughout history. Even today those who on the one hand promote local farm-to table economy for food production and consumption usually also think it is an abomination *not* to "think globally." As regards the Homeland Art Movement, its general passions and loves should have caused it to stand against the homogenizing effects of the Nazi movement, but its antipathies overcame it passions, and tragedy ensued, as it always will when one is no longer *primarily* motivated by what one loves, but rather by what one hates.

As important and long-lasting as the effects of Homeland Art were during the actual time period of the zenith of the Reform Movements, other art forms and theories met with far more international acceptance and enthusiasm.

One of the most widely influential artistic trends was that of *Expressionism*. This has roots that go back to about 1905, but it becomes more widespread in post-WWI German painting and graphic arts. In literature and graphic arts Expressionism presents life and events not as they might appear to the objective (natural) eye, but rather in ways that the author or artist *perceives* reality to be. Art is a lens and objects and events are often "distorted" in order to represent the object as it is *subjectively* perceived by the artist or a character in literature. The subjective, inner reality is pressed outward (ex-pressed) into objective artistic creations. Masters of Expressionist literature include Franz Kafka, Alfred Döblin, Robert Musil and Heinrich Mann, among many others. Expressionist art *forces* the viewer or reader to participate in the subjective universe of artists by presenting the world as they perceive it to be (or pretend to perceive it for the sake of art).

Several literary artists who might not have considered themselves members of the Reform Movements nevertheless either touched on Reform themes or were greatly influenced by Reform ideas or in some cases were very influential on them. These included Gerhard Hauptmann (*Eulenspiegel-Epos*), Thomas Mann (*Der Zauberberg*), Rainer Maria Rilke and even Franz Kafka (various thoughts on the reform of the Reform Movements). (Rasche 2018: 11)

Culturally, one of the greatest triumphs of German art in the Weimar period was found in the art of cinema—motion pictures. In America, great strides were made in transforming a carnival stunt (nickelodeon) into an art form, but it was in Germany that the whole industry was turned toward artistic expression on the cutting edge of artistic culture.

Films were first shown commercially in booths at fairs or amusement parks. In 1895, the first nickelodeon type presentations came out in Berlin. Films eventually began being shown in theaters, and finally in theaters specially built to show them. The first truly *artistic* film is said to have been *Der Student von Prag* (The Student of Prague, 1913), a sort of Faust-tale based on the Poe story "William Wilson" and created by the "decadent" author Hanns Heinz Ewers. The first truly great German film, from an artistic standpoint, is *Das Kabinett von Dr. Caligari* (The Cabinet of Dr. Caligari) filmed in 1919—a masterpiece of the Expressionistic art form.(25) The golden era of filmmaking in Germany was contained entirely within the Weimar period. From an art-critical viewpoint the *silent* film is the highest form of the art-form known as the *motion picture*. The theoretical reason for this is that it is there that the art is in its purest form: narratives told almost entirely through moving images alone. The artistic quality of silent pictures is often measured in the number of "titles" (the written explanatory texts which were inserted to explain the story). The fewer of these the higher the quality of the art. The addition of sound in the late 1920s somewhat diluted the theoretic purity of the art-form.

4.7.2.1. Friedrich Nietzsche

One of the major philosophers who influenced the development of the Reform Movements was the German thinker and writer Friedrich Wilhelm Nietzsche (1844-1900). He perhaps became best known in popular culture, both then and now, as the man who declared that "God is dead" and who coined the term "superman" (*Übermensch*). But he is much more than that and in fact his ideas transformed the world in many ways and on a variety of levels. His most famous work was entitled *Also sprach Zarathustra* (Thus Spoke Zarathustra [1883]). His philosophy was not presented in a systematic way, such as we might find with Kant or Hegel, and in many ways is more akin to poetic literature or even a new religion.

Nietzsche's visionary period spanned from August of 1881, when he received the vision of the eternal return during a walk near Sils Maria in Switzerland, to January of 1889 when he becomes either insane or divine in Turin, Italy. One of his last works was one called *The Antichrist* [1888] which was a full-force frontal attack on Christianity, in which he writes:

> What is good? Everything that heightens the feeling of power in man, the will to power, power itself.

> What is bad? Everything that is born of weakness.
>
> What is happiness? The feeling that power is growing, that resistance is overcome.
>
> Not contentedness but more power, not peace but war, not virtue but fitness (Renaissance virtue, virtù, virtue that is moraline-free).
>
> The weak and the failures will perish: first principle of our love of man. And they shall be given every possible assistance.
>
> What is more harmful than any vice? Active pity for all the failures and all the weak: Christianity.

His attack on conventional morality is clear. This provided a certain kind of energy to anyone who read his words, or, more typically, heard about his ideas. It should also not be missed that he did have strong ideas about what is good as opposed to the bad. Nietzsche's robust attack on the weak, ineffective and powerless in life was inspiring to generations.

The comprehensive philosophy of Nietzsche is too complex to discuss extensively in this context. Because of the visionary and poetic style in which he wrote, many different interpretations of his words are often possible. Nietzsche's words moved people from (almost) every political and philosophical band of the spectrum: anarchists, fascists, members of the Left or Right all felt his words to have deep meaning. His cosmology appears to have been focused entirely within this manifest world, on *Diesseitigkeit* ("this-sided-ness").

This focus does not mean that Nietzsche's own intellectual underpinnings were crudely "materialistic" in the conventional sense. Perhaps most mysterious of Nietzsche's ideas is his doctrine of Eternal Recurrence or the Eternal Return-- *ewige Wiederkunft or ewige Wiederkehr*. It was this idea which he himself thought was the essence of his teaching. Three ideas—the Will to Power, the Overman and Eternal Recurrence—are bound together in a triad: Recurrence is the law, Will is the method and the Overman the aim. Essential to the technique of Nietzsche's active philosophy is the *Umwertung aller Werte*: "the Revaluation of all Values." This virtually defines a modern school of secular antinomianism instituted for the sake of the evolution of the Will into a unique and potent entity. This radical ideology made his writings very attractive to any and all who dared to take upon themselves the act of Reforming the individual self or society.

A list of thinkers and writers influenced by Nietzsche in one way or another from the late nineteenth to the early twentieth century is a formidable one and included such names as the philosophers Martin Heidegger, Ludwig Wittgenstein, Ernst Jünger, Theodor Adorno, Georg Brandes, Martin Buber, Karl Jaspers, Henri Bergson, Jean-Paul Sartre, Albert Camus, Leo Strauss, Michel Foucault, Julius Evola, Ayn Rand, Rudolf Steiner, composers Richard Strauss, Alexander Scriabin and Gustav Mahler; the historian Oswald Spengler; writers such as Franz Kafka, Thomas Mann, Hermann Hesse, Stefan George, Rainer Maria Rilke, Knut Hamsun, August Strindberg, George Bernard Shaw, James Joyce, D. H. Lawrence, William Butler Yeats, Jack London and Joseph Conrad; painters Pablo Picaso, Salvador Dalí and Wassily Kadinsky; psychologists Sigmund Freud, Carl Jung, Alfred Adler and Abraham Maslow; and not least of all the mage Aleister Crowley.(26) Nietzsche affected thinkers directly and indirectly through a vast network of influences.

4.7.2.2. Hermann Hesse

Hermann Hesse (1877 - 1962) can be considered the poet laurate and world-wide intellectual and spiritual ambassador of the Reform Movements to the world. This was not his intention, it just happened. He was a German-Swiss poet, novelist and painter who wrote major works between 1904 and 1943. He received the Nobel Prize for Literature in 1946. His works consistently explore the individual's quest for authenticity, self-knowledge and some form of spirituality—as such his works mirror the times especially with regard to Reform-minded young people in the German-speaking world. Only later did his works become widely influential in the English-speaking world where they once more worked their magic.

Hesse grew up in a well-educated pietistic household, which meant that he was surrounded by religion, but not of an overbearing or dogmatic kind. Little Hermann was an energetic and willful child, but was depressed in his early years of schooling. He began writing stories almost as soon as he could write at all. His grandfather was a PhD fluent in several languages, who gave access to his library to the young boy. He had decided he wanted to be a writer by the time he was about twelve. Hesse did not take a traditional pathway in his education, so, although he became very learned, he never attended the university. He concluded his formal education in 1893 at a college preparatory school (*Gymnasium*) near Stuttgart. His continuing education came in connection with his apprenticeships with prestigious booksellers. He studied religious writers and Greek mythology, as well as Goethe, Lessing, Schiller and most especially Nietzsche after 1895. Later he concentrated on reading the Romantics: Brentano, Eichendorff, Hölderlin and Novalis. Hesse wrote constantly, and his breakthrough novel came in 1904 with the publication of *Peter Camenzind*, which became widely popular. From then on he made his living by writing. In the following years, his interest in Buddhism was renewed. At the same time, he developed deep interest in Schopenhauer and in conjunction with him Theosophy.

Hesse took a long trip to the East and visited India, Sri Lanka and Indonesia, all of which added to his knowledge later used in *Siddhartha*. But the actual experience of these countries left him depressed, his East was an East of the mind not the physical reality of today.

When the Great War broke out Hesse joined the German army and saw duty caring for prisoners of war. He was not caught up in the rabid nationalism of the day, and really took neither side in his heart.

He left military service in a depressed state. Over the years, Hesse had bouts of depression and certain emotional problems. In seeking treatment for these he became a patient and friend of Carl G. Jung. Interestingly, the Nazi sympathizer Miguel Serrano maintained friendships with both Hesse and Jung and carried out correspondence with both.

Hesse wrote his next great novel, *Demian*, over a period of three weeks in 1917. It would be published after the war in 1919 under the pseudonym Emil Sinclair. He resettled to southern Switzerland after the war and lived there for the rest of his life, gaining Swiss citizenship in 1923. In the prior year, he published another of his best-known works: *Siddhartha*. In 1927 he published one of his major masterpieces *Der Steppenwolf* (Steppenwolf) followed in 1930 by a completely new turn with *Narcissus and Goldmund*.

From his home in Switzerland, Hesse observed the rise of Nazism in his native Germany and quietly opposed it, but was not vocal in his condemnation, as he maintained a studiously apolitical attitude. He helped artists, such as Berthold Brecht and Thomas Mann, escape Germany through Switzerland. Hesse annoyed the Nazis enough that they eventually banned his works in Germany. He worked on his last major work, *The Glass Bead Game* throughout the years of the Nazi regime. The book was published in Switzerland in 1943.

Hesse remained active throughout his life, devoting himself greatly to correspondence in his latter years—he penned as many as 150 pages a day writing letters. He died at the age of 85 and is buried in the cemetery of Sant'Abbondio in Gentilino, Switzerland.

During his lifetime, Hesse attained a high degree of popularity among young people in the German-speaking world. Beginning with his first novel *Peter Camenzind* (1904) his work moved the younger generation seeking a more natural life amidst industrialization. *Demien* (1919) spoke to the generation having just returned from fighting on the fronts of the Great War (1914-1918). Similarly, *The Glass Bead Game* (1943) would eventually help shape the post-WWII generation in Germany.

Hesse was both a living product of the Reform culture of central Europe and one of the greatest influences on its development and legacy in the world. On a deep level he documented the yearnings of the spirit of Reform in such a way that his works seem to manifest the feelings and thought patterns of the ideology itself—without ever consciously intending to do so.

Hesse influenced the youth of Germany from the time he first started writing and was both an influence upon the Reform Movements as well as a living exponent of many of its principles. Beyond this also Hesse became a fixture of the late twentieth century American counterculture movement and his works were to be found in many a backpack of Hippies everywhere.

4.7.3. Fidus, the Artistic Face of the Reform Movement

Anytime the subject of the Reform of Life and its culture is discussed there will usually be an illustration or several by the artist known by the name Fidus. The themes and style of his graphic art is clearly an expression of the spirit of the Reform Movements on many levels. Fidus was born Hugo Reinhold Karl Johann Höppener (1868-1948), and received the nickname: Fidus, which means "loyal" or "faithful" from his teacher Karl Wilhelm Diefenbach, in whose cause young Hugo served a short prison sentence for public nudity. He met Diefenbach when he was around eighteen years of age and became his student. He eventually settled near Berlin and set up a commune there and worked as the illustrator for a variety of publications including *Sphinx*, *Jugend* and the early gay journal *Der Eigene*. Between 1900 and 1918 he was one of the best-known painters and illustrators in the German-speaking world.

Poster for the Congress for Biological Hygiene in Hamburg 1912

Like so many others of his generation, Fidus was influenced by Theosophical ideology and this was turned more and more onto Germanic-oriented themes as times went on. He was also ideologically influenced by writers such as Arthur Moeller van den Bruck and the Brothers Hart (Heinrich and Julius). Fidus was a staunch Reformer and anti-materialist. He was interested in designing structures and even cities (e.g. garden-cities) of the future. Although Fidus was primarily a graphic artist, he did write a number of works himself as well. An anthology of these is found in the volume entitled *Fiduswerk*. But as the article translated below demonstrates, his attitudes toward the written word and its relationship to his graphic expression was complex and well-considered.

During the earliest phase of his popular artistic works his style was more abstract and dream-like than it later became. His style can be understood with in the Art Nouveau movement and especially also the Sezessionist style which had its home in Austria.

After the end of WWI his style was less in vogue and fell out of the high demand it had formerly enjoyed. Fidus was an early admirer of the ideals of National Socialism, but like so many other original thinkers fell afoul of party orthodoxy. He became a member of the NSDAP in 1932, but he did not receive support from the party that he expected. In fact, his work was eventually banned by the Nazis and ordered seized in 1937. When he died in 1948, his work had been virtually forgotten for a number of years. He was "rediscovered" by artists in the 1960s in California and his works influenced a whole generation of graphic artists in the Hippie Movement

The following text by Fidus is drawn from the seminal volume entitled *Fiduswerk* (1933: 145-153) and it explains the artist's own attitude toward his craft.

The Language of Images by Fidus 1923

Now put all of your feelings in your eyes! And perceive what an artist of visible things wants to tell you, no, wants to show you. Look only with your eyes and do not impertinently try to inquire about words, about what the artist "wanted to say." Least of all ask him directly; for he has already expressed everything in his heart in a visible language, in his language of images. Or do you wish to offend him and act as if he has spoken, i.e. depicted things, in an unclear or imprecise manner? If you ask others [about it] at least determine that they have been able to perceive his language clearly, because they have seriously looked at, and contemplated, things and you admit that you have not done so. But what would it help you anyway if someone else told you in words what you could have seen for yourself in visible forms and colors if you had really looked and contemplated for a long enough time. And above all what would you get from a visible work of art, for what purpose was it created, if you only want to hear one idea about it from someone else instead of beholding and enjoying it yourself? For a work of visible art is supposed to be seen, to be enjoyed, and not to be known by hearsay, and its animating forces can only be perceived by being viewed and received. Certainly, it is also possible to speak about a visible work of art in a manner so beautiful and true that its particular powers can be conveyed and thus it becomes superfluous for the listener, but in such a case the narrator has to be just as much of a poet as the original creator of the artwork had to be. But for all of that he certainly could not be too enthusiastic about this audible representation if the visible one were not seen by him, or if it did not even exist.

But visible works of art exist, and they are real things in themselves and they cannot be replaced by any audible art, much less by any dry speech, because they are actually primeval revelations for the eye, just as music is for the ear. Neither is it in this instance sufficient for the narrator to talk about it in beautiful words, rather one must hear it and wants to hear it with one's own ears. But whether this is understood or not?—People are generally no longer thought to be able to do this with music—and why: it provides everything by means of tones and rhythms. Every "musical" person perceives quite clearly what the musician, the composer, of audible art "wanted to say." Does not the lover of visible art acknowledge himself to be unartistic when he constantly asks about its "meaning"? <u>A visible work should not mean anything beyond what can be seen.</u> This has also been preached a thousand times more recently, but unfortunately this has been done mostly by those who are far too superficial.

How then did it come to pass that people of today, no, really of yesterday, begin asking such questions about art? This happened simply because in fact the art of "yesterday," i.e. really the visible arts of all times of decadence, developed an art of interpretation in which all visible things were not used in the sense of direct and natural meaning, but rather in a conventional language of riddles. This was called allegory. In it an owl does not mean a nocturnal bird of prey, but rather wisdom itself, the equally unfortunate snake is to be degraded to meaning deceitfulness. An overturned torch has been seen as indicating a life extinguished and a nude human figure—ugh, for propriety's sake always means something mythological, or if this is not possible it implies a time when people were ignorant or at least uncultured. An artist too only received permission to give expression to his thoughts, feelings, or even his sensuality under these conditions. In any event, visible nature always has to bear the brunt of alluding to invisible or even merely conceptual things. Even today this is where the fear felt by all viewers of art comes from—that they will be thought of as uneducated if they do not know what is "meant" by every work of art in its details as well as in its overall composition. O what a ghastly aberration of the most exalted taste; of artistic taste—at least as far as the visible arts are concerned!

If only this art had always been called visible art, which it really is, then this most childish naïveté would not have been ascribed to it, and it would have been understood that it is supposed to portray, and indeed only can portray, things which can be seen. But it was actually called graphic art, and despite the fact that scholars specializing in all this understood and emphasized that designation—intended in an entirely materialistic way—only related to its technical aspects and that with these words it was not, unfortunately not meant to imply that one should form one's own soul around it, nevertheless the guileless common folks, who always take things in a deeper way than science does, assumed that people were supposed to educate themselves by means of this art. All the more, since people do not obtain new knowledge by listening to music. And thus both people and artists fell into the erroneous practice of entertaining themselves with desolate conceptual riddles in pictorial form instead of gazing with a sense of awe and terror upon the miracle of Nature created by God or the innate spirituality of the soul condensed into a visible likeness.

Yes, condensed! The artist of visible things must also be a poet if he wishes not only to capture things which happen but also to give shape to the emotions; but to give this shape purely by means of natural, earth-based and familiar envisionings. And if he makes these clear and palpable to all people who are similar to him and belong to his country, then his picture will need no explanation, not even a name alluding to its meaning. Certainly, for practical reasons each work has to have a name, but when the artist gives it one, here too he will show whether he is a poet, or a conceptual hair-splitter, or merely a copycat. In this regard one can see in catalogs of art how much or how little true artists, poets of the visible, lose themselves among the "thousands in Israel." But—true artists almost never show up in "catalogs," they pay no attention to the annual markets which serve these things. And almost as rarely they are to be found during their lifetimes in the junk rooms of art history, today called "museum," because these, like the whole of the contemporary history of art and criticism, in turn suck their knowledge out of the offerings of the market. They forget the waring, in a free interpretation of the saying: "If you wish to understand an artist, you have to go inside his workshop." But back to the language of images, that is to the language of images itself.

Visible art speaks to us in images, in signs. We could therefore just call its artists drawers of signs, if this designation as merely used to express a technical definition of what they do, but what has happened, sometimes more recently at least, is that this term is used to slander the very creative people who go out beyond such things and put them back into a narrow standard. The signs of the creative will can be buildings, sculptures, or two-dimensional pictures—if this will is great and all-encompassing these works will be, as with the greats of all times, all of these in one: they would be works of spatial art to which the last two types of art named may be of helpful service. But this "total art" comes out of spiritual visions and impulses and if it places itself in the service of a spiritual community, then it can grow into being a form of temple-art. The artist, however, always speaks with purely visible, even tangible substances and does not require anyone to believe or even see something that he has not made visible. For art and talent give and bless, they do not require anything of anyone, there should therefore be a quiet preparedness to be able to receive and view on the part of the observer.

The visible signs in all three types of art are form, material and color, and these again mutually condition one another. The true artist does not torture a form out of material substance that does not easily yield that form, and, since he only should use natural materials, they will already have their particular colors. He does not over-refine things, but rather follows the way of the least expenditure of energy in his materials; for the man who is creative spiritually produces something more important than skillfully crafted baubles, only admirable in the technical sense, and for every visible sign, whether it is a part of a structure, a sculpture or decorative surface, he chooses the material that is correct in character, suppleness and durability. Therefore in spatial art he uses natural materials as much as possible or those artificial ones which preserve their form and color. He will limit as much as possible the use of "painting" which is the least durable sort of art and provide for the chromatic atmosphere of the space as much as possible by means of construction materials and "inlay work" or by means of the conduction of light. In pictorial art he will make an important and basic distinction which in more recent times has been confused, simply because there is a struggle for a new style and there is conflict over such things, things which are actually always more correctly worked out over time in the history of art. <u>The distinction in question is the difference between decorative work and experiential work.</u> Increasingly these two elements in the arts are being developed exclusive of one another in order to be reunited once more in a total work of art in the service of spatial art, but only after they had been intentionally separated and developed to their greatest possible individual functions. In the ancient periods of style, e.g. in Indian or Egyptian temples, the massive walls and columns were almost completely covered with decorative work which was as much mere surface-animation without regard to the structural element of the building as it was conceptually an indicator of holy places and therefore of something belonging to the experience of the soul. In the Greek temple, which kept its actual structure free of pictorial bombast, the ornamental decoration of the walls is also markedly distinguished from experiential images, that is, painted or sculpted forms. And this distinction grew ever more consciously in all subsequent stylistic ages. Semitic culture condemned "image and likeness" and so entirely banned natural depictions; thereby it arrived at an especially strict and fine development of pure ornamentation.

In our modern time, however, which intentionally strives for new styles, emotions are, as always, confused where intentions drive them. Once people had had enough of the necessary new natural studies, Naturalism, the word "decorative" was taken up; and when youthful up and comers get to know something new they like to swing the pendulum toward the other extreme: they now condemn everything that merely alludes to the experience of nature. And so not only was the representation of nature "overcome," but so too was the representation of the soul, which was in any case earlier more theatrically idealized than it was deep in emotion. "Decorative" was now the battle-cry and the "colored spot" was the sanctuary of wall ornamentation, if pictures were still allowed at all. We idealists were counted for nothing, for we were even giving form to "inner experiences"; the "true art which was finally recognized," however, only allowed for "stimulation of the retina." That the truly creative ones had long since met all of these challenges in their works was simply not recognized due to blind jealousy—even Boecklin and Feuerbach, the poets of decorative depiction (v. Marees had become unknown by that time), were rejected: they painted that which I call experiential pictures and were therefore not at the height of the "purely decorative." Since no new spatial art had yet been arrived at, the need could not be felt that both kinds of art have to be present in order to animate a space meaningfully, not merely to decorate it in a meaningless manner. And so it came to be that even those artists, who despite their best intentions, were not decorative talents, but rather those of the naturalistic or psychological experiential depictions, desperately tried at least through technique to give the appearance of ornamental images made up of "lines and flecks of color." The less soul or even spirit they had the easier it was for them to achieve this. Genuine German hearts, who always want "everything all at once," were not satisfied with this art. Snobbish "society," however, was soon persuaded to celebrate as modern, and pay for, such narrow-mined works.

Great spatial art, and especially temple-art, requires, however, everything all at once: matter, soul and spirit. It provides the great spiritual symbol in the form of a temple with all its articulation of space and its perceived and intuitive lines in architectural features and ornamental work. Mathematical signs, which indicate purely spiritual perceptions, the circle, square, triangle, cross, spiral and other things, may and can be included here, for they can be sufficiently taken up again in emotional experiential images and made visibly intelligible in graphic fateful images and brought closer to humanity through the passion of emotion and color. But in no way should such experiential images, as they formerly did in the ancient temples, dogmatically overrun all architectural features, or scream out from every wall either. No, true architecture only speaks in great architectural lines and sensible ornamental art true to its material basis; but real experiential images are only presented in niches and chapels, which we only confront after stepping through a curtain, and invite us to a very solitary, intimate or admonishing dialog. People make pilgrimages to them, experience them and depart from them again; they do not scream at us from the walls and gables! Therefore, they in no way disturb one another or upset the unity of the principal space; here too no work is to be squandered by its not being appreciated or enjoyed due to its excess or distance from the eye or due to accidental disadvantages of lighting making it so it cannot be seen clearly.

In spiritually innate spatial art not only is everything derived from a living idea, but rather also everything, from the largest to the smallest, is also open to being experienced visually and all elements are mutually supportive of one another, the formation of space, conduction of light and articulation of imagery. No formation goes unappreciated due to unforeseen circumstances or absurdities.

All temple structures were intended to be unified in this way, even those of antiquity, even if the composition of individual works displayed a more conscious awareness of the distinction between decorative and experiential work. Chaos, variations overwhelming the basic composition, always added a secondary ostentatiousness, as with the baroque proliferations in the Gothic churches, which even led to the mangling of the main architectural features. But in the temple art of the future decorative and experiential work will be increasingly conscious of the heart and soul of the matter. Both will become increasingly less dogmatic and conceptual and more lively and sensual. Great linear symbolic images will be increasingly derived from the "art-forms of nature," but the experiential images will increasingly correspond to the general human destiny of the soul and therefore will be more and more "understood" to the degree that individual souls have experienced reality.

But all of the glory will be enjoyed by everyone purely in a visible way through the clarity of its formation, the authenticity of its materials and the splendor of its colors. For the Word shall become Image and the Image shall become Flesh and Blood, and Beauty shall redeem the Earth.

Woltersdorf near Erkner in Scheiding (IX.) 1923 Fidus

Reform ideas emerged from the artistic and literary underground of the Romanic Movement in the early nineteenth century and then found further expression in the literature of the later nineteenth and early twentieth centuries. The ideas in question went from the visions of a few to the motivations of the many. In the hands of the culture at large these concepts acted as a form of explosive cultural action—not always in the best interests of the whole. The effects of Reform ideology have not yet been fully played out in our culture. Much of what makes our world interesting and exciting stems from Reform ideas, but also the seeds of self-destruction and unhappiness can be found embedded in Reform concepts which have not yet been gainfully assimilated.

4.8. Animal Rights and Anti-Vivisection

The formalization of the concepts of "animal rights" and the prevention of cruelty to animals on a philosophical or legal basis did not occur in the Christian West (or anywhere else for that matter!) until the nineteenth century. The first laws were passed in this direction in England in 1822, especially to prevent the mistreatment of horses. Shortly thereafter, a pastor from Stuttgart named Albert Knapp formed the first German society for the protection of animals (*Tierschutzverein*) in 1837. By 1871 actual laws were enacted to prevent the torture or mistreatment of animals, and in 1881 the German League for the Protection of Animals (*Tierschutzbund*) was established. Clearly all of these efforts occurred in tandem with general attitudes prevalent among the Reformers.

A general overview of animal rights and antivivisectionism among the Reformers is provided by Zerbel (1998: 35-46).

The impetus behind new attitudes toward animals, like so much else in connection with the Reform movements, was rooted in the effects of urbanization. The increase in the number of house pets in the urban environment led to an increased awareness of the experience and understanding of the existence of a soul in animals. Animals, wild or domestic, began to be seen as parts of a holistic natural environment, deserving of care and protection. Especially native wild animals in nature were beginning to be understood as symbolic parts of the whole natural environment with a virtually *spiritual* meaning. Only after about 1920 did the fauna of a region begin to be understood in an entirely ecological context.

To some extent the human attitude toward animals was historically conditioned by two contrasting viewpoints. The Bible expressly, and from the very beginning, states that the animals of the Earth are placed here for humans to *use*. This attitude, of course, led to a license for much animal cruelty. On the other pole, exists the (pre-Christian) Indo-European attitude that animals are exponents of the gods and goddesses and that they deserve respect and kindness. Even in the process of animal sacrifice the animals were to symbolically give permission to be sacrificed, according to ancient Greek evidence, and that according to Germanic thought the animals were to suffer no fear or pain in the process of slaughtering, for to cause such things would be an affront to the divinity which had given the animal to mankind and would actually cause the god or goddess fear or pain. This is because the animal was seen as a visible and manifest exponent of the divinity itself. Taking this evidence into account, the very idea of "animal rights" can be seen as a sort of return to paganism. The very idea of having "pet" animals, sometimes called a *familiaris* (servant, domestic, household companion) in Latin, was seen by Christian theologians as tantamount to devilry or a sign of witchcraft. This is the origin of the concept of the witch's "familiar." The medieval Christian attitude toward animals was not unlike the general animal-hating culture promoted within Islam. Note that Greek, Germanic or Celtic lore is full of men having loyal companions—dogs or horses—there are no "famous animals of the Bible."

From early on there was a link between the natural healing movement and vegetarianism, of course, but this phenomenon was also immediately connected to the idea of a special link between animals and humans. This linkage, generally discouraged by Abrahamic religions, was another byproduct of the popular reception of Darwinian theories of evolution.

Beginning in the middle of the nineteenth century medical science increasingly began to make use of living animals in various experiments and in the training of physicians. Simultaneously, a movement arose from within the medical establishment itself to oppose the use of vivisection (literally the cutting into living beings) for education and experimentation. In 1879, the first manifesto was written about this subject: *Folterkammern der Wissenschaft* (Torture Chambers of Science) by Ernst von Weber (1830-1902). The antivivisection movement became a popular cause in Germany after this. It was supported intellectually and financially by Richard Wagner, for example.

Antivivisectionists were also more likely to be involved in other causes, such as vegetarianism (for obvious reasons) as well as natural healing and even anti-vaccination movements.

There existed a spectrum within the antivivisectionist movement. Some were totally opposed to any animal experimentation, while others sought only to moderate the practice as much as possible.

One dimension of the antivivisectionist movement recognized the link between animal cruelty and the likelihood of antisocial violence toward one's fellow man. Those who are cruel to animals in their youths are more likely to commit acts of violence against humans later.

Beginning in the late nineteenth century groups such as the Deutschsoziale Reformpartei (German-Social Reform Party) focused on the practice of kosher butchering which disallows the stunning or anesthetizing of animals prior to slaughter and demands the protracted bleeding out of conscious animals (in order to thoroughly drain them of blood). This ostensible animal-torture was made a central feature of this party's Anti-Semitic political platform.

I will return to the particular manifestation of the animal rights factor in section 6.11 which is concerned with the reception and use of Reform ideology in the context of National Socialism.

4.9. Economy

When viewed from a practical and down-to-earth level it can be seen that many, if not most, of the problems the Reformers try to address can be seen to be rooted in the advancement of science and technology on the one hand, but also in the financial system that provided the life's blood of capital to make these sometimes-deleterious innovations into concrete and widespread realities. This financial or economic basis was, of course, the target of proto-reformers such as Karl Marx. However, most Reformers had seen enough of the ways of Marxists and Anarchists to reject their solutions as being no more hopeful than those non-solutions of the Capitalists.

It should be noted that both capitalists and Marxists are entirely fixated on money. No real need exists to explain this about capitalists, but it should be noted that the magnum opus of Karl Marx was entitled *Das Kapital* ("Capital," 1867) In the doctrinaire, materialistic philosophy of Marx money substituted for God. Capital as an ersatz God was something that had to be monopolized and distributed by the state "from each according to his means, to each according to his needs." Just as the medieval church had monopolized God, distributing the Holy Spirit though the ritual of the Eucharist only to those loyal to the Church, the communist party would possess and control all means of production and the results of that production would be redistributed according to the party's own agendas.

Typically, the Reform-minded individuals who made up the various branches of the Reform Movements did not share either of these approaches, capitalist or communist. The main reason for this is that they were typically philosophically anti-materialist. This idealism may lie at the root of many of the general failures of Reform ideology to become a unified force for change. Directing and marshalling Reform ideologues would be something akin to the attempt to herd cats.

A few brave souls undertook the task of coming up with alternative theories for an economic system which would be more in keeping with the ideals of Reform ideology. But because the reform of the system of finances was so tied to the existing governmental structure the possibilities for individuals to take actual practical action in this field were extremely limited. Because the practical side of Reformism was rooted in its ability to be expressed on an *individual* basis or in the context of *smaller groups* (whether separate communities or in certain organizations) the possibilities for any Reform-based macro-economic solutions to be tried were for the most part doomed. The entrenched establishment of the government-finance-industry triangle was too strong to challenge without violent upheaval. For the most part the Reform-minded people were not predisposed to any violent solutions.

The history of the concept of economic reform is long and complex. Such a history reaches back into antiquity with the Mazdakite movement in Persia by which the society was to be reformed according to certain economic principles: redistribution of hereditary land and wealth (including wives!), and other cultural reforms, e.g., free love, hedonism, vegetarianism, a rule of no-killing, and very liberal customs of hospitality. In doing all this the Mazdakites were applying principles first established by the prophet Zarathustra whose Gathas promote the care of the poor and of animals, as we have seen. Within the European world, there is a continuous debate from at least the time of Adam Smith whose book *The Wealth of Nations* initiated new ideas on the subject. Philosophers such as John Locke and Thomas Paine devoted a good deal of attention to the ethics of economic development. Many Reformers looked to the American economic philosopher Henry George (1839-1897) for inspiration. Of course, the ideas of the German philosopher Karl Marx formed a fundamental touchstone in such debates. In many regards, economic Reformers of the nineteenth century were still dealing with questions surrounding the financial remnants of medieval feudalism.

Johann Silvio Gesell

An important Reform-minded economic theorist and activist was the German-Argentine Johann Silvio Gesell (1862-1930). Gesell was forced to earn his way in the world from an early age. He first worked for the postal system, then did an apprenticeship as a merchant with his brother in Berlin. He worked as a correspondent in Malaga, Spain for two years. In 1887 Gesell moved to Buenos Aires in connection with his brother's business. It failed due to economic difficulties, and he began thinking and writing about theories of financial reform. He returned to Europe in 1892, where he began farming in Switzerland. In 1900 he started the journal *Geld- und Bodenreform* (Money and Land Reform) and later another journal called *Der Physiokrat*.

Gesell returned to Argentina between 1907 and 1911. There he lived in a vegetarian commune near Buenos Aires. Upon his return to Europe he lived in the famous commune *Obstbausiedlung Eden* in Oranienburg near Berlin. In 1914 his writings were shut down by censors in the interests of wartime security and control. He returned to his farm in Switzerland, but was recruited by the National Bolshevik leader Ernst Niekisch to join the government of the Bavarian Soviet Republic in 1919. This revolution lasted only a few weeks before being suppressed. Gesell was arrested and tried for treason, but was acquitted after an eloquent speech he made in court in his own defense. His final years were spent both in Germany and Argentina before his death in 1930.

Gesell's Reform economic philosophies were highly developed and complex. His own attitude toward himself as a "citizen of the world" colored his ideas. He supported the idea of abolishing national borders and that the land should be owned in common allowing for free trade and competition between and among equal individuals. This abolishment of the private ownership of land was due to his belief that benefits obtained from welfare are diminished by the proceeds workers gain through their labor on private land. This idea is at the root of his free-land reform concept.

It is noteworthy that Gesell took into account the idea that individuals are motivated by their own self-interest, and that this must be realized and incorporated in any economic reforms. This self-interest was seen by him to be perfectly natural and healthy. He clearly saw that if this aspect were not accounted for the system would surely fail miserably. This stance placed him firmly against orthodox Marxism, which he considered to be against nature, and therefore impossible to sustain.

Gesell was the founder of what is called *Freiwirtschaft* (Free Economy) which he put forward in 1916 as what he called the *natural* economic order. *Freiwirtschaft* had three main components:

> *Freigeld* (free money)—money issued on limited basis with constant value.
>
> *Freiland* (free land)—land commonly owned, must be rented from government.
>
> *Freihandel* (free trade)—trade across national borders, borders which were to be abolished in time.

It was Gesell's aim to have a system in which those with the greatest individual talent and work-ethic would prosper most, as all sorts of inherited legal and financial benefits and privilege would be removed allowing for the emergence of the "natural economic order." At the same time, average incomes would rise and broaden resulting in more spending power for the masses and this would act as fuel for economic growth. The "free money" concept disallows the hoarding of money, thus keeping money in circulation in the actual productive economy and taking it out of the hands of bankers who lend the hoarded money for their own profits through interest.

Gesell rejected the validity of the value theory in economics, generally a theory used by Marx, although he called it the *Wertgesetz der Waren* (value-law of goods) also called the labor theory of value which states that the value of a good or service is calculated according to the total amount of socially necessary amount of time spent in labor to produce it.

Obviously influenced by some of Gesell's ideas, was another German writer and ideologue who rose to prominence named Gottfried Feder (1883-1941). Feder was a founding member of the National Socialist German Workers' Party whose theories and writings much influenced Hitler early on. Feder consistently fought against the ides of lending money for interest and what was called "high finances." His ideas were consistent with Reform ideas on many levels, but because it was also based on an Anti-Semitic theory, it was initially attractive to the Nazis. I will address Feder's ideas in some more detail in section 6.

4.10. Environmentalism and Ecology

One of the greatest and most enduring legacies of the Reform Movements is the idea of *ecology*, natural or environmental preservation and the whole concept that now finds expression under the (usually politicized) code-word "Green."

It might better be understood that the concept of ecology as we understand it today had its deep roots in the Monistic scientific philosophy of those such as Ernst Haeckel and in the various interests of the Reformers of the late nineteenth century. However, the full application of ecological theory would not find its popular home until after the mid-twentieth century.

Interest in the natural world is a feature directly linked to the heritage of the Reform Movements in the German Romantic Age with its key concepts of *Naturphilosophie* (Natural Philosophy) and the scientific concept of *ecology*. This interest in Nature was viewed from two sides: the direct and sensory and the scientific. On the one hand Nature is seen as something which the human being experiences with all the five senses in a three-dimensional framework. The meaning of nature is absorbed and experienced in this way, but the mystical meaning of this experience of Nature is a matter of poetic reality. By the time of the inception of the Reform Movements the understanding of Nature had itself evolved into a more scientific and practical model. The science of ecology was aimed at describing the complex interactions of a healthy balance of elements in nature, identifying disruptions in these interactions and arriving at solutions to problems posed by the mistreatment of the natural balance. The word "ecology" and in large measure essential aspects of the whole concept were first shaped by the great German scientist and evolutionist Ernst Haeckel in the nineteenth century.

A convenient overview of the concepts of the protection of nature and the landscape are offered by Gröning and Wolsche-Bulmahn (1998: 23-34) and Klueting (1998: 47-57). The connections between German Romanticism and environmentalism are many. These range from the direct and sensory appreciation of the natural environment and the desire to preserve and promote its experience on a spiritual level to the scientific theories of researchers such as Haeckel.

The main differences between the Reform concepts of ecology and the conservation of nature and that which is often understood as ecology in present-day jargon is that Reform-minded individuals and groups were not firmly in the grip of entirely materialistic philosophies and thus they had a more holistic view of nature and the environment which included an emotional connection to the land and the connection of the people (*Volk*) to their immediate natural environment.

Naturfreunde

An organized, grass-roots movement for the protection of the environment was formed in 1895 by a circle of enthusiasts around Georg Schmiedl in the Vienna Woods. Its original aims were to provide the working people with the opportunity to enjoy nature and to promote its preservation. This was the *"Die Naturfreunde"* (Tourist-Club: The Friends of Nature). This organization expanded mainly over the Alpine regions and in 1897 instituted a scientific study section focusing on botany and minerology. The organization grew rapidly to a few thousand members and became engaged in guided hikes in various regions and the production of hiking maps and books to guide the members in the mountains. In 1905 the Friends of Nature went international and by 1933 they had a total of about 200,000 members. The organization was then outlawed in the Nazi period and their properties were confiscated. In the post-war years, the organization was reconstituted and it has since come more and more under the principles of the so-called Green movement with about 350,000 members world-wide.

The greeting of the Alpine clubs of the day was originally "Berg Heil!" However, that of the *Naturfreunde* was and remains "Berg frei!" (Gröning and Wolsche-Bulmahn 1998: 23-34).

What began in the Reform Movements as a level-headed and reasonable desire for clean air and water and the preservation of the natural environment was soon politicized and "weaponized" by professional politicians, at first especially by the National Socialists in Germany and then later by the global Left in the post-war years. As noted in section 1 of this book, after the fall of the Soviet Union in 1991, its last General Secretary of the Communist Party of the Soviet Union, Mikhail Gorbachev, turned his attention to the foundation of the Green Cross International the next year. This appears to be a global initiative meant to arm the governments of the world to be able to reenact the kinds of uses of "ecological ideology" first pioneered by the Nazis (sanitized and re-packaged, of course!). The Nazis used "the protection of nature and the environment" as a moral cover for everything from land confiscation to mass-murder. (27) When any government can claim to have a vital interest in the total environment, then the door is open to programs designed to control and even own the entire environment itself—not just the land, but the water and air, as well. It does not take much of a student of history to realize what this can mean to the life and liberty of individuals.

In section 6.12, I will review in some more detail the question of Nazism and the "Green Movement," as the whole question of "How Green were the Nazis?" is a question that is always guaranteed to excite all sorts of controversies, and so deserves to be discussed and analyzed further.

5.0. Detour: The Sexual Revolution

We are fond of thinking that "the sexual revolution" was something belonging to Anglo-American culture of the 1960s-1980s, but as we have already seen the first general sexual revolution belonged to the Reform culture of German-speaking central Europe from the late nineteenth to the early twentieth centuries. The two capital cities of this revolution, or Reform, of sexual mores and customs seem to have been the German-speaking metropolises of Vienna and Berlin.

A convenient overview of the subject of sexual Reform is provided by Ulrich Linse in his article "Sexual Reform und Sexualberatung" (Sexual Reform and Sexual Counseling) (1998, pp. 211-226).

In many ways, it is probably difficult, especially for younger people today, to realize just how repressed people were with regard to matters of sexuality and sexual experiences before quite recently. In a bourgeois world that has embraced transsexuality as the latest "thing," and in which drag queens read stories to little kids at the public library and television sitcoms regularly feature gay characters, the old world still conditioned by Victorian mores seems light years away. But all that was not that long ago, and it would be a mistake to assume that such repressive norms have been put permanently behind us. Reforms can liberate, but if the results and experiences wrought by such Reforms are not handled with grace and decorum the backlash of convention and fear can be devastating.

The sexual revolution can be most comprehensively seen as one movement in two major phases. The first phase with its epicenter in Central Europe occurred between 1870 and 1933.

A hiatus was felt due to events of the Second World War and then the revolution was taken up in a second phase with its epicenter being in the Anglo-American world between 1960 and 1990. The phrase "sexual revolution" was in use in Germany and in Russia in the 1920s. In the use of the phrase Marxist undertones were present.

One does not need to be deeply educated in the history of European "morality" and sexual mores to realize that it was with the coming of Christianity that most of the overtly anti-erotic ideology entered the culture. Even in ancient times certain practices or relationships were considered "taboo," but these varied greatly from one European culture to the next. Greeks, Romans, Celts and Germanic peoples had very different ideas about things, one to the other. Generally, it should also be noted that the category of class played a large role in the variations between and among groups at different times. The sexual mores of upper class or aristocratic Englishmen or Frenchmen in the 18th and nineteenth century was a far cry from that of the developing middle class of this period. Testimony to this fact can be found in the erotic literature of the time!

In fact, of course, there have been many "sexual revolutions" in history. Some move society in a more liberated direction, e.g. the late 18th century in France and England, while others shift it toward a more repressive track, e.g. the Victorian culture of nineteenth century Britain. Such "sexual revolutions" in the past were laregley the result of tangential socio-economic factors more than they were direct and open reflections on the idea of sexuality itself. This is what makes the sexual revolutions in conjunction with the Reform Movements different. Sexuality did become the topic of conscious reflection and direct philosophical action. Perhaps a direct line could be drawn between the ideas of the Romantics, e.g. Rousseau, and the idea of *liberating* sexual feelings from an illogical and unhealthy repression.

Sexual Reform was in every way consistent with all other aspects of the Reform Movements. Just as with the religious reforms found in the embrace of alternative spiritualities in recognition of the fact that every individual person actually has, experiences and expresses his or her own particular attitudes in this realm of human existence, all the more is the same true for the most personal and intimate aspect of human life: sexuality. Sexual Reform stemmed from the recognition of this and the necessity of alleviating repression in order to establish true human health—emotionally, mentally and spiritually.

By way of deeper background, two very different sorts of men, the French nobleman, Donatien Alphonse François Marquis de Sade (1740-1814) and an Austrian, the Chevalier Leopold von Sacher-Masoch (1836-1895) each had personal sexual obsessions which later cause their names to be linked to certain forms of sexuality which attained great fashion in the early twentieth century: Sadism and Masochism respectively. These two individuals wrote a good deal of literary work in their lifetimes which had continuing effects after their deaths. Behaviors that fell into the realms for which these two became known became the subjects of academic or medical studies, as well as the stuff of imaginative recreational sexual experience. It should be recognized that these two gentlemen did not invent these forms of sexuality, but rather merely became articulate and artful exponents of the thoughts, feelings and behavioral patterns in question.

5.1. Sigmund Freud and the Psychoanalysts

No single individual is more associated in the general public's mind with human sexuality than is the Viennese physician Sigmund Freud (1856-1939). He is considered the founder of psychoanalysis and is best known for his theories on human sexuality, sexual development and the negative psychological effects of sexual repression.

Freud was of Jewish heritage and this made his ideas suspect in many "nationalistic" circles. Among Freud's most influential written works was *The Interpretation of Dreams* (*Die Traumdeutung*) published in 1899 and an abridged version of it entitled *On Dreams* in 1901. But Freud as not dependent upon written works to make his influence felt, as he was at the center of a medical organization called the International Psychoanalytical Association, though which his theories influenced medical practice around the world. The school of practice founded and promoted by Freud, that of psychoanalysis, made use of certain methods such as free association, word association, dream analysis and talk thearapy in which the patient delved into their lives to search for the causes of their neuroses. He developed a new psychological structure rooted in the concepts of the id, the ego and the super-ego.(28) Other supposed "discoveries" of Freud included the Oedipus Complex, the sexualized energy behind the libido and the death drive.

Freud developed also a theory of sexual development which included the stages of Oral, Anal, Phallic, Latency and Genital. These stages commence in infancy, progress into to puberty and continue after that. Individuals may become "stuck" at certain stages, or experiences and feelings associated with them may continue to manifest themselves throughout life. Freud based his theories on the study conducted on his clients over the years between the late nineteenth and early twentieth centuries.

Despite the reality that many of Freud's ideas have been subsequently rejected and seem rather idiosyncratic to many today, he did inaugurate a new serious phase in thought concerning the sexual life of human beings.

Eventually Freud had to flee Austria as the Nazis annexed the country in 1938. He spent the last year of his life in London.

Of course, many of Freud's theories have since often been outright rejected or called into serious question, but by the same token his ideas did cast a significant spell over the whole of the twentieth century and found expression in many auxiliary systems of thought, influenced literature, films, philosophy, politics and popular culture. The most fundamental aspect of Freud's thinking which has had the greatest lasting effect is that repression (especially of sexual feelings) is unhealthy for the individual, and that early experiences, even feelings can have a profound effect on a person's later life.

Two men who started out as disciples of Freud, but eventually broke with him due to their focus on the part sexuality could play in the liberation of mankind were Wilhelm Reich (1897-1957) and Otto Gross (1877-1920). Reich was a broadly influential and highly eccentric thinker who is credited with either coining or popularizing the very term "sexual revolution" (*Sexualität im Kulturkampf*). Reich wrote a book in German, published in 1936 with this title, which was published in 1945 with the English title *The Sexual Revolution*. The title, and the connotations of that title, had an impact on American popular culture. Due to Reich's later image in America (UFOs, orgone accumulators and the function of the orgasm, etc.) it is often missed that his ideas were originally steeped in Marxian philosophy. Otto Gross on the other hand succumbed to his indulgence in the excesses of post-WWI German culture even before Weimar got underway. Gross was, in his own right, an important personality and thinker, acknowledged by both Jung and Freud as having contributed important ideas to psychiatry.

The "sexual revolution" is one of those phrases which was subjected to redefinition by Marxist ideologues. This is a technique which they always seek to undertake in the cause of their Revolution. Normally, and on the face of it, the phrase simply refers to a time of profound changes in attitudes and customs surrounding sexual practices and norms. From a Marxist perspective, it is directly connected to the historical dialectic and is aimed at dismantling the norms of capitalist society, e.g. the nuclear family, marriage and child-rearing within that family. Already in the *Communist Manifesto* of 1848 Marx and Engels called for the abolishment of marriage and the nuclear family and promote the idea of the creation of a *Weibergemeinschaft*, i.e. that men should have "wives in common." Wilhelm Reich's original intent and message in his 1936 book *Die Sexualität im Kulturkampf* (translated into English in 1945 under the title "The Sexual Revolution") was in fact to further the socialist revolution.

5.2. The Beginnings of Sexology

A sort of cultural stereotype of the Germans is that, given any avenue of life or culture, they will try to study and systematize it into a *scientific* study. This is certainly the case with sexuality.

Besides Freud, whom we have already discussed, there also developed a whole school of what came to be called sexology (*Sexualwissenschaft*).

The three most important personalities involved with the pioneering scientific study of sexuality in Germany in the early twentieth century were Albert Eulenburg (1840–1917), Iwan Bloch (1872–1922) and Magnus Hirschfeld (1868–1935). There were many other significant physicians and scientists involved, e..g Sigmund Freud, Alfred Adler and Wilhelm Stekel, but here I wish to concentrate on these three perhaps less well known figures in the English-speaking world. Even this list of names hardly exhausts the field. Other important names include Ernst Burchard and Benedict Friedländer, who were gay rights activists and researchers. There was also Ernst Gräfenberg, whose name provided the "G" in the "G-spot," and he was also a pioneer in the development of the IUD contraceptive device.

The groundwork for the scientific study of sexuality had already been developed in the German-speaking world to a great extent by physicians such as Richard von Krafft-Ebing and Karl-Maria Kertbeny. An interesting personality in the foundation of sexology, who was not from Central Europe, was the Englishman Havelock Ellis (1859-1939).(29) His extensive studies published in two volumes as *Studies in the Psychology of Sex* (1905/1906) were every bit as groundbreaking as anything produced in Central Europe. But it is generally acknowledged that Krafft-Ebing's *Psychopathia Sexualis* (1886) forms the original foundation of the scientific study of sexuality.

The short-lived monthly *Zeitschrift für Sexualwissenschaft* (Journal of Sexology) began to be published in 1908 with articles by Freud, Adler and Stekel. In 1913 the academic *Society for Sexology* was established.

One advantage Germany enjoyed was that in the pre-Nazi period its laws were greatly conditioned by the Napoleonic Code of law, which was relatively more liberal with regard to sexual matters than, for example, Victorian England. A variety of factors, e.g. broad scientific and medical development and strong and inspired leadership, caused Germany to become the leader in all matters pertaining to the academic study of sexuality and causes affecting sexual liberation and variation in experience and expression. However, there was always a strong undercurrent of opposition to all of this in conservative circles.

As might be expected, Germany's leading role in research and activism regarding human sexual behavior on a global scale was almost entirely destroyed upon the advent of the National Socialist regime in 1933. Just a few months after the Nazi seizure of power, in May of 1933 Hirschfeld's institute was closed, his books burned and the building confiscated for use by the Nazis.

5.3. Magnus Hirschfeld: "The Einstein of Sex"

Without doubt the most important single figure in the foundation of sexology was Magnus Hirschfeld (1868-1935) who was a physician by training and during the Weimar period HE WAS BASED IN BERLIN. HIRSCHFELD WAS BOTH GAY AND JEWISH, which obviously made him and his work a particular target of the Right and of the Nazis in particular.

Hirschfeld was born into a learned Jewish family in Kolberg, Pomerania (now Kołobrzeg, Poland). He studied in Strasbourg, Munich, Heidelberg and Berlin earning his degree in medicine in 1892. Immediately after ending his studies he traveled in the United States and became involved with the gay culture in Chicago, Illinois. He was struck by the similarities between that culture and the one he found in Berlin, which sparked his interest and research in the idea of a universality of homosexuality as a global subculture.

Upon his return to Germany he set up a naturopathic practice, first in Magdeburg, then in Berlin-Charlottenburg. From a therapeutic perspective, he became especially interested in the problem of suicide among gay people. This problem, and his search for a solution to it, fueled a good deal of his activities, both scientifically and politically.

During his lifetime, Hirschfeld founded and managed two major organizations. The Scientific-Humanitarian Committee (*Wissenschaftlich-humanitäre Komitee*) founded in 1897 was an activist group with aims toward the legalization of homosexuality and a variety of other social causes. In 1919, at the inception of the Weimar Republic, Hirschfeld also founded the *Institut für Sexualwissenschaft* (Institute for Sexology), which was an academic and medical research institute for the study of human sexuality in all of its dimensions.

5.3.1. The Scientific-Humanitarian Committee

In his work with the Scientific-Humanitarian Committee Hirschfeld attempted to prove that homosexuality was found in all cultures all over the world. One of the ways he began doing this was by conducting interviews through interpreters with people from various German colonial regions. At the time there were over a dozen of these mainly in Africa and the South Pacific. Hirschfeld conducted his "field studies" in so-called Human Zoos at German international fairs where people from all over the empire were "displayed" in replicas of the "natural habitats" for Europeans to see.(30) Research conducted in this way served as a beginning for this 1914 book entitled *Die Homosexualität des Mannes und des Weibes* ("The Homosexuality of Men and Women") began writing what became his 1914 book *Die Homosexualität des Mannes und des Weibes* ("The Homosexuality of Men and Women"). The thesis of this book was that homosexuality occurs in every culture.

Hirschfeld, together with a number of colleagues, focused efforts, scientifically, legally and politically toward the purpose of repealing Paragraph 175 of the German constitution of 1871 which made male homosexuality illegal. The Scientific Humanitarian Committee was founded with this in mind. Not all of its members had the same attitudes toward gay life, but Hirschfeld was able to garner support from many quarters and a huge number of influential people in German culture signed his petition for the abolishing of Paragraph 175. Despite being introduced more than once, the bill to remove the paragraph never succeeded. As in England, homosexuality was only criminalized between men, lesbianism was not prohibited by law. (As it is said that Queen Victoria could not comprehend that such a thing was possible!)

As a physician and activist, Hirschfeld focused a good deal of effort on the problem of suicide among the gay population, which was identified as a significant problem then, and remains one today. He focused on the concept that society's condemnation of the behavior and feelings of gay people was at the root of the suicide problem, and the first and best solution to the situation was changing those attitudes and laws. A major effort to help prevent suicide among gays was represented by Hirschfeld's participation in the 1919 film production called *Anders als die Andern* (Different from the Others) starring Conrad Veidt. Hirschfeld appears in the film as himself.

Hirschfeld also allied himself to the feminist cause in 1905. Together they fought for women's suffrage, women's right to marry and have children in the professions of teaching and civil service as well as against the extension of Paragraph 175 to include lesbianism.

Hirschfeld became the face of sexual reform in Germany and became an international figure as well. On a 1931 tour of the USA the Hearst newspaper chain dubbed him "the Einstein of sex."(31) Currently in the USA the idea that there are "umpteen different 'genders'" is widely lampooned in conservative circles. This theoretical construct really stems back to Magnus Hirschfeld who attempted to categorize 64, and eventually 81, gradations of "gender intermediacy" (*Zwischenstufen*). He also coined the terms "transvestite" in 1910 and "transsexual" in 1923.

5.3.2. The Institute for Sexology

After the end of WWI and the institution of the more liberal laws under the Weimar Republic, Hirschfeld opened his *Institut für Sexualwissenschaft* in Berlin on July 6, 1919. It was housed in a large building near the Reichstag building. This building housed a large library and archive and the Museum of Sex. It became a center for sexual consultations and a haven for persons of various sexual identities and all income levels. Hirschfeld and his lover Karl Giese lived on the second floor of the building.

There was a research library and a large archive of materials relating to sexuality and homosexuality and it also housed medical, psychological and ethnological offices. It received as many as 20,000 visitors per year and conducted around 2,000 consultations on sexual matters. The poor were treated free of charge. The institute promoted the emancipation of women, advocated for the treatment of sexually transmitted diseases, and generally stood for widespread education in all matters dealing with human sexuality.

The Institute became a clearing house for medical treatments of transgender individuals and a meeting place for many celebrities of the sexual underground and gay scene in Europe. Visitors included W. H. Auden, Christopher Isherwood, Francis Turville-Petre, Gerhardt Hauptmann, Walter Benjamin, Ernst Bloch, Willi Münzenberg, Christian Schad, René Crevel, Andre Gide, Sergei Eisenstein and Elsa Gidlow.

Additionally, the Institute was a haven for patients receiving gender reassignment surgeries, which were just beginning at this time. Among these were Dörchen Richter and Lili Elbe. Transgender people were often given jobs, mainly as housekeepers, because they would have been otherwise unemployable. Richer was likely murdered by the Nazis when the Institute was sacked in 1933. Elbe, who had earlier been a successful Danish painter, died of complications of surgery in 1931. Her semi-autobiography was published in English in 1933 as *Man into Woman: An Authentic Record of a Change of Sex*.

The Institute also received official visits from the pre-Stalinist Soviets including a 1923 meeting with the Commissar for Health, Nikolai Semashko.

5.3.3. The Third Sex

Hirschfeld has become known for a variety of important concepts in the history of sexology. Among these are the idea of the "third sex," transvestitism, transsexuality and sexual intermediacy.

1901 Manifesto:
What the People Need to Know about the Third Sex!

The idea of the "third sex" was an early effort at establishing the idea that many homosexual individuals were characterized as having been born with an innate nature that was neither female nor male, but rather that they constituted a third sex that was in fact just as *natural* as either the male or female identity. This was a theoretical stage toward the ultimate recognition of sexual intermediacy. In 1905 Hirschfeld published the book *Geschlechtsübergänge* ("sexual transitions"). Here he further developed theories by earlier sexologists such as Benedict Friedlaender and Karl Heinrich Ulrich. Hirschfeld refined and developed his theories concerning the intermediate stages of sexual identity.

5.3.4. Sexual Intermediacy

Although the androgyny of the soul had been explored in psychology (see Jung's animus/anima dichotomy) and in literature (see Hesse's Harry and Hermine in *Steppenwolf*) nowhere else had the complexities of gender and sexuality been more thoroughly studied than in the work of Magnus Hirschfeld, who further developed theories of a "third sex" and introduced the idea of *Geschlechtsübergänge* (sexual transitions) and a classificatory system which involved the existence of gender *Zwischenstufen* (intermediate stages). The question of gender was seen not as a question of either male or female, but rather as a spectrum of possibilities. His theories held that one's sexuality was innate and inalterable. In 1908, the English writer Edward Carpenter wrote *The Intermediate Sex: A Study of Some Transitional Types of Men and Women,* no doubt influenced by the earlier German sexologists.

It was Hirschfeld who actually coined the term "transsexualism." He had transgender people on the staff at his institute and began research into the possibilities of doing gender reassignment treatments which included endocrinologic and surgical procedures. The first "gender affirmation surgeries" were undertaken in the early 1930s in Berlin. Hirschfeld negotiated with the local police the use of "transvestite passes" which allowed people to wear the clothing of the opposite sex in public. This was especially valuable for the free movement of certain kinds of sex workers in the city.

Among German male homosexuals of the day there was a pronounced anti-feminist tendency centering around the ideas of Adolf Brand and his journal *Der Eigene* (The Unique). Hirschfeld rejected these ideas and cooperated with the feminist movement, which is all explicable within the context of his theories of sexual intermediacy.

Even before the Nazis came to power the conservative Catholic Chancellor Franz von Papen began a crack down on the gay communities in major German cities. There was increasing political hostility to him and his efforts at repealing Paragraph 175, in the late 1920s, so Hirschfeld increasingly spent time abroad on world-wide speaking tours. Progress was made toward legalizing homosexuality, but the issue was complicated by the question of also legalizing homosexual prostitution. Hirschfeld consistently argued that homosexuality was natural, and that whatever is natural cannot be immoral. In the final analysis, the political landscape of the late Weimar period was simply too volatile and extreme to settle this issue rationally, and so it remained unresolved.

After only about three months from the time Hitler took power, Hirschfeld's institute was sacked, the library collected by the SA and made part of a public book-burning event. The sacking of the building also involved the murder of some of its residents, apparently including Dörchen Richer. The building was confiscated by the Nazis but it was virtually destroyed by allied bombs in 1944 and finally demolished in the mid-1950s. Its former location is memorialized by a plaque in the Berlin Zoo.

Hirschfeld went into exile first in Paris and eventually he moved south to Nice. He spent a good deal of effort attempting to reconstitute his institute with a new location in Paris. His research and writing continued, e.g. his book *Racism* (published in English in 1938).

Hirschfeld died suddenly of a heart attack while in exile in Nice, France on May 14, 1935. He is buried in the Caucade Cemetery where his tomb is engraved with the words *Per Scientiam ad Justitiam*—"Through Science toward Justice."

The importance of Magnus Hirschfeld to the study of human sexuality cannot be overestimated. Although he did not act alone in the work of establishing the idea of sexology his organizational work was important and his ideas continue to affect our culture today.

5.4. Other Sexologists

Another important researcher and sexologist was Iwan Bloch (1872–1922). His qualifications included being a physician (dermatologist and psychiatrist). His researches also led him into the field of literature and philosophy. For example, he rediscovered and published the manuscript of the Marquis de Sade's fragmentary novel *Les 120 Journées de Sodome ou l'école du libertinage*. This work was thought to have been lost. He used a pen-name, Eugène Dühren in conjunction with this project published in 1904. Previously, and under the same pseudonym, he had published a book entitled *Der Marquis de Sade und seine Zeit. Ein Beitrag zur Cultur- und Sittengeschichte des 18. Jahrhunderts. Mit besonderer Beziehung auf die Lehre von der Psychopathia Sexualis* (*The Marquis de Sade: His Life and Works*) in 1899.

Freud credited Bloch with the development of an anthropological theory of human sexuality. This helped free homosexuality from the pathological model.

Although Bloch wrote an impressive body of literature his *magnum opus* was to be the *Handbuch der gesamten Sexualwissenschaft in Einzeldarstellungen* (Comprehensive Handbook of Sexology Presented in Separate Studies). Only three volumes of this appeared before his untimely death at the age of 50. There were two volumes on prostitution and one on homosexuality. He also wrote *Geschlechtsleben in England* in four volumes (1901-1903) translated in 1936 as *A History of Sexual Morals. Das Sexualleben unserer Zeit in seinen Beziehungen zur modernen Kultur* (translated as: *The Sexual Life of our Time in its Relations to Modern Civilization*). This was an encyclopedia of the sexual sciences as they related to modern civilization. Other works included *Der Fetischismus* (Fetishism) in 1903; Bloch often wrote under pseudonyms such as Eugen Dühren, Gerhard von Welsenburg, Veriphantor and Albert Hagen.

The third pioneer considered here was the Berlin-born neurologist Albert Eulenburg (1840-1917). He was a professor of both pharmacology and neurology. Eulenburg's magnum opus was the multi-volume *Real-Encyclopädie der gesammten Heilkunde* (The Subject-Encyclopedia of Complete Therapeutics). Eulenburg was the first to recognize the rare genetic disorder known as paramyotonia congenita which became known as "Eulenburg's disease." It was only later in his already distinguished career that he began to publish on the subject of sexology. He was co-editor of the *Zeitschrift für Sexualwissenschaft*. In 1899 he delivered an address to the Psychological Club in Berlin on the subject of the Marquis de Sade. Then in 1902 he published an influential study: *Sadismus und Masochismus* (Sadism and Masochism), the English translation of which appeared in 1984.

These three great figures of German sexology, Hirschfeld, Bloch and Eulenburg, banded together in 1913 and founded the the *Ärztliche Gesellschaft für Sexualwissenschaft und Eugenik* [Medical Society for Sexology and Eugenics]. It was mainly these three figures who created the scientific context for the study of sexuality as a separate specialty known as sexology.

One of the most unique figures of the world of sexual Reform in Weimar Germany was Dr. Ernst Schertel, who has been mentioned several times in this book already. His range of activity was very broad and intense. He was an artist and magician, a scholar and an organizer. He was a doctor of philosophy, not of medicine, and taught his conceptual models through the magical use of dance (in front of audiences), publications (he ran one of the most influential publishing houses in the Weimar avant-garde called Parthenon) and promoted "free-body culture" not through a therapeutic or political model, but through a psycho-sexual one. Where Hirschfeld preached and taught sexual tolerance and diversity, Schertel evoked sexuality from within the subjects of the highly sexualized Weimar society.

The sexual revolution was one of the most impactful aspects of the Reform Movements and different dimensions of this impetus found influence in many of the other phases of the movement—the religious, psychological, health-related and political. I will return to considerations of the sexual revolution of the Weimar Republic in the section below on Reform's influence on our own contemporary society.

6.0. Sons of the Swastika

It is widely believed and taught that the ideology of the Reform Movements came to an abrupt end with the Nazi seizure of power in Germany on January 30, 1933. This is generally true, mainly because the essence of the Reform Movements was individual freedom and freedom to explore various possibilities in life, and the regime of the National Socialists brought that freedom to an end quickly. However, there is more to the story than that. It will be seen upon closer examination that the culture implied by the Reform Movements greatly affected the culture of Germany and the attitudes of many individuals within that culture, and that these elements did greatly shape the ideological mixture that was National Socialism.

A more global and contextual study of alternative ideas at the root of, in the midst of and in the aftermath of the National Socialist period in German history is provided in my book *The Occult in National Socialism* (Inner Traditions, 2022).

In so many regards National Socialism—as a brutal political movement—ran in ways contrary to the very spirit and essence of the Reform Movement. But on the other hand, because the leaders of the NSDAP were after all children of the Reform-Age many of their ideas and programs aimed for things almost identical to the final *aims* of Reform ideology. However, their methods and *modus operandi* were obviously contrary to the Reform ideology. Primarily it is the element of hate, so fundamental to the motives and soul of National Socialism, which is almost entirely lacking in the Reform Movements.

The biographies of the leading Nazis in Germany reveal that many of them were in one way or another devoted to the ideas contained in one or another part of the Reform of Life Movement. Many people are shocked to hear that Hitler was himself a teetotaler, a vegetarian and a devout antivivisectionist. The Reform ideology was a powerful and profoundly influential, if now often forgotten, force in German and world history. Most of the National Socialist revolutionaries of the early 1920s were veterans of WWI and most were born sometime during the 1890s. This means that they grew up in a Germany or Austria well-steeped in *Reform* ideology on several levels. They did not have to seek these ideas out so much as they were just "in the air." Had the Great War of 1914-1918 not occurred, certainly there would have been no Nazism and the Reform ideas would have found their normal and natural functions in the culture. But the wartime traumas, coupled with the post-war experiences of humiliation, poverty and chaos, led to a particularly toxic mixture of ideas of radical reform and violence as a solution to problems.

As is well-known, the swastika (German: *Hakenkreuz*, "hook-cross") was widely taken to indicate a symbol of the sun in the early twentieth century. Therefore, the connection between the followers of Hitler (who personally designed the swastika logo for his organization) and the children of the sun is actually a natural, but complex, one. Numerous book-length studies have been devoted to this engaging and fascinating symbol. (32) Most obviously, it was a sign used by the Aryan Indians and throughout Europe as well, leading many to the conclusion that it was the symbol of the "Aryan" folk. It also figured prominently in the symbolism of the Theosophical Society.

In this section I will attempt to review some of the elements found within the programs and leadership of the NSDAP

(Nationalsozialistische Deutsche Arbeiterpartei), or the National Socialist German Workers' Party that pertained to, or grew out of, Reform ideology. For more details on some of this I refer readers to my book *The Occult in National Socialism* (Inner Traditions, 2022). It will be found that the Nazis had a National Socialistic answer for almost every aspect of the Reform Movements.

As we have seen though the course of this book, the movements connected with the reform of life in Germany from the late nineteenth century forward were mostly applied in the spirit of adventure and for the purposes of improving the lot of humans on the planet. In the next sections, we will discover how these ideas led to the better parts of the so-called Hippie Movement in the USA. But as is true with all great and powerful ideas, they can be used for purposes that were never envisioned by the originators. At the same time, we will discover how these ideas can be transformed in the minds of those who hold them, transformed in ways that are both unexpected, yet quite understandable once the empathetic link has been forged with the ideas in question. The Reform of Life Movement in Germany was a radical impulse that opened the minds of people to extreme solutions to profound problems. In this section, we will examine closely how Reform ideals were directed toward the aims and goals of National Socialism.

It is often forgotten that not all "Nazis" were *real National Socialists*. Many were drawn from the ranks of Communists and Socialists who got on the band wagon as the Nazis gained power. Also, the original ideology of National Socialism was not that far removed from Marxist Socialism. The SA, or *Sturmabteiling* (Storm Detachment) was especially full of what the Nazis themselves called "Beefsteak Nazis"—brown on the outside but red inside. The German form of the term is *Rindersteak Nazi*. The storm troopers may have been ready for violence, but ideologically they were often "questionable."

For the cause of Reform the role of young people was always important. Therefore, youth organizations were also important in the political and cultural struggles that went on during the early twentieth century. Because most German-speaking youth organizations of the time, e.g. the Wandervogel, can be characterized as romantic, idealistic and moral the organizations tended to be if anything right-leaning as far as politics are concerned.

As National Socialism tried to see itself as a new philosophy of life in general it is no wonder that the Reform ideas often so dear to so many individuals who became leaders in this movement would find their way into Nazi ideology and propaganda.

6.1. A National Religion

Many observers over the years have seen National Socialism as much as a *religious* movement as it was a *political* one. I outline in some detail the religious and magical dimensions of the regime of the NSDAP and its leaders, especially in chapter 7 of my book *The Occult Dimensions of National Socialism* (Inner Traditions, 2022). There we see that the Nazis were not, as is so often assumed, exponents of some sort of a *pagan* ideology, and certainly were not involved in anything remotely resembling "Satanism." As we have seen elsewhere in this book, religious streams of thought that were pagan, and others that were *völkisch* expressions of Christianity (e.g. the so-called Deutsch-Christen) were popular among Germans in the years leading up to the inception of the Third Reich, and these sorts of elements did play some role, albeit a minority one, in the affairs of the Nazi regime. However, no outside influence, that is an influence from an ideology outside that of the apparatus and personalities of the NSDAP itself, were ever seriously entertained by the Party itself. The way of National Socialism was intended to be a comprehensive view of life in all its aspects and all aspects of life were to be understood within a National Socialist perspective. In other words, National Socialism was not intended to have a religious dimension, it was rather intended to subsume all those parts of human life that were related to any sort of "religious" impulse. In all of this Hitler and his minions were largely following a pattern of practice and ideology first set out by the Bolsheviks in Russia.

The National Socialist regime did not seek to create another religion, but rather the National Socialists sought to replace religion with their own political ideology. At the same time, Hitler did conclude the Konkordat (concordance) with the churches in Germany which made them essentially part of the government. Instead of the churches having to raise money from the congregation, the state taxed the populace and distributed funds to these churches. This arrangement both saved the churches financially and brought them effectively under governmental control. Essentially the Konkordat continues to define the church/state relationship in the Federal Republic of Germany.

The Reform Movements, as we have seen, did not particularly embrace any one religious point of view: there were Christians (of various sorts), pagans, those tending toward Eastern religions, atheists (*Freidenker*) and a wide variety of new thinkers, what we could later call "new agers." This latter group included, of course, Theosophists, Anthroposophists and others. For the most part the Nazis, contrary to popular notions currently, were for the most part officially Christians. Very few of them resigned from the Church, which was and is an option in Germany. Among notable Nazi leaders who did so are Heinrich Himmler and Rudolf Hess. At the same time, the hostility of the NSDAP toward the organized *churches*, both the Roman Catholic and Lutheran, is unmistakable. Clearly Hitler had in mind the eventual replacement of the churches with his own kind of Party-based faith rooted in *völkisch* ideas (not necessarily "pagan" ones) and in science and progress. National Socialism represented a reform of religious ideas in a new direction, focused on race, eugenics and a new German empire which embodied a radically new way of looking at all aspects of life. These ways have in time come to be understood as repugnant to the ideals of Western republics founded on individual liberty and free market economies, but nevertheless the path of National Socialism must be historically recognized as just one of the pathways that was opened up to people's minds by considerations of the ability of humans to reform life in a fundamental way under the aegis of the human spirit.

6.2. Politics and Economics

One of the most important underpinnings of National Socialism was its economic opposition (philosophically) to the practice of usury, the idea of charging interest on monetary loans. The main Nazi ideologue on this topic was Gottfried Feder, who was a member of the Party from the beginning. In the Party Program of 1920, commonly called the "Twenty-Five Points," the tenth and eleventh points read:

10. It must be the primary duty of every citizen to work mentally or physically. The activities of the individual may not conflict with the interests of the general public but must be carried on within the framework of the whole and for the good of all.

WE THEREFORE DEMAND:

11. Abolition of income unearned by labor or effort;

BREAKING THE BONDAGE OF INTEREST

The abolition of usury was both an influence from medieval Christian attitudes and ultimately an inheritance from Indo-European customs. This was nothing more than a dream and a philosophical idea as put forward by the NSDAP. In practice the financial institutions of the Third Reich limped along for the duration of its time in power with no major reforms. Germany became a military regime on the order of the Roman Empire, exploiting for financial gain all of its conquests. Hitler was supported and controlled by industrial and capitalist interests from an early time, and these were debts that could not be easily dismissed for more radical philosophical predilections. The "25 Points" demonstrate the idea, but history lays out the fate that awaited the conclusion of one more diabolical deal.

Hitler's view of how the German state was to operate was in many ways contrary to the natural character of Germany historically. It was from time immemorial to the dawn of the Third Reich a collection of tribal states with no overriding sense of greater nationalism—Germans were Prussians, or Bavarians or Alemannen first, Germans second. Hitler wanted to change this and to this end in 1935 he instituted what was called the *Gleichschaltung* ("coordination"). The ultimate aim of this was to forge a hierarchical centrally commanded state: *Ein Volk, ein Reich, ein Führer!* The *Gleichschaltung* operated on the level of politics and law, but first and more importantly on the level of symbolism: This involved making the symbols of the NSDAP the same as those of the German state, so the swastika flag became the national flag of Germany and on a practical level the system of administering the state was subsumed by the administrative structure of the Party. Other parties were outlawed. Hitler was the absolute dictator of a single and united greater Germany. Again, this would appear to be contrary to the spirit of Reform, which would have more ideally taken the natural cultural differences of the various German tribal regions into account, as had, ironically, the Second Reich—the Holy Roman Empire which had maintained the independent kingdoms and principalities of ancient Germania.

One might expect that the National Socialists would have a unique attitude toward economics, but as opposed to Marxist Socialism the Nazi attitude was not one totally devoted to economic concerns in any sort of theoretical way. At least that is the way it turned out. Originally the movement was more concerned with economics, but Hitler brought a highly pragmatic, power-oriented and militarily organized attitude which set economic ideals to the side.

Gottfried Feder

Gottfried Feder (1883-1941) was among the original small group that founded the German Workers Party in January of 1919, which then became the National Socialist German Workers' Party under Adolf Hitler's influence. Feder's interests were essentially economic and related to land-reform. It was his speech which first inspired Hitler to join the group. He was a civil engineer and commercial builder. Events of WWI led Feder to a deep interest in the problems rooted in the financial establishment, banking, etc. He developed a passion for "breaking the servitude to interest" (*Brechung der Zinsknechtschaft*). It was his wish that the banks be nationalized and that the charging of interest be abolished. In his mind, as well as in those of many Europeans of the time, "usury" was thought to be connected to nefarious "Jewish bankers." He continued to write works on economic ideas such as *"Kampf gegen die Hochfinanz"* ("The Fight against high finance") and a pointed anti-Semitic tract *"Die Juden"* ("The Jews,") both in 1933 and in 1934 he was named *Reichskommissar* (Commissioner), but he was quickly moved to the side as far as Nazi officialdom was concerned, as his ideas on economic affairs were at odds with Hitler's drift toward the bankers and industrialists.

Feder along with Hitler drafted the original "25 Points"(33) document which outlined the basics of National Socialist ideology, a document which remained the official stance of the Nazis for the duration of their existence.

A fundamental principle of idealized Nazi economic theory was that of autarky—the belief that cultural systems (economic, ethnic, etc.) should be independent of one another and as self-sufficient as possible. Feder published a work in 1939 entitled *Die Neue Stadt* (The New City) which proposed the development of "garden cities" of approximately 20,000 inhabitants, divided into nine semi-autonomous zones encircled with adjacent agricultural areas. Each city was to be entirely self-sufficient and self-sustaining. Not only were new cities to be established in the countryside, but the system was also to be implemented in urban environments where existing large cities would be reconstructed into self-sufficient neighborhoods according to this theory.

Hitler tried to retain the old guard member, Feder, in a position of power, but Feder's philosophy simply was not practical for Hitler's advance to power. Hitler required the support of the industrialists and capitalists, and the application of Feder's philosophy would utterly destroy the banking industry by abolishing the earning of interest. After the Nazis assumed power Feder was removed from the government and made a professor for Settlement Policy at the Technical University of Berlin.

In the end, the National Socialist movement enacted very little of the Reform-minded economic policies that it had begun with. The so-called Anti-Capitalist wing of the Party was largely purged in one way or another.

6.3. Nazi Education

One of the main principles of Reform pedagogy, the idea of an orientation toward the student and the motives of the student, rather than the authority of the teacher or the curriculum is fundamentally at odds with basic authoritarian principles of National Socialism. In the NS ideology the student is there for the most part to be indoctrinated into the attitudes of the Party and government. The individual will or motives are minimized. All organizations structured under the concept of Reform Pedagogy were formally shut down as the NSDAP tightened its grip on German culture in the *Gleichschaltung* process. Many of the concepts and practices at home in Reform Pedagogy were incorporated into Nazi educational programs, but the name "Reform" was not ideologically pleasing to the Nazi mentality. With this being said, however, several important representatives of the movement for Reform-Pedagogy did become members of the NSDAP and ideas connected with the Reform Movements did find their way into the educational organization of the Third Reich. The Nazi officials seemed most concerned with the fact of whether educators were or were not Jewish than anything else. Many of the Reformers, and this was true of most endeavors during the Third Reich, probably thought that National Socialism was just another passing political fad. In this they were right, I suppose, but its passing did involve the unter destruction of the country.

Several Reform educators signed on to the educational establishment under the Nazis, but not all. Certain Reform-oriented schools, e.g. the Odenwaldschule and Wickersdorf retained or incorporated Reform ideas in their curricula. Reform ideas may have only been used in a superficial way. Certainly the idea that a more natural form of education for young people, in close proximity with nature and away from the bourgeois world governed by adults was incorporated into the camping education (G. *Lagererziehung*) used by the Hitler Youth and the League of German Girls. The head of the youth organizations in Nazi Germany, Baldur von Schirach coined the philosophical phrase: "Jugend führt Jugend" (Youth leads the Youth). Ideally education would be a far more direct and physical experience than that provided by the establishment schools. Critics could easily make note of the appearance of these systems really being experiences tailor made to harden the youth for the vicissitudes of war.

The authoritarian drift of the educational programs in the USA can clearly be identified in that the school system, teachers and their unions, etc., increasingly claim the authority to design the curriculum and teach what the student *ought* to learn as regards social and cultural issues. Obviously, in the case of the educational programs in the USA, this trend has a Left-ward leaning orientation, but its authoritarian, and anti-Reform ideology is nevertheless clear.

6.4. Fashion and Clothing

As most people are aware, the Nazis were great aficionados of uniforms and every detail of their design and styles. As regards Reform Ideology, this would again seem foreign to the proto-Hippie fashion sense of men such as Diefenbach, Fidus or Gräser! But there is a connection, nevertheless. A uniform is an *equalizer*. Everyone who wears the uniform belongs equally to the group, the rich are not differentiated from the poor. (The positive effect of the wearing of "school uniforms" in institutions of education has long been noted.) The only differentiation between and among those wearing the uniform lies in the *insignia* which signal differences in rank or accomplishment, as measured by the hierarchy of the organization. Hitler's own self-styled uniform conveyed a contemporary aura of the ordinary, humble and unassuming soldier of the folk. (This can be contrasted with the flashy and gaudy uniforms worn by Hermann Göring.) In general, the propagandistic effect of the wearing of uniforms sent a signal to the population as National Socialism was on the rise that the NS members and supporters were forces of law and order in contrast to the "rag-tag" appearance of those on the Left. Famously, Hugo Boss designed the SS uniforms, among others. In their effort to "brand" their movement every detail of NS regalia was designed and given form in a "Nazi manual of style"—the *Organisationsbuch der NSDAP* compiled by Robert Ley.

6.5. Health and Nutrition

Because, as we have seen, the leading Nazis were all for the most part children of the Age of the Reform Movements, the idea of natural methods of healing, and so on, were well accepted by many of them. After 1933, the whole apparatus of the Reform Movements was systematically incorporated into the apparatus of the NSDAP in the *Gleichschaltung* process. Most of these aspects were amalgamated into the governmental program known as the *Reichsarbeitsgemeinschaft der Verbände für naturgemäße Lebens- und Heilweise* ("State Study Group of the Associations for Natural Ways of Living and Healing"). It seems to have been the aim of the Party to discover and promote a naturally, and hence racially, based theory and practice of health, vigor and well-being. A "German Medicine" (*Deutsche Heilkunde*) with the incorporation of various folk-remedies and natural healing methods were sought to displace the established forms of medicine which were seen as foreign influences. This "New German Medicine" was, however, generally resisted by the powerful medical establishment in Germany and made only marginal progress. As was typical of National Socialism, many governmental agencies were created to absorb popular ideas previously freely purpued by individuals and groups. Other examples of this include the *Deutsche Gesellschaft für Lebensreform* ("German Society for the Reform of Life"), Julius Streicher's *Forschungs- und Prüfungsinstitut für biologische Heilmittel* (Institute for the Research and Verification of Biological Healing Methods") and the *Forschungsinstitut der Deutschen Lebensreformbewegung* ("Institute for the Investigation of German Reform of Life"). In 1942 Werner Kollath published the seminal National Socialist document on the subject *Die Ordnung unserer Nahrung* ("The Regulation of Our Nourishment"). Kollath assessed "civilized fare" as an inferior semi-nourishment, while raw foods were seen as "full-valued" or a complete form of nourishment

Famously, Hitler was a teetotaling vegetarian. Rudolf Hess was an enthusiast for "health food" of all sorts as recommended by the Reform Movements. The Führer led an ascetic life: non-smoking, non-drinking, vegetarian and an anti-vivisectionist. His source for these ideas appears to have been the works of Theodor Hahn, who had influenced Richard Wagner to take up vegetarianism. Wagner wrote about this in his work entitled *Religion und Kunst* (Religion and Art) in 1881. There Wagner characterized the consumption of meat and even cooking as a Semitic, un-Aryan trait! This influenced some other Nazis as well.

6.6. Anti-Alcohol Aspects

As a part of Hitler's ascetic image, he was known not to indulge in the drinking of alcohol. This was apparently early on a part of his *modus operandi* in manipulating the masses—first the members of his own party and then the general population. He famously held his early rallies and meetings in beer halls, where he was likely the only sober man in the house! This being said, as time went on Hitler was far from sober. Through his personal physician, Dr. Theodor Morrell, Hitler was "prescribed" the state of the art drugs of the day, as many as thirty-two of them, including cocaine and methamphetamine.(34) When it came to the armed forces of the Nazis, it is interesting to note that they were often fueled by the recently synthesized methamphetamine. This was a key to the initial successes of the Blitzkrieg in France when the Germans fought for days without rest. This drug was available over the counter under the brand name Pervitin and called "Stuka-Tablets." The situation in France was further exacerbated by the fact that the French had supplied their troops with ample bottles of *wine!* (Miserable memories of the trenches in the war of 1914-18 led the generals to think that the boys might need a bit of wine to help them get through it all.)

6.7. The Naked Nazis

The concept of nudism in connection with National Socialism at first glance seems to be a far-fetched one. But, as seen elsewhere here, the Nazi cults of physical beauty, health and strength were actually natural outgrowths of Reform Ideology. It can be seen that theoretically the holistic idea of "healthy mind, healthy body," the unity of body and soul and the curative power of nature in air, water and sun could be seen to have strong links to the *völkisch* concept.

The idea of *Freikörperkultur* spanned many political and cultural interests of the right and left. Because it was at home on the Left and among many "decadents," especially in the Berlin area, the practice was at first forbidden by the Nazis (by a decree of March 3, 1933). It was soon transformed into an official National Socialist institution as the Kampfring für völkische Freikörperkultur (Militant Ring for Racial Free-Body Culture). Under leadership of Hans Surén and supported by Walter Darré, nudism even found a place among members of the SS itself. Restrictions against nude swimming were relaxed in 1942 and rules concerning the practice were ones kept in place in post-war West and East Germany.

Americans may be used to seeing images of "nudists" from about the 1950s forward. These were as often as not photographed as overweight and "ordinary" individuals engaged in "wholesome" activities, such as playing volleyball. In Germany, the image and purpose tended to be different, and the emphasis was on healthy, strong and *beautiful* bodies, as we have seen. For the Nazis, this impulse was directed toward eugenics (racial purity), the establishment of racially coded standards of health and beauty and all of this was more or less directed toward the organization of a martial body of warriors and women designed to be the mothers of this future generation of German fighters. All this would seem to be unique, if we did not know so much about ancient cultures, such as that of Sparta.

6.8. Sexuality and Reform

In the area of sexual liberation and reform the Nazis officially shared little of the spirt of the Reform Movement's attitudes, aims or philosophy. But because the Reform ideas had actually become cultural realities among the population, there was nevertheless a good deal of the alternative sexual lifestyle among the Nazis themselves, but it was something that had to be secret and hidden from any acknowledgement. Famously, some of the members of the SA (*Sturmabteilung*), including its leader, Ernst Röhm, were gay (Ger. *schwul*). But this was one of the "charges" brought against the organization after the so-called Night of the Long Knives (30 June 1934), when Röhm and the leadership began to be purged.

As pointed out by Mel Gordon in his wonderful book *The Voluptuous Panic* (Feral House, 2006), there were in fact night clubs in Berlin which catered to the eccentric tastes of members of the NS movement.

The term "sexual magic" as used by the predecessors of the Nazis, such as Lanz von Liebenfels or Maximilian Ferdinand Sebaldt von Werth for the most part boiled down to a spiritual or mythic attitude toward the practices of eugenics, in order to engineer a more beautiful, healthy and strong race of future Germans. Although most people today look back on the various features of the Reform Movement in terms of what they find of value in it at present, and the whole idea of "eugenics" has been thoroughly discredited in the public eye due to the excesses and radicalism of the Nazis on this subject, such a dimension does seem to have had a hold on the Reformers of the day, as it would have been a way, in their minds, to ensure a healthier and happier future for the members of the whole culture, eliminating problems in an organic way before they ever arose.

Under the Nazi regime there was a general liberalization of sexual mores and pre-marital sex and out of wedlock births were tacitly approved. Girls were not supposed to refuse the sexual advances of SS-men, for example. All of this was approved in the name of both "eugenics" and to increase the birth rate for the sake of the expansion of the German people biologically and to ensure that men would be available for the wars of the future!

6.9. Urban Planning and Settlement Programs

From the beginning of the Reform Movements in Germany visionaries, such as Diefenbach, sought to create communities of people as self-sufficient as possible and set apart from the bourgeois world. In such laboratories theories and ideas that ran the gamut from social experimentation to living spaces, to food production could all be engaged in. We know that leading Nazis such as Heinrich Himmler, Walther Darré and Rudolf

Höss were enthusiasts for the *Artamanen*-theories of Willibald Hentschel. For the Nazis, these ideas were seen as something to be virtually *weaponized*. Colonies of Germans would be sent out to the East and vast agricultural communes would be established, principally under the aegis of the SS. The lands would be colonized and the indigenous local populations would be replaced and/or enslaved.

The design of such settlement communities actually influenced the shape of what became concentration camps where the deplorable or undesirable parts of the population would be separated from the body politic of the German people. As we know these quickly evolved into facilities for actual mass murder.

In a footnote or ironic horror, the concentration camp at Dachau was also fitted out with an herb garden, apparently one of Himmler's ideas, so that the prisoners could grow medicinal plants in an effort to cure themselves of the afflictions being instilled in them directly and indirectly.

One of Hitler's main obsessions (he had so many) was the redesign of cities. The Austrian town of Linz was one he had a plan for, but his major project was the redesign of the city of Berlin, to be renamed "Germania," and to be the capital of a worldwide empire. Clearly here, as in so much else, the Führer was imitating the patterns set forth by Roman emperors. Emperor Trajan famously reconfigured whole sections of the Eternal City during his reign. The great congress hall depicted below is a clear imitation of the temple known as the Pantheon in Rome. In many respects the Nazi obsession with Rome and Roman ideas and patterns of thought and aesthetics ran counter to the principles of Reform ideology.

Conceptual Model of Hitler's Vision for "Germania"

In general, the attempts to form communities or communes independent of government design and control were almost completely eliminated by the National Socialist regime, the formation of virtually independent political groupings in the countryside was theoretically unthinkable. It is interesting to note that the Eden Community was allowed to continue operation, as it had early one become dedicated to *völkisch* principles at the time of the First World War.

The Artamanen Movement set into motion by Willibald Hentschel at the end of the nineteenth century had a direct effect on certain developments in the Nazi organization regarding the development of settlement programs in the east. Hentschel even became a member of the Nazi Party for a while, and maintained good relations with the organization. Certain Nazi leaders had been involved with his movement in their youths, these included Heinrich Himmler, Walther Darré and Rudolf Höss, who held posts at various concentration camps, eventually taking command at Auschwitz. The Artamanen organizations that developed in the 1920s were eventually incorporated into the apparatus of the Nazi Party in keeping with the general program of *Gleichschaltung*, whereby elements of culture beneficial ot the Party were incorporated in National

Socialist form, and those elements antithetical to Party interests were targeted for elimination.

In the late 1960s there was an attempt to revive the organization and ideology of the *Artamanen* in Germany, with mixed success. Hentschel's basic idea appears to be a good one, but its involvement with racial obsessions and hostilities doomed it from the beginning.

6.10. Art and Literature

A well-researched and illustrative book entitled *Art in the Third Reich* by Berthold Hinz (Pantheon, 1979) provides the basic information we need to make a general assessment of the topic.

Art, as it came to be understood in the nineteenth and twentieth centuries, is antithetical to the totalitarian and authoritarian philosophy of Fascism, National Socialism or Marxist-Leninist Bolshevism for that matter. If artists are required to give expression to the ideology of the party in charge, and are not free to express the contents of their own souls, art as we know it today is impossible. This political direction is in principle no different than the guiding principle of art in the Middle Ages when most artistic expression was limited to the purposes of the Church. Art is always created for the sake of something. Historically this has usually been for the sake of the king, the religion or for the ruling political authority—the idealistic dictum of "art for art's sake" is actually a historical anomaly. So, art in the Third Reich really represented a reversion to historical norms, as dreary as that might have been.

Because both art and literature fall in the Nazi mind under

the aegis of propaganda, and the main agendas of the NSDAP involved the marshaling of the population into compliant, obedient believers in the message of National Socialism, aspects of both art and literature we usually associate with the Reform Movements were generally repressed. The ultimate rationale for this repression and lock-step direction of art, literature and even architecture can, however, also be seen to be a (misguided and inaccurate) interpretation of the Reform message. The Nazis, as the "25 Point Program" makes clear, were oriented toward what was supposedly only good and protective for the health and well-being of the German nation, as understood as a natural and organic entity. Much as an ecologist today would think of an endangered species, the Nazis thought of the German nation. All of the repressive measures of the state were intended to protect and promote that natural entity, or so the underlying theory might go. The facts show that the regime was more interested in the maintenance of maximal power for the political leadership, which should not be surprising, as this is usually the case universally when it comes to political leadership.

One feature was a constant in National Socialist ideology as regards art: localism. Things were favored which seemed rooted in the locality in which the art was produced. This idea extended to literature and to representational art. Hitler, as an artist himself, often spoke about art and the philosophy of art. He favored a return to the realistic traditions of the nineteenth century. Socialist Realism as practiced in the Soviet Union was singled out as decadent simply because it strove to be internationalist and universal in its approach.

Perhaps the greatest theoretician on the topic of this concept of localism in literature was the Austrian Josef Nadler (1884-

1963). His magnum opus on the subject was *Literaturgeschichte der deutschen Stämme und Landschaften* (Literary History of the German Tribes and Landscapes, 1912-1928). He studied how literature and landscapes interacted with one another. He concluded that this relationship was determinative, that the Germans and Romans had become a mixed race in Germany and that this "race" preserved the best traits of both of these worlds. Literary traits were, according to him, determined by *tribal* affiliations. Nadler became a member of the NSDAP after Austria had been annexed by Germany.

Nazi Art

In general, the art world suffered greatly under the Nazi regime. The free and vibrant, if often chaotic, world of Weimar art was all seen as a representation of degeneracy (*Entartung*) by the Nazis. All art, graphic, cinematic, literary, etc. was bought under the control of Hitler's artistic tastes in programs largely administered by the Minister of Propaganda, Joseph Goebbels. All this seems rather ironic as Hitler saw himself as first and foremost an *artist* himself. But this might be the result one could expect when one puts an opinionated artist in control of the art world!

As is well-known, Germany was the epicenter of film-making, especially experimental, artistic and ground-breaking cinema in the time after WWI. Much of this artistic production dealt with imaginative, outré themes and quite often many Jews were involved in the industry as well. Immediately after Hiter became chancellor, his Propaganda Minister, Joseph Goebbels marched to the centers of film-making, most especially to UFA studios, and informed the employees and management that the studios would be brought under the control of the National

Socialists and that Jews would be excluded from participation. This heralded a great creative drain from the German film industry to Hollywood. (35)

Fidus, that artist whose works and whose style has come to most exemplify the whole Reform Movement (see §4.7.3.), had his own involvement with the National Socialists. The story of his involvement is in many ways a microcosm of the way in which millions of Germans were drawn into the Nazi movement. He joined the NSDAP in 1932, during a time of severe economic hardship in Germany, but his style and everything else about him was found to be an anathema to Nazi ideology, so his works were banned and forbidden by the Party in 1937. The Fidus style was targeted by later Marxists critics and held up as somehow exemplary of Nazi aesthetics, but nothing could be further from the truth.

6.11. Animal Rights

It is one of those ironies of the Nazi period that while monstrous experiments were being carried out on humans in concentrations camps and humans whose lives were considered unworthy of life, due to mental or physical deficiencies, the most stringent laws regarding animal experimentation known up to that point were passed with National Socialist sponsorship. This animal rights movement was a general part of the Reform Movements in Germany, as we have seen, but the idea of animal rights, not based on an anthropocentric, but on a nature-centered basis was an integral part of National Socialist ideology. The laws came under the rubric of the German word *Tierschutz* ("animal protection").

Animal rights activists at the end of the nineteenth century focused on protests against the use of animals in medical and scientific experiments ("vivisection") and against the practices of kosher slaughtering and butchering of livestock, which was seen to be inhumane because it was thought to amount to torturing the animal to death rather than the traditional European methods focused on the quick and painless death of animals. Curiously, secular modes of animal slaughtering developed in Europe actually go back to pagan methods of animal sacrifice, which was really a sacralized version of the slaughter and consumption of animal flesh.(36)

Before the Nazis ever came to power they were proposing laws in the Reichstag against animal cruelty and experimentation on animals for scientific purposes (e.g. vivisection). For example, in 1927 an NS representative proposed a ban on kosher butchering (which involves prolonged agony on the part of the animal) and in 1931 there was a call for the ending of vivisection. Most of these proposals went nowhere because the Nazis were only a small minority party at the time. But once they came to power all such legislation was quickly passed and enacted.

It was on November 24, 1933, that Germany enacted a law called *Reichstierschutzgesetz* (Reich Animal Protection Act). This was the most wide-ranging such set of laws ever established in history. This included provisions against inhumanly slaughtering animals (without anesthetic) and animal experimentation in science, as well as even regulating the slaughter of cold-blooded animals. This was followed on July 3, 1934 with the *Reichsjagdgesetz* (The Reich Hunting Law). This not only limited hunting but also included a provision for an educational program for teaching hunters about how to hunt ethically. In general laws were passed against trapping wild animals for commercial purposes, the wolf was placed under legal protection. Nazi Germany was the first state to ever pass laws to *protect* the wolf. Other measures were overtly taken to restore lost habitat for wild animals. This included re-forestation programs.

Among the leading Nazis it was the "minister without portfolio," Hermann Göring, and Hitler who were the most dedicated to the idea of the protection of animals. Himmler also attempted to pass laws against the hunting of animals.

Writing in his personal diary, Propaganda Minister Joseph Goebbels (1948: 679) said of Hitler that much of Hitler's animosity toward both the Jewish and Christian religions had its origins in the strict distinction both religions make between humans and animals and the resulting mistreatment of the animals. It was this that was at the root of Hitler's vegetarianism. At the same time, Goebbels states that the Führer was planning to abolish all slaughterhouses after the war was over. Göring was especially enthusiastic in his promotion of the cause of the protection of animals. He was also an avowed conservationist. Already in 1933 he declared in a radio broadcast that those who think they can treat animals as inanimate property would be confined to concentration camps until a final punishment could be assessed. Famously he promulgated the law that prohibited the boiling shellfish (lobsters, crabs, etc.) in a slow manner. He even went so far as to ban the use of animals in filmmaking, show business, etc., in ways that might cause the animal pain or be detrimental for its well-being. Animal rights became a part of the official educational curriculum in German schools and universities as well.

As is the case with many radically new laws in any sort

of society, including that of Nazi Germany, the entrenched establishment resisted these laws and they were not uniformly or completely enforced in every instance. Scientists could apply for and receive exemptions, for example. Those who are highly motivated today to deny any and all positive aspects of National Socialism obviously tend to emphasize this lack of enforcement of these laws without comment on the philosophical roots of such laws and the motives behind them. There were many examples also, however, of people being sent to concentrations camps for violations: Göring sent one fisherman to one for cutting up a frog for fishing bait!

Because these and other aspects of the National Socialist regime were really expressions of long-standing and widespread sentiments among the German populace stemming from a time before the Third Reich, many of these types of laws remain in effect in Germany today.

6.12. Environmentalism (Ecology)

As we have seen (§4.10) the ideas we today associate with the Greens, the science of "ecology" and the philosophy of environmentalism were all big parts of the Reform of Life Movements. These too found an important place in the ideology and policies of the NSDAP. Much of this was outlined in some detail by Anna Bramwell in her book *Blood and Soil: Richard Walther Darré and Hitler's 'Green Party'* (Kensal, 1985). Subsequent scholars have tried to obfuscate and deny the environmentally based ideology of the Nazis. This was because they used this ideology to promote, further and substantiate their racist and xenophobic program. Environmentalists of the time identified the deleterious effects on the ecosystem of so-called invasive species (of the variety of plants or animals). However, the Nazi mind applied this idea to cultural issues and identified so-called non-German persons (which in their minds most especially included the Jews!) as a cultural form of "invasive species." This line of thinking was also expressed in NS economic ideology where the idea of *autarky* was extolled as the ideal.

The Nazis only barely grasped the use of ecological ideology was a mode of controlling the masses. If a consensus could be arrived at where the masses agree that the environment should be controlled, and the population of humans can clearly be considered a part of that environment, then it only stands to reason that the human population should be strictly controlled as a part of the ecological system.

6.13. Conclusion

The relationship between National Socialism and the Reform Movements is complex. Because they shared the common idea of transforming society according to a set of ideological principles the two movements were similar in their kind. What those principles were tended to be very different from one another. The drive to achieve reform in radical ways cannot be entirely discounted as a precursor to the events in Germany at the dawn of the Third Reich, nor can the fact that all of the men who led the Nazi movement were generational children of the age of Reform. With all of that being factors, no one should make the colossal error of ascribing to the Reform Movements some sort of "Nazi" interpretation. The Reform Movements were almost entirely motivated by positive and healthy intentions. The Reform Movements all have their roots in a time long before the events of WWI and the negative repercussions of that event. The radical political, social and cultural changes ushered in by the National Socialists had the way prepared for them by the far-reaching dreams outlined by the Reformers. Many people's initial willingness to go along with Nazi excesses were of course fueled by the extreme state of chaos and widespread despair of the time of the Weimar Republic. Sadly, that level of despair was but a prelude to far worse things.

7.0. Children of the Sun
Naturmenschen and the Origin of the American Hippies(37)

The California "Nature Boys"
In Topanga Canyon 1948(38)

The philosophies of *Lebensreform* have had a tremendous effect on the world we live in today. One of the most interesting things to consider is how these German movements helped to build up, and/or give shape to, the popular counter-culture of the 1960s, especially in the USA. It is not too bold to assert that *Reform* is the mother of the American Hippie Movement. For this connection, we are most indebted to the American writer and researcher, Gordon Kennedy, who in 1998 produced a ground-breaking book project entitled *Children of the Sun: A Pictorial Anthology; From Germany to California 1883-1949*. One of the chief differences between the American Hippie Movement and the German Reform Movements is the former's enthusiastic use of intoxicants or psychoactive drugs as an essential part of its culture. Some conspiratorial types have even seen the introduction of drugs into the Hippie counter-culture a governmental plot to destroy or derail the possible political development of that movement into something that would have disrupted the political and economic establishment. In spite of any such efforts, the influence was nevertheless felt, for good or ill.

It is also interesting to note that in personal conversation with me, Kennedy reported that counterculture shops in California often refused to carry his wonderful book because the connection between the *German* and American movements was seen as unsavory. By the late 1990s certain political and cultural interests had succeeded in stereotyping anything German or Germanic as "uncool, man." However, serious investigators and historians have widely acknowledged his "theory" to be fully vindicated. Also, the wider public does not share the general attitude that Germans and things Germanic are "uncool," as we saw in section 2 the annual BBC survey continuously ranks Germans as the most positively thought of national group in the world.

Reform ideas from the German-speaking world entered the USA in three main ways: the immigration of young people who had been influenced by early twentieth century Reform ideology, immigration and/or travels of German thinkers and practitioners to America and finally, through readings of German-language literature on the subject (or translations of them). As we discuss various fascinating personalities in this section, examples of all of these avenues of ingress of Reform ideas will become apparent.

One thing that might not be obvious to contemporary readers is the degree to which things such as nutrition and even medicine were topics that were not as "fixed" and "orthodox" as they appear today. People could practice medicine with a minimum of qualifications, or none at all until after the time of WWI. Laws pertaining to drugs and other treatments were much laxer just over a hundred years ago—remember that "Coca-Cola" actually contained cocaine and until the time of prohibition most drugs such as cannabis were legal.

The system of alternative medicine that came to be called naturopathy originated in Germany, perhaps to some extent rooted in folk-medicine and the traditions of the early pioneer of medical science known as Paracelsus (Theophrastus Bombastus von Hohenheim, 1493-1541). The philosophy of naturopathy is rooted in the idea that the body is naturally healthy and can heal itself and maintain a healthy state with the aid of diet and natural remedies free of poisons and aggressive medical procedures. This, and all other such "alternative" forms of medicine, has been consistently opposed by the medical establishment, especially in the United States. As the naturopath might see it, the medical business establishment has become dedicated to profit at the expense of natural health. By the same token, the naturopathic philosophy often puts itself at odds with the advancement of medical science based on unsubstantiated concepts. The friction between the medical establishment and the alternative forms of health care is far more pronounced in American culture than it is in Germany, where a more holistic, non-adversarial, approach remains acceptable. As in all aspects of human life and thought, polarization can lead to radicalization and entrenchment in unreasonable and extreme positions.

Benedict Lust

Benedict Lust (1872-1945) was born in Michelbach, Germany. As a young person he was chronically ill and was cured by Father Sebastian Kneipp, who practiced a method of the "water cure." In 1892 Lust moved to the US as a representative of Kneipp's method. He continued his education and aquired several medical degrees, the last from the Eclectic Medical College of New York in 1914. Already in 1896 Lust undertook practice as a naturopath and opened a health food store in New York City. Lust was an advocate of many alternative healing methods, massage, chiropracty and hydrotherapy. He published works in both English and German.

Lust was also a follower of the famous German naturopath Adolf Just, whose best-known book was translated into English as *Return to Nature; the True Natural Method of Living and Healing and the True Salvation of the Soul: Paradise Regained* in 1903. Lust even established a version of Just's famous institute, the *Jungborn* (= Yungborn), in Butler, New Jersey.

Lust was an energetic publicist and practitioner of his ideas and those of Just, such that he was recognized by some as the "Father of Naturopathy" in America. He also introduced concepts from the traditional medicine of India, such as Ayurveda and yoga. Notably, Lust was an opponent of the whole "germ theory" of disease and the practice of vaccination. He like most Reformers was also an opponent of the practice of using animals in medical research and experimentation. All human maladies were to be cured by a healthy lifestyle, natural therapies and diet.

Lust's fame and notoriety led to him becoming the target of controversy and persecution by the American authorities and the still-fledgling American Medical Association. At one point, he was convicted of "practicing medicine without a license"—and fined $100.00.

Arnold Ehret, whom I discussed in section 5.4 above, was influential on the American scene as well. He made several lecture tours in the US, going back to a time before the First World War. In America he made connections with the Californian horticulturalist Luther Burbank and German expatriate Benedict Lust. The outbreak of WWI is said to have hindered his return to Germany. Ehret remained in the Los Angeles area until his death in 1922 when he fell outside a hotel where he had just given a lecture on "Health Thru Fasting." The fall resulted in a fractured skull and he died as a result.

Ehret's works and ideas once again became influential in the USA in the 1960s. His system of fasting and a diet of fruit and fruit juices were taken up by many, including the co-founder of Apple, Steve Jobs.

In the western part of the United States, the most active proponent of alternative medicine and naturopathy was the German immigrant and medical doctor Carl Schultz (1849-1935). He was widely qualified in a number of areas. He came to the US as a medical doctor from Germany, but devoted himself to naturopathy, became a doctor of chiropractic, and osteopathy—and he became a lawyer as well! Schultz generally followed in the footsteps of Benedict Lust, but was very active in setting up institutions of training in Los Angeles and in attempting to gain legal recognition for these which involved getting bills passed in the California state government. His institutions trained a whole generation of naturopaths all along the West Coast in the early twentieth century.

These German and German-American practitioners of naturopathy brought their own brand of alternative medicine and health regimens to America, to be sure. However, it must also be realized that the US had its own cadre of self-styled health and diet experts such as John Harvey Kellogg and Sylvester Graham and alternative systems from osteopathy to chiropractic. The American expressions of such things were often caught up in puritanical anti-sexuality and religious extremism. A whole different direction was given to the idea of a healthy and natural lifestyle not by professional practitioners (some would say "quacks") but by individuals and groups who actively engaged in living in a way seen as more directly connected to nature. These people were greatly influenced, and to some extent even shaped, by writers and thinkers such as Lust, Schultz and Ehret but their approach was more free-form and "laid back" than the professionals.

Friedrich Wilhelm Pester
[= Bill Pester]

Bill Pester Outside His Cabin in Palm Canyon

One of the most important figures in the development of the movement that was to evolve into what became known in America as the Hippies, was a German immigrant named Friedrich Wilhelm Pester (1885-1963) who came to the US in 1906 and eventually settled in the Palm Springs area of California in Tahquitz Canyon in 1916. There he became known as William Frederick Pester, or simply Bill Pester. Pester was already a dedicated apostle of the ideas of *Lebensreform* when he came to America, and he seems to have been determined to live out the principles of the movement in the ideal climate of southern California. Bill built a hut out of palm trees and lived the idyllic natural lifestyle in the Palm Canyon. He explored, wrote, collected Indian artifacts, played the slide guitar and taught the tourists about the local culture and natural features. He ate raw fruits and vegetables and spent his time naked in the California sunshine. To make what money he needed he sold walking sticks he made from palm trees, postcards with *Lebensreform* tips printed on them and charged people ten cents to look through his telescope while he gave lectures on astronomy. It is proven that Bill had extremely good relations with the local natives of the Cahuilla tribe, and spoke Spanish with them. His hut was built on their tribal land, and his collection of artifacts seems to have been done with their agreement, as they were eventually donated to a local museum. Pester's fascination with the American Indians certainly stems back to exposure to the enormously popular writings of the German novelist Karl May (1842-1912) who inspired the whole generation of Reformers among German-speaking youth, these ranged from Albert Einstein to Adolf Hitler.

Most importantly, Bill became a sort of living icon of a radically new and strange life-style which was on display for all to see for a long time in an area which had a significant population of influential people. Bill was not a random eccentric, but rather was a true exponent of the ideas of Reform. He was visited by many celebrities such as the writer Zane Grey and the actor Rudolph Valentino. Throughout the 1930s he was himself a sort of attraction to the area, and hundreds of people a day might pass by his hut.

Among those who became acquainted with him at this time was the song-writer and compatriot in the *Lebesreform* lifestyle, eden ahbez. It is not unlikely they met at the home of the Richters (see below). In any event, ahbez seems to have written his iconic song "Nature Boy" inspired by Pester. The song was recorded and released first by Nat King Cole in 1948, and became a big hit. As a side note, the moniker "Nature Boy" was used by the professional wrestler Buddy Rogers [= Herman Rohde] beginning in the early 1950s and later the moniker was taken up by Ric Flair [= Richard Flier] who is thought by many to be the greatest American wrestling performer ever.

As war with Germany approached, Pester's German background caused him suspicion. It is well-known that even the Jewish-German expatriates in Hollywood had to hide their actual German backgrounds to avoid prejudice. An example of this is Peter Lorre, who was thoroughly Austrian-German in culture and language, but claimed Hungarian affinities to avoid this "suspicion." Some locals suspected Pester of being a "German spy" and that he was sending secret radio messages to Hitler from a transmitter on top of the San Jacinto Mountains. In any event, Pester was arrested in 1940 on charges of "sexual perversion" and spent the duration of the war in both San Quentin and Folsom Prisons. He was released in 1946. After that he moved to Los Angeles, subsequently married and moved to Arizona where he died in 1963 at the age of 78. He is buried in Yavapai County Cemetery in Prescott, Arizona.

Pester was the dean of the Nature Boys it seems. These men formed a very small and localized subculture which spread throughout the southern California region and influenced others directly and through points of congregation, such as "health food stores." Examples of these are the Eutropheon owned by the Richters in Los Angeles and the Sexauer's Natural Foods in Santa Barbara. Later Gypsy Boots opened the "Health Hut" in Hollywood.

The location of Pester's cabin in Palm Canyon was subsequently turned into an "Indian trading post" and then into a store which became known as "Hermit's Bench." Millie Fischer published a booklet in 1985 about the history of Palm Canyon that had a chapter on Pester and there is also a full biography: *William Pester: the Hermit of Palm Springs* by Peter Wild (2008).

John and Vera Richter

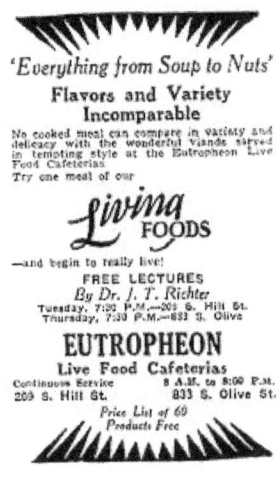

An important meeting place and conduit for the introduction of German Reform ideas into the United States was the natural food restaurant called the Eutopheon ("good nourishment") in Los Angeles, California. It was run by a married couple named John and Vera Richter. John Richter (1863-1949) was the son of German immigrants in Illinois. Richter's father, Frederik, was a pastor but also a natural healer and "physician." John Richter trained in the school of John Harvey Kellogg using natural healing remedies and a vegetarian diet. He eventually became a qualified naturopathic physician. Around 1911 he began using the theories of Benedict Lust regarding raw foods. After the death of his first wife, John remarried Vera (née Weitzel, 1884-1960). The couple moved from the Midwest to Los Angeles around 1917 and opened the Eutropheon at 833 South Olive Street. The building is long since demolished, but the location is just around the corner from Whole Foods store today! Vera published a book *Mrs. Richter's Cook-less Book* in 1925. Their establishment received much publicity and they lectured widely in the area on the theories of German experts such as Arnold

Ehret, Louis Kuhne and Adolf Just. They were so successful that they opened several more such restaurants. As proponents of the dietary path of the Reform Movement the Richters opposed cooked food, refrigeration, dairy products, meat, salt, sugar, coffee, alcohol, while they promoted beliefs and practices such as naturism, sun bathing, sun-gazing (meditative viewing the sun at dawn and sundown), massage, iris diagnosis, and even barefoot walking. In 1936 John Richter published the book called *Nature the Healer*, which proved very popular.

Politically, the Richters were known to be socialists who even supported the ideals of the Bolshevik Revolution as well as the American socialist leader Eugene Debs. The Eutropheon was a meeting place for many of the "Nature Boys," such as Bill Pester, Gypsy Boots, eden ahbez and others. The restaurants were sold in the 1940s and soon thereafter went out of business. But the seed had been planted, so to speak, for natural and healthy food stores in southern California.

Hermann Sexauer

Hermann Sexauer (1883-1971) was born in Teningen, Germany and immigrated to America in 1906. He made his way to California where he lived an alternative lifestyle. This involved the eating of raw foods and the advocacy of pacifism. In California, he became something of a magnet for young Americans open to the general message of social and cultural Reform. He and his wife, Frieda (an academic hortoculturalist) opened a health food store in Santa Barbara in 1934 called Sexauer's Natural Foods. Sexauer was not alone in his general activities, several other Germans around the country opened such stores inspired by the *Reformhäuser* back home.

Maximilian Sikinger

For what little we know about this influential figure in the southern California proto-Hippie world we are indebted to the work of Gordon Kennedy (1998: 165). He was the author of a now-obscure pamphlet in 1946 entitled *Classical Nutrition*. Sikinger was born in Augsburg in 1913, but is reported to have lived on his own among various groups (often children) from the age of six. He wandered throughout Europe practically living off the land, apparently. In 1935 he immigrated to America and made his way to California in hobo style. He was a merchant marine until 1941 after which he settled permanently in California, living part-time in Tahquitz Canyon and Sonoma in the summer. His pamphlet in 1946 gained him a following in the area and he was part of the network of *Naturmenschen* in the region. His philosophy and practice included meditation, massage, the eating of live plant foods and living in the sunshine. Sikinger passed away in 2004 at the age of 91.

eden ahbez

Another of the "Nature Boys" was one eden ahbez (= George Alexander Aberle [1908-1995]). It was ahbez who wrote the song *Nature Boy* which became a number one hit song for the singer Nat King Cole in 1948. He spent his early years in the Brooklyn Hebrew Orphan Asylum and was adopted in 1917 and given the name George McGrew. In the 1930s he lived in Kansas City where he worked as a pianist and dance band leader. He made his way to Los Angeles in 1941 and hung out at the Sexauer's Health Shop and the Richters' Eutropheon and began to be involved in the Reform ideology. His name was changed to eden ahbez, the lower-case initials were to signify that only God and Infinity deserved to be capitalized. Also, eden became one of the Nature Boys in the Palm Springs area. Throughout the late 1940s and all the way into the early 1990s, eden was active as a song-writer and performer. He wrote hits for several recording artists of the day and it would appear that he was an influential presence in the community of musicians in California from the late 1940s onward. It also seems clear that the direct inspiration for the song "Nature Boy" came from the life and ways of eden's friend Bill Pester.

Gypsy Boots
(= Robert Bootzin)

A man who commonly went by the name Gypsy Boots (= Robert Bootzin, 1915-2004) was a key agent in the transmission of the German philosophies and practices of Life-Reform as exemplified by individuals ranging from Pester to Sexauer to Ehret to Sikinger to Lust to the wider American culture. Gypsy Boots was a charismatic figure of popular culture in Southern California, outlandish sports fan, musical performer and enthusiastic and gregarious representative of his ideas and of the others he admired.

Bootzin was a home-grown Nature Boy, born in San Francisco to Russian-Jewish parents. His mother, Mushka, was an eccentric vegetarian who fed the homeless with her homemade black bread. Bootzin dropped out of school in 1933 and took up a wandering—"gypsy"—lifestyle, mostly hanging out with fellow "tribesmen" or Nature Boys in the Palm Springs area.

Gypsy Boots was an outlandish character who loved the spotlight of the world of showbusiness. He appeared in several television shows and was widely interviewed and due to his location in Hollywood he also had many opportunities to make propaganda for his health food, organic, vegetarian life-style.

Gypsy loved to hobnob with all sorts of celebrities in the world of show business and sports. He also wrote two fairly well-known books *Barefeet and Good Things to Eat* and his memoir called *The Gypsy in Me*.

All this led the researcher Gordon Kennedy to conclude that "[Gypsy Boots] was the most important living link between the old *Naturmensch[en]* and the surfers and flower children of the hot generation. He passed the torch into a new era and reached more people than nearly all of his predecessors [in California]." (1998: 178)

It is widely surmised that there was another artistic and aesthetic connection between the German Reform Movements and the genesis of the alternative life-styles of the original California Hippies in the form of the art of Meister Fidus (see section 4.7.3.). An artist, or consortium of artists, working in the San Francisco Bay area somewhere discovered Fidus artwork and were inspired by its principles to create new styles for the poster-art of the time.

In so many ways the Nature Boys of California represented an extension of some of the best elements of German Romanticism set in a world that was free of the centuries of political and cultural baggage that Central Europe represented. It is another tragedy of history that this movement was eventually diverted into a world of politics and the use of drugs. They were part of the cultural mosaic that for a short time (1945-1995) turned California into a cultural oasis of freedom, creativity and free education. The California Dream was spoiled by political and governmental mismanagement akin to the conditions that precipitated the demise of the golden age of the Reform Movements. The California Dream, like its sister epoch in Central Europe is now a culture gone with the wind.

8.0. Influence on Contemporary American Society

Even a cursory glance at the contents of this book would demonstrate to the reader how much our contemporary culture and its mindsets owe to the Reform Movements' influences in broad swathes of our society today. To a great extent the heroes of the Reform Movements have receded into obscurity, but their activities still echo in many of our everyday actions and attitudes. One of the main roles of this book is to introduce and re-introduce many of these heroes of the movements to the general public and especially to the English-speaking public. In this section I will concentrate on the influences of Reform ideology on contemporary Anglo-American culture.

At the root of Reform ideology was the desire and willingness to undertake radical re-envisionings of the most profound aspects of human existence. In this one of the first topics that comes into focus is that which is commonly called "religion." By this term, I intend to denote the broadest spectrum of beliefs and attitudes individuals might have toward themselves and their own beings and place in the world, as well as what they think of communities of like-minded individuals with whom they might cooperate in an organized manner. Today we are used to hearing that a person is "spiritual," but not *religious*. The old orthodox confessing religions, Catholic, Protestant and Jewish have had to change radically to keep up with changing mores and attitudes in the public—or fall behind in popularity in the Western world. Certainly, the individualizing tendency of Reform spirituality may be seen to have its roots in earlier times, in movements such as Romanticism, Pietism, Transcendentalism, etc. But the particulars of the new spiritualities, including the creation of whole so-called New Religions appears clearly linked to the mindset of the Reform Movements as found not only in Germany, but the Anglo-American world as well. One of the most important features of the Reform Age, i.e. the introduction of exotic religions (e.g. Buddhism, Hinduism, Sufism) to individuals and groups in Western society, is a trend that has only grown in significance in more recent years. The liberty persons feel to approach the most profound dimensions of human existence based upon their own individual beliefs, thoughts and experiences, unbound by the opinions and values of their families, neighbors or fellow citizens is something that is clearly rooted in the ideals of Reform ideology. In the Anglo-American world, there was a significant wave of interest in alternative spiritualities roughly contemporary with the Reform Age in Europe, but this really only became a mass movement and feature of what could be called popular culture beginning in the 1960s and becoming more pronounced in the 1970s—the advent of the so-called New Age Movement or the Age of Aquarius. Although there are many demographic and theoretical differences between these two social phenomena, there is also much that binds them together

Significantly, features of the esoteric world of the German-speaking neo-pagans and runosophers of the early twentieth century made their way into the Anglo-American neo-pagan (or "heathen") scene with roots going back into the early 1970s. These are outlined in some detail in my book *The Revival of the Runes* (Inner Traditions, 2021: 152-190).

In the area of politics there is an obvious and significant divide between the underlying attitudes and experiences which conditioned the German-speaking world of the late nineteenth and early twentieth centuries and that of the adjacent and subsequent Anglo-American society. It is in the area of politics that the Reform ideology has most profoundly failed. If we equate Reform with a more rational and healthy manner of thinking about human problems and the freedom to act upon this more rational approach to improve the lives of human beings both individually and collectively, then we cannot look upon the present political and cultural landscape and see these dreams as having been fulfilled. We are probably further away from these goals than we were in the recent past.

One of the most obvious direct connections between the political ideas shaped in the Reform Movements and present-day politics is found in the so-called Green Movement. In Germany, this developed into a separate political party, *Die Grünen*. As a political movement, the Green agenda is multifaceted. It begins with environmental protection. This is a concept that finds almost universal appeal (with the exception of fundamentalist religious fanatics who believe "the Lord" is coming soon). The agenda extends into the development of "Green energy" which attempts to avoid those forms of energy that put carbon dioxide into the air. What they have against allowing the plants to breathe remains a mystery! It would appear that this movement has long since been coopted by Leftists and many of the apparent anomalies in their philosophy can only be explained in these terms. If it can be thought that the natural environment is something that the state has an interest in "protecting," then the state (i.e. political operatives) have a clear pathway to control of everything and all human behaviors. A pure and principled Green movement remains an essential part of the future of Reform.

One of the great errors of recent popular culture is the tendency (based on too much watching of television) that it is "politics" that matters and that "political" thought is the highest and most profound pursuit in contemporary human life—ignoring what is really far more powerful than *politics*—i.e. **culture**. A quick comparison of the caliber and nature of individuals involved in politics before the middle of the twentieth century and the average politician today cannot fail but to allow us to understand the problem. The Reformers who are the objects of our study in the book generally understood that change must be made at a cultural level, and be rooted not in a commonality of opinions, but in a Reformation of the personality of the individual.

A major, if perhaps fleeting, direct impact of the Reform Movements in American history lies in the foundations of the so-called Hippie Movement so identified with the '60s counter culture. This historical aspect is more fully treated in section 7, The Children of the Sun.

One area that all people feel and experience in the most common and everyday way that is a result of Reform ideology is that which resulted from the new attitudes toward clothing. Both men and women as late as the nineteenth and early twentieth centuries suffered under the yoke of *fashion*. Restrictive and uncomfortable clothing was the norm. In the Reform world, these fashions and the necessity for them were questioned and as a direct result people today at least have the ordinary option of dressing in a more comfortable way on a daily basis. Men still often have to wear ties around their necks and many women still feel it necessary to wear high-heeled shoes, but in general people can, if they desire, dress in comfortable and healthy ways—or at least this is the trend that was first set in motion by the Reform ideology.

Among the several clear connections between the Anglo-American "New Age" movement and the German Reform Movements was the common obsession with things organic and holistic with regard to matters of diet and health. Here, as section 7 of this book shows, there was a clear and historical link between German Reform and the American movement in this direction beginning in the mid twentieth century. By the time the whole country was prepared for this kind of interest, beginning in the 1960s, many ideas had been instituted with direct connections to the German Reform ideology, e.g. environmentalism, anti-vivisectionism, health food, vegetarianism, nudism and liberated sexuality (the so-called sexual revolution).

The development of the health food movement and alternative ideas on diet and nutrition in America are covered in some more detail in section 7.

The ideal of highly localized economies along with political structures to support these was a basic one in the Reform ideology. Eating foods that are locally raised and grown, with short supply chains that are more local and geographically limited would certainly seem to be the ideal of economic and physical health. Everyone knows this now, thanks to Reform thought. However, in general we are far away from this ideal today. Foods are imported from distant places, and some that are locally produced are sometimes sent half way around the world to be "processed" and then re-imported into our local areas! The deleterious effect on the quality of that food, not to mention the amount of pollution that is created by the transportation involved (by truck, plane or ship) is obvious. Nevertheless, corporate and government interests have created this situation and continue to promote it for their own reasons, contrary to the interests of the general population or the environment. The "Green" movement extols the virtues of "locally sourced" foods, and we are urged to "buy locally"—but the system has made this virtually impossible and it all becomes more impossible with each passing year. The tension between "thinking locally" and "thinking globally" extends from practical economic fields into profound spiritual and cultural concepts.

In the post-war years in Germany the whole movement toward the acceptance and use of natural healing methods actually increased. During the 1970s it was estimated that about half of the population made some use of natural healing methods, while a survey in 2013 revealed that the number had risen to about 70%.

Another of the marked differences between the general spirit of the German Reform Movements and the Anglo-American "New Age" and Hippie Movements is the role played by intoxicants. Within the German culture, especially in the Weimar Era, drugs did exercise an important recreational role, but in general they lacked the virtually religious dimension they would enjoy in the 1960s and following.

A notable exception to this is to be found in the work of the sexual magician Ernst Schertel who did not shy away from suggesting the use of various drugs for magical exercise and operational engagement. The English mage, Aleister Crowley, certainly promoted drugs, especially at one point peyote. The chemical designation for this drug was *Anhalonium Lewinii*, which he abbreviated AL or by the coded reference with the numeral 31 (= 1 + 30) the value according to gematria of the two Hebrew letters *alef* and *lamed* (= A + L). Crowley's most important theoretical work is called *The Book of the Law*, to which he also gave the designation *Liber AL*. The psychoactive component, mescaline, was first isolated and identified (1897), then eventually synthesized (1918) by the German chemists Arthur Heffter and Ernst Späth. Crowley had his direct link to Reform Age magic in his connection with the German order O.T.O., and his *bona fides* as a figure in the Hippie counter culture is testified to by his appearance as one of the many "heroic" figures depicted on the Beatles album cover for *Sgt. Pepper's Lonely Hearts Club Band* (1967).

8.1. Nudism in America

The nudist movement in America was directly influenced by the FKK ideology found in Germany. Kurt Barthel (1884-1969) founded the American League for Physical Culture in 1929 and advertised it in German publications. They had their first gathering on leased farmsteads in Westchester County, New York. Other groups, such as the American Gymnosophical Association and the American Association for Nude Recreation grew out of the ALPC. In 1932, Barthel established the first American "nudist camp," called Sky Farm, in New Jersey. Other groups and camps began to spring up. One of the early camps, the Rock Lodge Club, continues to operate today.

Barthel named Ilsley Boone (1879-1968) as his successor in much of the organizational work for the promotion of nudism in America. Boone was an ordained minister and envisioned a Christian rationale for the practice of nudism, which would be effective in America—"the Land of the Bible."

Boone also traveled to Germany to visit nudist resorts such as the Freilichtpark ("Free-Light Park") near Hamburg. In 1936, he opened his "Sunshine Park" near Atlantic City, New Jersey.

Boone was also a publisher and put out a variety of nudist publications including *Sunshine & Health* which was the most successful nudist magazine in the US continuing to be published into the 1980s well after Boone's death. Part of Boone's work for nudism included court battles to allow for the publication and distribution of his literature through the US postal system. He also constantly fought local officials to allow for the establishment of nudist camps in their regions. In the early 1950s Boone renamed the ALPC the American Sunbathing Association, which in turn became the American Association for Nude Recreation.

Subsequent American nudist movements during the twenty-first century, such as the Young Naturists of America, did not have the sustainability that those organizations with their roots in the German Reform scene possessed.

It is astounding to observe how what appeared at the time to be a strange and isolated phenomenon pioneered by a few elite physicians and thinkers in the Weimar period—that of transgenderism—would come to almost dominate popular culture and political discourse in 2022. The profound difference between the transgender issue in the Reform-minded Weimar era and that of the 21st century is that the former was oriented toward the freedom, self-expression and happiness of *individuals* whereas the latter seems to be connected to a partisan political operation oriented toward cultural change or social or societal "transformation" rather than individual authenticity. Despite this, it is clear that the question of transgenderism has its roots in Weimar-era culture and that we can count the phenomenon as something inherited directly from Reform ideology.

In the US, toward the middle of the 1960s the works of the Nobel Prize winning writer Hermann Hesse were discovered by publishers who began to issue more translations of his works and they proved right for the times, just as they had been in the German-speaking world many decades earlier. This American phenomenon also had the effect of generating a renaissance of interest in the German-speaking world in the 1970s. The enlightenment-seeking attitudes of many of the Baby Boomers of the 1960s and 1970s were wonderfully reflected in the works of Hesse: *Siddhartha, Journey to the East, Narcissus and Goldmund* and *Steppenwolf* all struck a deep chord. The passages regarding the "magic theater," "for madmen only," in *Steppenwolf* were thought by the Hippie generation to be based on some psychedelic experience. There are theaters whose names are inspired by this literary reference both in San Francisco and Chicago. The American counter-culture figure Dr. Timothy Leary (1920-1996) considered Hermann Hesse to be a "master-guide" to the hallucinogenic experience. Despite all this, there is no evidence that Hesse ever experimented with any sort of drugs of the kind Leary is referring to, such as LSD. Another alternative philosopher, Colin Wilson (1931-2013) wrote a book devoted to Hesse. Hesse also finds his way into the rock and roll culture of the 1960s—a quote from Demian on Santana's 1970 album *Abraxas*. The name of the rock-band Steppenwolf was, of course, inspired by Hesse. The rock-band Steppenwolf, founded in 1968 and led by John Kay (= Joachim Fritz Krauledat) took its inspiration from Hesse and his novel of the same name. In general, there seems to have been a profound symbiotic relationship between the works of Hesse and the so-called Hippie Movement based on the similarity of themes and interests connected to the search for enlightenment and counter-cultural ideas. The American embrace of Hesse even inspired a renaissance of interest in his work in Germany.

The movement toward attention to animal rights and against experimentation on animals for medical purposes had its genesis in the Anglo-American world—the first was established in Great Britain with the Cruelty to Animals Act, 1876. But the movement found an enthusiastic home in Germany. There it is today more powerful than anywhere else on Earth. One commonly sees billboards with images of sick people and sick animals with the phrase: "We make them sick, they make us sick." It is difficult not to conclude that this northern European attitude is rooted in the ancient Germanic belief that animals (especially those which are sacrificed, and hence consumed, by humans in holy rites) are physical extensions of the indigenous gods and goddesses themselves. Hence, cruelty shown to these creatures is a direct offense toward the divinities themselves.

Perhaps the greatest single influence of the German Reform Movements and their earlier foundations in the German-speaking world, on our own present-day culture is the obsession with the natural environment as a resource understood globally within an "eco-system," and as something that must be preserved and cared for. The German biologist Ernst Haeckel had coined the term "ecology" (G. *Ekologie*) in the nineteenth century, but with the Reform Age ideas related to this were popularized and accepted in a broad spectrum of the population. This popularized view was then imported as a virtually finished product into the American ecological movement in the mid-twentieth century. The most important event in this popularization of the cause of environmentalism was the publication of Rachel Carson's book *Silent Spring* (1962).

Although concepts rooted in ecology would be influential in the ideology of National Socialism, as we saw in section 6.10, the same ideas appear to have been used in what appears to be a more benign context, but using the same underlying theories when the concept of "indigenous peoples" or "first nations" are considered in the contemporary North American political ideology. In an eco-system those species, kinds or types which are considered indigenous are marked for preservation and their interests are seen as worthy of promotion, whereas "invasive species" are seen as undesirable. This model then takes on a *moral* and even political component beyond straightforward biological science. This ideology could be used by the Nazis against the Jews, but by the same token is also employed to imply that "indigenous peoples" are the "real Americans," etc. This binary or polarized, some might say dualistic, model is obviously flawed in real life. As we know Europe was historically a maelstrom of migrations and invasions of peoples over every millennium, and this process continues. The same can be said of the Americas. In fact, or course, there is no people truly indigenous to the Western Hemisphere, we are all invaders—it is just a matter of who was here earlier. Using the logic of "earlier" is "superior," although those groups usually identified as native American would be the "highest," but would that same logic deem that the Spanish, English and French are "more native" than the Germans, who are more native than the Africans, who are more native than the Italians, etc.? The whole matter becomes absurd in the "moral" sense.

8.2. The Sexual Revolution in the Industrialized West

It would be a mistake to think that the events of the Reform Age in Germany were the beginning of something that had no roots as far as the liberalization of sexual mores is concerned.

Western culture has gone through many "sexual revolutions" over the centuries, some allowed for more freedom others moved in a more restrictive direction (e.g. the advent of Christianity and the morality of the Victorian Age).

The study of sexuality on a scientific basis and the wave of sexual liberation that swept society in the 1920s on both sides of the Atlantic were the most direct roots of the so-called sexual revolution or sexual liberation movement that reached an intensive phase in the Anglo-American world from the late 1960s through the early 1980s.

The attention, even obsession, German-speaking Europe showed toward sexuality in the early twentieth century exercised a tremendous level of influence on the English-speaking world. This came through a variety of avenues. The work of Sigmund Freud swept from the scientific world directly into the level of popular culture. The message received from Freud was that the repression of sexual feelings led to mental and emotional sickness, and the discovery and expression of these feelings could have a health-bringing and liberating effect. This constituted a profound psycho-sexual revelation. It went from the message of "repression is good," to "repression is sick." It was a message the world was ready and eager to hear and act upon. The German psychologists, psychiatrists and sexologists from Freud to Adler, from Jung to Reich up to and including the sexology of Magnus Hirschfeld would have had its effect regardless, but the Nazi take-over of Germany in 1933 led to a mass exodus of many of these (often thought of as 'deviant") thinkers farther to the West. Part of this wave of immigration also included the Reform-minded youth we see in section 7.

The German psychiatrist Wilhelm Reich is credited with coining the term "sexual revolution." His book *Die Sexualität in Kulturkampf* ("Sexuality in the Culture-War") was translated with the title *The Sexual Revolution* in 1936. Reich would become famous, or infamous, in the USA as a sort of "mad doctor" with experiments having to do with the orgasm and the accumulation of an energy called "orgone." He would eventually be hounded to death by the American Food and Drug Administration in 1957.

A theoretical and cultural context for this revolution was set in the 1950s and early 1960s through the reception of sexual studies (e.g. Alfred Kinsey), expansion of sexually-themed media (e.g. magazine, literature with sexual content and art films from Europe) coupled with growth in political and cultural movements (e.g. the hippie movement, popular music and women's liberation). All of these influences and trends came to a head around 1970 in the context of general social upheaval over the Vietnam War when what had been a movement among the cultural elite in major urban areas spread out into the population at large via the mass media. So, by the early 1970s in America 75% of the population thought that pre-marital sex acceptable behavior, oral contraceptives were universally available and the then-known sexually transmitted diseases (with the exception of non-lethal herpes) were treatable.

The most intensive phase of the sexual revolution in American culture can be marked from its inception by the widespread availability of oral contraceptives for women in the very early 1970s to its demise with the rise of widespread awareness of AIDS in the late 1980s. This movement had deeper roots that go back to the German Reform age as well as more directly to the works and writings of people such as Wilhelm Reich, Alfred Kinsey and even Hugh Hefner in the late 1940s and early 1950s. Of course, this sexual revolution, like the ones before it, left an indelible mark on the culture in which it occurred. The characteristics of this revolution were: more acceptance of sexual experience outside marriage, the normalization of contraceptives, increased explicit representations of sexual behavior and nudity in the media and literature and expanded sexual experience with alternative forms of sexuality, e.g. homosexuality, open marriage, mate swapping, swinging, and group or communal sex. The overriding message was that sexual repression stemming from religion, state and family authorities was unhealthy and that sex should be a form of self-expression and fulfillment.

Oral contraceptive pills were perfected by 1961 and became more widely available in the mid-1960s, with universal availability for all women (married or unmarried) in all states did not come until 1972. Besides disease (syphilis, gonorrhea and herpes primarily) pregnancy had been the main "risk factor" connected to "free love." The use of the new drug penicillin reduced mortality from syphilis in the 1950s forward.

As I have already noted the work and influence of Sigmund Freud was decisive in the popularization of the idea of healthy sexual thoughts and feelings world-wide. This new attitude stemmed from the general reception of his ideas as pertaining to the unhealthy results of sexual repression. Freud also influenced a whole generation of psychologists and writers including Otto Gross, Carl Jung and Wilhelm Reich.

Reich coined the term "sexual revolution," which was marked by Marxist and Anarchistic overtones. He viewed sexual energy as a source of revolutionary social and cultural transformation. Although sexuality played a large role in the very early years of the Bolshevik Revolution in Russia, Stalin soon instituted a rather puritanical attitude toward sex. It would only be with the new Sexual Revolution in the beginning of the 21st century in America that the use of alternative sexualities would be effectively used as a mode of breaking down bourgeois social norms as a method of causing a shift in political power-centers. It is likely that this is what was at the deepest level of Reich's notion of the Sexual Revolution, but it was too dangerous to express the program openly.

A work, first published in 1928 by the American anthropologist Margret Mead called *Coming of Age in Samoa* had a tremendous effect on sexual attitudes. This was initially a scholarly work, but its findings permeated the academic world and hence began to influence popular culture over the ensuing years. Dr. Mead was a frequent guest on late night talk shows in the 1960s. Her findings suggested that Samoan society permitted the adolescent youth to experience sexual activity at a young age, which she pointed out as a contrast with our 'civilized" Western sexual repression. Her writings helped support a certain sexual revolution that took place (at least in certain circles) in the 1930s. As a matter of fact, her findings were later called into serious question by another anthropologist who used more current methods to gather a new set of data from the same population. It seems that to a great extent the Samoans behaved in ways that Mead seemed to suggest to them with her questions. It became an example of the observer being a causal agent.

In many ways following in the footsteps of Magnus Hirschfeld, Wilhelm Reich and others in the Weimar Republic, in America certain pioneers in sexology such as Alfred C. Kinsey in the late 1940s and early 1950s followed by William H. Masters and Virginia E. Johnson not only did groundbreaking work, but became quite well-known and popular in doing so!

Another important figure in the American sexual revolution in the post-war age is one Hugh Hefner (1926-2017) who began publishing a magazine called *Playboy* in 1953. Its pages were most famous for the photographs of beautiful women in various stages of undress, but its real message was what Hefner came to call the Playboy Philosophy. The magazine became a cultural icon and Hefner built an economic empire with it.

Around 1960 the world of literary expressions of sexuality underwent a liberation. Literary works which had been suppressed in the United States, e.g. James Joyce's *Ulysses* (1922), D. H. Lawrence's *Lady Chatterley's Lover* (1928) and Henry Miller's *Tropic of Cancer* (1934) and even John Cleland's *Fanny Hill* (1750) were finally published in uncensored forms in the US, especially by the Grove Press in New York.(39)

"Marriage manuals" went back to a time before WWII, but their influence was not widespread. There was even one by Margaret Sanger *What Every Girl Should Know* (1920). Beginning in the 1960s more popular and liberated works began to be produced, e.g. Helen Gurley Brown's *Sex and the Single Girl* (1962), Dr. David Reuben's *Everything You Always Wanted to Know about Sex* (*But Were Afraid to Ask)* [1969], "J" (= Joan Garrity) *The Sensuous Woman* (1969) and its companion by "M" [= Joan and John Garrity] *The Sensuous Man* (1971). These were guidebooks to sexual experimentation which did not shy away from topics such as oral and anal sex. One of the most culturally subversive books of this time-period was *Open Marriage* by Nena and George O'Neill (Evans, 1972). This last book, to the authors' later regret, in part suggested in practical terms that marital partners could be free to pursue sexual liaisons apart from their marriages.

Erotic literature and films became more popular and more accepted as legitimate art-forms in popular culture from the late 1960s forward. The literature of the so-called Victorian era (such as *Fanny Hill*) started to be published by Grove Press in New York. Works by authors such as Henry Miller (*Tropic of Cancer*) overcame legal battles. In the world of cinema, Andy Warhol's *Blue Movie* (1969), *Last Tango in Paris* (1972) and the more extreme *Deep Throat* (1972), *The Devil in Miss Jones* (1973) and *The Opening of Misty Beethoven* (1976) became cultural icons. 1975 also saw the release of the film version of *The Story of O* based on the 1953 French novel (*Histoire d'O*) by Pauline Réage (= Anne Desclos).

The emancipation of women, recognizing their rights in a legal sense as full citizens, has been a long and hard road in all of European society as well as in America. The German Reform Movements had little influence on the Anglo-American story of the evolution of women's rights, but the struggle here and there was a parallel development with suffrage coming at about the same time and the ability of women to study at major universities was something that developed unevenly in European and American societies. German women gained the right to study at universities in the Weimar period (after 1919) whereas, for example they only could study at Oxford in

1920 and Cambridge in 1948. Women were not admitted to the major "Ivy League" schools in America, Yale and Harvard until the early 1970s. The constitution of the Weimar Republic recognized the legal equality of men and women, but this was modified by the National Socialists. During the Weimar period women made up about eighteen percent of the university student body, but the Nazis sought to keep the amount of female students to about ten percent.

The political dimensions of sexual liberation, related to, but not identical with what is seen as something purely sexual, are the women's liberation movement and the gay rights movement. Both of these, of course have their antecedents in the German Reform Movements, although the direct American connections are certainly more with Britain than with Germany.

There is has always been a connection between the causes of women's rights and gay rights. This is because the "establishment," dominated by heterosexual males, is seen to have to relinquish power to those outside their circles in order for them to obtain their rights and recognition. This whole issue is too complex to enter into here, but it always remains noteworthy that the questions and development surrounding these questions always appear to be related and run in a parallel fashion in various cultures. No doubt these worthy independent movements and causes have most likely been driven together under the banner of Marxist cultural theory which is obsessed with the analytical paradigm of dividing all individuals and groups into classes of "oppressors" and "oppressed" so that racial minorities, women and homosexuals can conveniently be categorized as belonging to the oppressed class. The validity of such theories remains highly questionable, as in reality it appears to be part of an occult political "divide and conquer" strategy.

From its inception, the American women's movement of the 1960s was closely connected with ideas of sexual liberation for women as individuals and as a gender. Books such as Betty Friedan's *Feminine Mystique* (1963) and Anne Koedt's *The Myth of the Vaginal Orgasm* (1970) were battle cries in the women's struggle. Feminist thinkers urged women to discover, assert and actualize their own ideas about sexual experience and fulfillment. Women were encouraged to be free to initiate sexual advances, feel free to enjoy sex as men had historically done and explore new kinds of sexual expression. In all of these things there were echoes of the phenomenon of "Girl Power" of Weimar Germany.

The development of an organized and philosophically grounded movement for the rights of gay people was well-developed in the early twentieth century in Europe, whereas such an organized response to the situation only developed much later in the USA. An organized gay rights movement in America first comes into being in obscure corners after 1940. The Mattachine Society (or the International Bachelors Fraternal Orders for Peace and Social Dignity) was founded in Los Angeles in1940. This group also included a socialistic (or even communist) agenda as well. In 1955 the Daughters of Bilitis(40) was founded to support lesbian women.

The contemporary gay rights movement has its beginnings in 1969 in the wake of the Stonewall Riots in New York. Following patterns established by the civil rights movement in the 1950s and 1960s LBGT people began to organize to assert their rights in ways quite different from those pioneered by Magnus Hirschfeld in the early part of the twentieth century.

The concept of "free love"—to engage in sexual relationships without regard to marriage and allowing one's mutual attractions guide one's behavior—was not a new one in the twentieth century. English Romantic and radical circles, such as that around William Godwin, Mary Wollstonecraft and their daughter Mary Shelley with her husband Percy Bysshe Shelley were predecessors in the late 18th century.

Following in the wake of the general public becoming aware of the AIDS epidemic, coupled with the rise of the use of the Internet, a form of sexuality, generally thought to be the "Last Taboo"(41) was Sado-Masochism, which came to be known with the somewhat Internet-based moniker "BDSM." This type of sexuality had deep roots and was widely experienced in the European world of the late nineteenth and early twentieth century, especially in England and Germany-Austria. In the Age of Reform its leading exponent was Dr. Ernst Schertel. In the context of the American Sexual Revolution, this form of sexuality had remained relatively unpopular, perhaps due to the confusion between its expression and notions of "violence," which was a significant misunderstanding. The rise of interest in "BDSM" came only slowly. The French book *Histoire d'O* was translated into English and widely published in America by Grove Press in 1965. The book was banned or put on indices in many countries, e.g. Germany and Great Britain. In the late 1960s this book stimulated the imaginations of many in the US. It was published in German in 1967 and gained a certain "cult" following there. The 1975 French film by Just Jaeckin, released in the US under the title *The Story of O*, opened a much wider awareness of the phenomenon. The book and film then also gained a certain cult following in the US between 1975 and the late 1980s.(42) Because BDSM sexuality could be effectively practiced as an art-form separate from practices of conventional sexuality which involved the exchange of bodily fluids, it was quickly fixated upon by many more people in the Age of AIDS as an alternative sexual "life-style." Before the time of the Internet BDSM was a quasi-philosophical phenomenon encoded in literary references, e.g. de Sade, Sacher-Masoch, and most especially *Histoire d'O*. As BDSM became a relative mass-movement this deep heritage became more obscure, and has subsequently been largely lost.

The story of the Western Sexual Revolution which began in the middle of the twentieth century has not yet fully played itself out. The age of the Internet has been the most recent development in its history. This digital universe has provided every individual with the words and images surrounding the most explicit sexual acts (some might even call them "stunts") and has also provided avenues for individuals to communicate with potential partners and make connections in order to live out our darkest fantasies. The long-term effects of the revelation of information and images regarding the mysteries of sex to everyone regardless of age, education and income have yet to be understood and processed.

The contemporary manifestations of reform or alternative views of life found in twentieth century Anglo-American culture have strong connections and/or analogs with German ideas of Reform. But it would be a great mistake to see the path between the two as always linear and direct and an even bigger mistake to ascribe all of these ideas to the culture of Central Europe. The connections between the British Isles and Germany had been intimate from the very origins of England itself with its inception in the early Middle Ages as a mass migration from northern Germany and was a continuing process. Many "German" ideas had their origins in England and visa-versa.

The future of reforms and innovations in contemporary English-speaking societies could be greatly enhanced and improved by a thorough understanding of the successes and failures of the German Reform Movements in the late nineteenth and early twentieth centuries. In some small measure that is the underlying goal of this book.

9.0. *Ausblick*: The Future of Reform-Ideas

Clearly the ideas that we have identified as those belonging to the Reform Movement of Central Europe in the latter nineteenth and early twentieth centuries had historical antecedents. Those, and the new shapes and directions that came into being about a hundred years ago, continue to have an effect on our society and culture today. Those ideas radically reformed our attitudes toward almost every aspect of life. But since most people appear today unaware of this history, these cultural features have become a part of the unconscious flow of events in ways that are actually rather contrary to the spirit of the Reform Movements themselves. We are very much in need of a mid-course correction on the historical flow of Reform. The possibilities of such a correction come from three main sources—awareness of history (which necessarily affects our understanding of events yet to come), a re-assessment of the goals of Reform and the setting of new goals for such a movement. When we look back we can ask ourselves certain questions: What has been achieved? What has not been achieved? What ideas were wrong-headed or counter-productive? In all honesty, it appears to me that as a culture we are not in a very heroic or visionary position at present the way we were in the middle of the nineteenth century when the Reform ideas were first rising in people's consciousness. As we saw in the history of the Reform Movements, there were two very different aspects to the movement: Self-Reform and World-Reform. It would appear for the most part that the English teenager, Mary Shelley was correct in her vision that humanity's ability to make things happen has far outstripped the wisdom possessed by the species to make any substantial improvements. As a species, we are at present so unwise as to make it most likely that whatever we come up with, the cure will be far worse than the disease. This situation stems from a species-wide narcissism, selfishness and orientation toward immediate gratification. It appears to me the wisest course is to study the past and the heroes and villains of days gone by as a part of a program of education in preparation for a deeper-level attempt at self-reform, or *initiation*. Only once this process has matured in enough people can the project once more reliably be undertaken anew. Any RE-Form undertaken by the dominant personalities in the present culture would only lead to further decadence and decay of essential qualities. At present our (American) culture seems trapped between those dominated by superstitions of the past on the Right (Christianity) and utter unsubstantiated and tyrannous madness on the Left. Without radical and substantial self-directed and authentic re-education (or *initiation*) there is no room or space for common sense and pragmatic ways forward. In the language of Reform, Self-Reform must come before Cultural Reform. Additionally, Self-Reform must have an authentic basis and not be a matter of indoctrination by inauthentic thought-patterns. One must become what one truly is and then undertake activity to modify the environment in harmony with that being and vision.

Historically, the process of reform has in fact been an ongoing and constant one in human history. Things are always changing and most individuals or groups of individuals are interested in guiding such change in ever increasing quality toward a happier and better tomorrow. Absolute conservatism, i.e. a society that is unchanging in all its particulars over time is just as unthinkable as is an utter chaos in which no elements are retained from moment to moment and no guiding principles are employed to help direct events or developments. Even the Optimism of Leibnitz, who is famous for coining the idea that we live "in the best of all possible worlds," does not advocate that we should do nothing to make the world better. Anarchy posits that people should destroy everything, and let Nature recreate things according to Her design, whereas Messianic Millenarianism passively awaits the coming of a Savior to "make everything right." The Golden Mean in all of this is the idea of *Reform*. The Reformer says that things are basically good, but could be better. The means by which improvement is gained is a rational way, although also one often inspired by irrational or intuitive sources. Reformers believe that the individual and groups can make a difference in the world and can be active agents in the betterment of the cosmos.

The word "reform," as a *brand* has a powerful appeal. The idea of a "*Reform* Party" has been around in the political landscape of North America for a long time, and can be found in Europe as well. When the American political insurgent Ross Perot used the term for his presidential campaigns the brand name could be seen as lending the movement some credibility. In general, Americans love the idea of reform more than revolution, although that attitude may be changing. Reform implies that things are basically on the right track ideologically, but that the particulars of cultural change have to be "tweaked" to make them more rapid, complete or effective. At the same time the soul of the idea of "reform" is always open to insidious forces of entropy and is not deeply inspiring to most.

Called by whatever name, the basic view appears obvious that if one is trying to promote developmental change in the political and cultural landscape *Reform* is usually better received than many alternatives, e.g. Communist Revolution, capitalist greed run amok, totalitarianism in whatever form, or any system that is extreme and intolerant of the liberty of individuals or smaller social groups.

As the Reform Movements of over a century ago can safely be seen as a response to the cultural challenges posed by urbanization and hyper-industrialization, the current social problems can substantially be understood as ones caused by the digitalization of culture. Social media and the destruction of the contextual past in order to make a more malleable social structure have substantively deteriorated the culture of the West. Just as the Reform Movements responded to those challenges, a new impetus of Reform is needed to respond to the present troubles.

At present, the West is mired in controversy over reforming the ways in which we produce energy. It is a given that our society is heavily dependent on the production of energy, the question is how it is to be produced and distributed and by what means is this to be effected. The idea of renewable energy is a concept near and dear to the hearts of Reform-minded people. It is a great and wonderful idea. Its implementation is dependent on a number of factors. Among these factors is not the government forcing people to use what the government (now seen to be divorced from identity with the people) thinks is "best" for the population. For a culture to embrace something so profound, the people have to make this happen and they have to embrace the new reforms enthusiastically and voluntarily. Coercion will always fail in the end. The population recognizes that where coercion is found, the idea behind it is usually something that benefits primarily the one who is doing the coercion. To see how profound cultural change can take place, and do so relatively quickly one only has to review the history of how a horse-based culture was superseded in the West by an internal combustion engine-based over the time span of about thirty years. The government did not slaughter people's horses, try to starve them or force people to buy cars. It just happened because the engine did the job better and more cheaply than did the horse. (Although as a nod to history, engine power was still measured in "horsepower.") It took 30 years for motorized vehicles to overtake horse. This took place between 1900 and 1930. Propagandists for alternative energy often point to the idea that horses were rejected because of the pollution they produced (dung). But social and economic facts make this a weak effort. The motorized vehicle proved itself to be a cheaper, easier, more convenient—not to mention *faster*—mode of getting the basic job done. That job, simply put, was getting a person (or freight) from point A to point B. With the innovation of Henry Ford the car became more affordable to the average Joe than the horse was. (remember that we had been a horse-based culture for *six thousand* (6,000) years by the time the car came along! The story of how the car overcame the horse in our culture demonstrates the story of how the new technologies will replace the old ones in the near future. One option overcomes the other because it is either faster, better or cheaper than the present option. If all three are present, as it was in the case of the car and the horse, change will come quickly and easily.

One of the main road-blocks to continuing and expanded influence from the concepts of Reform ideology is the enormous level of ignorance about history and ideology among the average citizens in the West today. Because history and philosophy, as well as the very utilization of actual *critical* thinking (not Marxist "critical" indoctrination) has increasingly fallen by the wayside in the education curricula in the West (and especially in the USA) people can feel the stresses of failed government and economic programs, but they are ever more hard-pressed to understand what is oppressing them, and even more flummoxed about possible solutions to their problems.

In the natural history of the Reform Movements in Germany (or in England or America) the story was most usually told by what might be characterized as "special interests," each of which had in mind to Reform some segment of culture: economics, health, sexuality, etc. There was no centralized and coherent movement which represented this underlying feeling. For Reform to succeed in the future, the development of just such a centralized philosophy would seem likely to be necessary. The unfortunate aspect of this is that the very act of centralizing such a movement and forcing it to conform to a consistent ideology betrays the individualistic and small-scale nature of the very root concept of Reform. Reform ideas were typically coopted by political interests of the Left or Right—until the final and most devastating of all such acts of coopting occurred under the Nazis. This was called *Gleichschaltung* ("coordination") in the jargon of National Socialism. Through this program any and all "special interests" were either eliminated or given an ideological form that coordinated with NS ideology. As many are aware, there were similar movements present in pre-Revolutionary Russia. These too were treated to a similar fate under the Bolsheviks.(43) The Reform Movements became the systematic victims of Nazi *Gleichschaltung* in the 1930s and the impetus behind many Reform ideas (ecology, health sexual reform, etc.) have recently shown themselves to be easily exploited by a new band of collectivist, big-government and big-business power grabs. If the true spirit of Reform is to have a future it must find a home and expression in the hearts of individuals and it is these folk who must find one another as kindred spirits to form communities which manifest an alternative to the mass-culture of our day. The key lies in the accomplishment of an internal principle of unity based not on an external partisan political ideology but on one true to the spirit of Reform itself. The great tactical handicap that is inherent in most Reform-minded individuals is that they do not easily *hate*. Political or cultural movements toward radical aims most often are given their energy not so much through love or hope, but through hate and animus. The Bolsheviks used the nobility, capitalists and the church, Hitler used the Jews. But if the heart refuses to hate the majority of potential members of a mass movement cannot be motivated—it is a challenging aspect of human nature.

History is full of lessons as to how this has been done in the past and how these efforts can go terribly wrong. A good outcome is dependent upon true knowledge and the pure will to enact the lessons learned.

Occasionally during the course of this study I have made reference to the idea that the kind of cultural phenomena that were common during the intense activity of the Reform Movements in the German-speaking areas of Central Europe could be compared to parallel phenomena found in the Anglo-American world in the 1960s and 1970s. If this was indeed so, what have been the possible results, historically and culturally, of this movement in the English-speaking world? I am afraid that just as the reform ideology found in Russia and in the German-speaking areas of Central Europe where the end results of the movements were tragic, so too have the results of Reform ideas in the American context been disappointing. The hopeful hunger for radical change that fueled the spirit of the 1960s has resulted in the increasing manifestation of a sort of "soft tyranny" and attachment to unthinking and unreflective use of individual liberty. We too have sunk into an abyss, perhaps not one equipped with a system of gulags and concentration camps, but nevertheless one far, far away from what had been dreamed of for the Age of Aquarius.

The study of the history of such cultural phenomena as the Reform Movements helps remind us of the depth of cultural life that could so often be found in the past. At present, Western culture finds itself in a maximally shallow condition. The media-driven and "virtual" state of experience has reached a critical state. Perhaps the study and appreciation of life of a more profound nature can be some small step in the reawakening of a sense of culture and of life itself. At least that is my own, perhaps vain, hope.

The best strategy, as I see it, is to return to the roots of the Reform mindset, but to do so in a way that is informed by the lessons of history and with a realization that what is needed is an authentic and integral mythology which explains the aims and modes of what we actually hope for and what exactly the vison of the transformed society would be. Too often the naive are simply led in the directions ordained by just another cabal of materialistic or superstitious mobsters dedicated primarily to their own personal empowerment at the expense of the average person. Knowledge, understanding and a will to act coupled with the ability to do so in an effective manner is the only way out.

The questions that plague the West today are not so much different from those that perplexed the Reform generations. We are caught as they were between the forces of collectivization (guided by tyrannical hands, e.g. communism or fascism) and that of consumer capitalism. The graphic icon drawn by Master Fidus seen in section 3.4 illustrates the position of Reformism in this context. Reformers then as now, reject the choices offered to the masses and chose to go a separate way. It must be recognized that the crushing forces present in the current culture of the West—fueled by poor education, limited imagination and a paralyzed will to act—make the future appear bleak. But keeping the dream alive is all we can attempt to do at this point. Focusing on one of the main principles of Reform, rooted in the idea of the holistic vision of the body-mind-spirit as interconnected realities we can more clearly see what moves us forward and what hinders us from making any sort of progress. For example, it is clear that anything that promotes the direct physical interaction with symbolically meaningful ideas which in turn become material for the mind to contemplate meaningfully move us forward, while substitutes and shams replacing these experiences move us further away from the goals. There is a place for technology in a Reformer's universe, but it must be made to serve the purposes and goals of Reform, and not become a substitute for reality itself.

Beyond just being an exploration of a fascinating chapter of cultural history, the underlying purpose of this book is greater. Its greater aim is to clarify this particular set of movements in the context of actual historical and cultural events to shed light on the full scope of human motivations and activity which give rise to truly *revolutionary/evolutionary* change. It can be seen that awareness of the history of such ideas deeply affects our understanding of the present and creates a channel for possible future activities. A flawed, incomplete or ideologically bound view of history warps the present and derails any hope of healthy change in culture or society. The German Reform Movements certainly suffered from being hijacked by an ideology (National Socialism), just as Russian Cosmism(44) was deformed and spoiled by Marxism-Leninism. In some small way, I hope the contents of this book will help arm future Reformers against similar diversions of purpose by such ideological gangsters.

Notes

(1) These groups were often couched in religious terms but all of them had both political and religious dimensions it seems. One of the most influential of these were the so-called Brethren of the Free Spirit active in Germany, the Low Countries and Bohemia in the fourteenth and fifteenth centuries. In the 1600s we find the Levellers and Diggers who promoted popular sovereignty and equality of all men before the law. Later in the wake of the First Industrial Revolution we have the Luddites, an oath-based, secret organization which attempted to turn back the encroachment of technology. All of these groups laid the deep cultural foundations for Reform.

(2) Among Romantic critics of the modern world the term "civilization" came to be understood in its etymological meaning: it is a Latin word that is tantamount to the concept "citification," i.e. urbanization. The Mediterranean world (and the early Christian one) equated urban existence with an orderly life-style and the rural life with barbarism, hence the notion of pagans and heathens being synonyms for non-Christian or un-civilized. Romantics developed the concept of *culture* as a more well-rounded and valid description of the good in society. "Civilization" can be understood as synonymous with cultural tyranny.

(3) A new religious movement, also known as a new religion or an alternative spirituality, is a religious, spiritual or magical philosophy with a group that has modern origins and remains peripheral to the dominant religions of a given society or culture. These can be seen to arise and proliferate when a culture is under stress and seem to constitute a universal and perennial human phenomenon. In the nineteenth and early twentieth centuries these rose to prominence, and did so again in the 1960s in Western cultures. But in point of historical fact all religions that are not rooted in folk-traditions, e.g., Greek religion for Greeks, Germanic religion for Germanic peoples, Japanese religion for the Japanese (i.e. Shinto) are all actually "new religions." This includes all religions that have a historical personality who founded them, e.g. Zarathustra for Zoroastrianism (ca. 1700 BCE), Siddhartha for Buddhism, Jesus for Christianity or Mohammad for Islam.

(4) In large part as a reaction to the modern developments of mechanization, mass-production and urbanization found in the industrialized counties and regions of northern Europe and certain parts of North America, a variety of youth-oriented organizations or movements were developed. Besides the Wandervogel movement in Germany discussed here there were also groups in Great Britain and North America. The most important such organization in the Anglo-American world is Scouting founded by Robert Baden-Powell in 1907. This was historically connected to the "Woodcraft" movement of Ernest Thompson Seton, with the Woodcraft Indians, Order of Woodcraft Chivalry and the Woodcraft Folk. Most such groups made use of imagery taken from the Indians of North America as they had been understood in the fictional literature of the time. Out of this also grew the Kindred of the Kibbo Kift led by John Hargrave in 1920. This latter group was also linked with the political social credit movement based in part on the ideas of Silvio Gesell and had similarities with fascism. In the Soviet Union there developed form the remnants of Scouting an official organization called the Pioneers (1922) as an adjunct to the Komsomol (Communist Youth).

(5) Anti-Semitism was a fundamental part of Christianity from shortly after its inception. The Church Fathers wrote against the Jews as an "evil race." Anti-Semitism even went back to pagan times among the Romans. The pagan Roman historian Tacitus wrote against them in his book *Histories* (5.2-5). Lutherans were just as Anti-Semitic as the Catholics, as Luther had written against them. The role of the modern Papacy against the Jews at the time of the Reform Movements is well-documented in David I. Kertzer's book *The Popes Against the Jews* (Knopf, 2001).

(6) The Kalmyks are remnants of the Golden Horde of Genghis Khan who settled in the region after the demise of the Mongolian Empire in the fourteenth century.

(7) Note that Indian religion and philosophy is largely derived from deeper common Indo-European roots which are shared by religious systems from India to Iran and from Ireland to Greece and from Rome to the Germanic world. Although India may have on the surface appeared exotic, in its philosophical essence it is deeply attached to the mythological worlds of Europe due to their shared roots.

(8) *Karma* is a Sanskrit word that suffered greatly semiotically at the hands of "New Agers" and Hippies. Here is a straightforward definition from an anthropological and religious-historical perspective provided by Stephen A. Tyler (1973: 56): "Karma (literally, action) refers to the inevitable consequences of action, the resolving of one's good or bad actions through many forms of existence. Bad actions incur rebirth in the bodies of lower beings. Good actions incur rebirth in the bodies of higher beings. One's thoughts and deeds in one earthly life have their fruition in a subsequent embodiment. A man's body, character, status, happiness, and sorrow in this life are the consequences of past deeds and knowledge.

(9) To date only the first volume of the *Northern Dawn* series has been printed. It is a projected three volume study encompassing the reawakening of indigenous Germanic culture from the earliest time to the dawn of the Age of the Internet to be published by Arcana Europa.

(10) The best general introduction to the life and times of Guido von List is Eckehard Lenthe's *Wotan's Awakening* (Dominion, 2018.)

(11) For a general introduction to *Armanentum* see my books *The Secret of the Runes* (Destiny, 1988) and *The Religion of the Aryo-Germanic Folk* (Lodestar, 2014).

(12) See my books *The Occult in National Socialism* (Inner Traditions, 2022: 104-120 and my critical analysis of the ideology of Lanz von Liebenfels and accurate translation of his book *Theozoology* in the book entitled *Lanz von Liebenfels and Theozoology* (Lodestar, 2023)

(13) This is in stark contrast to the general historical character of American political parties which, at least until recently, seem to resemble more arbitrary political teams with little real discernable ideological differences. In the latest phase of history American parties have perhaps become more ideological, or at least the Democrats have started to manifest principles of overt socialist and perhaps even Marxist-Leninist influences. This may be a temporary trend. In former times, American politics had been characterized (at least since the middle of the nineteenth century) by general ideological consensus on major questions, with the parties fulfilling their major function by the creation of an illusion of

a "two-party" system. The main purpose of American political parties appears to be to gain and maintain power for individual members of the club in question. The great common-sense middle ground of American politics remains largely unrepresented in the world of political parties.

(14) Montmorillonite is an extremely soft phyllosilicate group of minerals. They become what is known as clay when they precipitate from water solution as microscopic crystals. The name is derived from a location in France, Montmorillon.

(15) It is tempting to draw some sort of connection between Just's "Luvos" and the references in the Old Norse *Edda* to earth or mud with magically healing properties, e.g. the Old Norse word *aurr* which is a water/earth mixture that nourishes the cosmic tree and references to "earth" exercising a healing property against drunkenness in the poem called the Hávamál.

(16) Macrobiotics is an old idea discussed by the ancient Greeks such as Herodotus and Hippocrates of Kos and in modern times was brought to light by the works of Christoph Wilhelm Hufeland in 1797. Although it was later expressed and "marketed" though a connection with Zen Buddhism, the term and idea had already had a long development in Germany in the early nineteenth century.

(17) It might be considered ironic that one of the earliest criticisms of the over-indulgence in alcohol came from Old Norse poetry. Poetic stanzas which may go back to the Viking Age found in stanzas 11, 12, 13 and 14 of the "Hávamál" in the *Poetic Edda* caution against over-imbibing (Old Norse *ofdrykkja*) in intoxicating drink, because it impairs the mind of men. It is remarkable that this very sentiment comes to the forefront of anti-alcohol propaganda in Germany in connection with the Reform Movements.

(18) A great and in-depth discussion of this world of dance performance is contained in the book entitled *The Empire of Ecstasy* by Karl Toepfer (California, 1997.)

(19) I have produced the first in-depth discussion and description of the life and work of Dr. Schertel in the English language in the book called *Dancing with the Demon* (Arcana Europa) which also includes an accurate and complete translation of his book *Magic* (1923).

(20) Certain writings containing information about the philosophy connected to yogic practices were translated into German in the eighteenth century. The next century saw an expanded interest, especially under the influence of Arthur Schopenhauer. Both Schopenhauer and Nietzsche undertook experiments in yogic meditation. With the advent of Theosophy study and experimentation in yoga became more widespread, e.g. meditation and hatha-yoga exercises in postures (asana), mantras and breath-exercises became part of the popular culture. The Russian refugee Boris Sacharow gave the first organized yoga-lesson in Germany in Berlin in 1927. Yoga was taught even more widely under his influence during the time of the Third Reich.

(21) Bernd Wedemeyer-Kolwe, "Runengymnastik: Von völkischer Körperkultur zu alternativen Selbsterfahrungspraktik." In: eds. G. Ulrich Grossmann and Uwe Puschner. *Völkisch und National: Zur Aktualität alter Denkmuster im 21. Jahrhundert.* Darmstadt: Wissenschaftliche Buchgesellschaft, 2009: 329-340.

(22) For an overview of the theories and practices of these rune enthusiasts of Germany during the early twentieth century, see Thorsson, *Rune Might* first published in 1989 The practice of rune-yoga was broadly and systematically first introduced into the English-speaking world in the book *Futhark* (Weiser, 1984)

(23) Literally this translates as "free-body-culture." The idea is that the body is *free* of the encumbering oppression of clothing.

(24) This was reissued in 1957, shortly before Schertel's death under a new title *Der Flagellantismus in Literatur und Bildnerei.*

(25) For a deeper exploration of the history and workings of Expressionism in Weimar-Era film, see the chapter called "Caligarism and the Trapezoidal Cinema" in my book *Gothick Meditations at Midnight* (Lodestar, 2023).

(26) One of the more curious manifestations of Nietzschean style and concepts is found in the book *Might is Right* written by Arthur Desmond under the pen-name Ragnar Redbeard. This text was then adapted by the American Satanist, Anton LaVey in the formation of part of his *Satanic Bible*. Nietzsche's concepts also found their way into the writings of other American writers such as H. P. Lovecraft and Robert E. Howard.

(27) The book *How Green Were the Nazis?* (Ohio University Press, 2005) constitutes an elaborate effort to demonstrate how what the Nazis were up to has "nothing" to do with the current "Green" movement. I leave it to the reader and student of history to determine if this attitude is accurate. A less polemic and more objective approach is found in Anna Bramwell *Blood and Soil: Richard Walther Darré and Hitler's Green Party* (Kensal, 1985).

(28) It should be noted that ancient Europeans, the Greeks, Romans, Germans, etc. had much more complex psychological theories and structures and that in many ways Freud was mimicking new categories with structural limitations inherited from the Judeo-Christian Middle Ages.

(29) Ellis was a thoroughly Victorian gentleman. He was a virgin until an advanced age, and was actually reported to have been impotent until the age of 60, when he discovered he could be aroused by the sight of a woman urinating!

(30) These research methods obviously did not meet the current scientific standards, but they were pioneering work. This is reminiscent of the controversies surrounding the field work of the famous American anthropologist Margaret Mead (1901-1978) whose methods were later called into question. The expectations and hopes of the researcher can often greatly affect the conclusions reached, but scientific breakthroughs must be recognized and usually provide major insights.

(31) See the German film entitled *Der Einstein des Sex* (English title: *The Einstein of Sex*) of 1999)

(32) A representative sample of the studies of this symbol in art and religion includes a classic "pre-Nazi" study by Thomas Wilson, *The Swastika* (Smithsonian, 1894), a recent study by Steven Heller, *The Swastika: Symbol Beyond Redemption?* (Allworth Press, 2000) and one from inside the Nazi mindset by Jörg Lechner *Vom Hakenkreuz: Die Geschichte eines Symbols* [On the Swastika: The History of a Symbol] (Kabitzsch, 1934).

(33) For a translation of this document and a commentary see my *The Occult in National Socialism* (Inner Traditions, 2022: 12-16).

(34) Norman Ohler's 2016 book *Blitzed: Drugs in the Third Reich* gives insight into the role of pharmaceuticals in Nazi Germany.)

(35) This is outlined in Ehrhard Bahr's book *Weimar on the Pacific*. (California Press, 2007). The so-called brain-drain ran across the board in all aspects of intellectual and creative life from academia to Hollywood and from the graphic arts to literature.

(36) Because in the Indo-European tradition animals were seen as physical manifestations of divine forces (gods and goddesses) which were considered gifts of the divinities to mankind, their slaughter was thought to necessitate a minimum or absence of "fear or pain" to the animal. Such trauma had to be eliminated as far as possible simply because it was seen as a direct affront to the free-will gift of the gods, who were to some extent actually incarnate in the animal which symbolized their divine essences.

(37) Clearly the word "hippie" itself had its ultimate origin in Black slang, Ebonics, or as it is most known in present-day academic circles African-American Vernacular English. It is derived from the word "hip" meaning "to be aware, clued in, etc." This etymology is doubtless accurate, but it does not explain or even help elucidate the movement to which the term was eventually attached.

(38) This photograph was, according to Gordon Kennedy, taken in August of 1948, and reproduced courtesy of Gypsy Boots. The men pictured are: (back row, left to right) Gypsy Boots, Bob Wallace, Emile Zimmermann (front row) Fred Bushnoff, eden ahbez, Buddy Rose and an unknown Nature Boy.

(39) I guess my own mother was a bit of a rebel, since she had copies of these books hidden away in our house. I found these when I was about 15 years old.

(40) Bilitis is the name given to a fictional lesbian contemporary of Sappho by the French poet Pierre Louÿs in his 1894 work *The Song of Bilitis*.

(41) An important non-fiction book published in the early 1970s was *S-M: The Last Taboo* by Gerald and Caroline Greene (New York: Grove Press, 1973). It preserved in its tone and approach the "old school" of "BDSM" steeped as it was in the literature, psychology and philosophies of the original traditions, without the Internet-based and more "blue-collar" style of the twenty-first century.

(42) The book *Carnal Alchemy* (Inner Traditions, 2013) constitutes a practical and poetic reception of this very cult following.

(43) See my book *The Occult Roots of Bolshevism* (Lodestar, 2022)

(44) This still little-known phenomenon has begun to make itself felt in recent scholarship, e.g. Boris Groys, ed. *Russian Cosmism*. (MIT Press, 2018) George M. Young *The Russian Cosmists: The Esoteric Futurism of Nikolai Fedorov and his Followers*. (Oxford University Press, 2012) and given a general overview in my book *The Occult Roots of Bolshevism* (Lodestar, 2022)

Select Bibliography

Bahr, Ehrhard. *Weimar on the Pacific.* Berkeley: University of California Press, 2007.

Baumgartner, Judith. "Antialkoholbewegung." In: Kerbs and Reulecke, eds. *Handbuch der deutschen Reformbewegungen.* Wuppertal: Peter Hammer, 1998, pp. 141-154.

Börner, Anna. "So träumt man wohl zuweilen zu tanzen" Diss. Lüneburg 2014

Bramwell, Anna. *Blood and Soil: Richard Walther Darré and Hitler's 'Green Party'.* Bourne End: Kensal, 1985.

Cusack, Carol. "The Contemporary Context of Gurdjieff's Movements." *Religion and the Arts* 21: 1-2 (2017), pp. 96-122.

Dörr, Evelyn. *Rudolf Laban: The Dancer of the Crystal.* Lanham: Scarecrow, 2008.

Ellwanger, Karen and Elisabeth Meyer-Renschhausen. "Kleidungsreform." In: Kerbs and Reulecke, eds. *Handbuch der deutschen Reformbewegungen.* Wuppertal: Peter Hammer, 1998, pp. 87-102.

Goebbels, Joseph. *The Geobbels Diaries.* (Trans. L. P. Lochner) New York: Eagle Books, 1948.

Gordon, Mel. *The Voluptuous Panic: The Erotic World of Weimar Berlin.* Los Angeles: Feral House, 2006, 2nd ed.

Grisko, Michael. *Freikörperkultur und Lebenswelt: Studien zur Vor- und Frühgeschichte der Freikörperkultur in Deutschland.* Kassel: Kassel University Press, 1999.

Gröning, Gert and Joachim Wolsche-Bulmahn. "Landschafts- und Naturschutz." In: Kerbs and Reulecke, eds. *Handbuch der deutschen Reformbewegungen.* Wuppertal: Peter Hammer, 1998, pp. 23-34.

Hinz, Berethold. *Art in the Third Reich.* New York: Pantheon, 1979.

Kennedy, Gordon. *The Children of the Sun.* Ojai: Nivaria, 1998.

Kerbs, Diethart and Jürgen Reulecke, eds. *Handbuch der deutschen Reformbewegungen.* Wuppertal: Peter Hammer, 1998.

Koch-Hillebrecht, Manfred. *Das Deutschenbild: Gegenwart, Geschichte, Psychologie*. Munich: Beck, 1977.

Koerber, Rolf. "Freikörperkultur." In: Kerbs and Reulecke, eds. *Handbuch der deutschen Reformbewegungen*. Wuppertal: Peter Hammer, 1998, pp. 103-114.

Kerbs, Diethart. "Erziehung und Bildung." In: Kerbs and Reulecke, eds. *Handbuch der deutschen Reformbewegungen*. Wuppertal: Peter Hammer, 1998, pp. 315-317.

Koerber, Rolf. "Freikörperkultur." In: Kerbs and Reulecke, eds. *Handbuch der deutschen Reformbewegungen*. Wuppertal: Peter Hammer, 1998, pp. 103-114.

Krabbe, Wolfgang R. "Naturheilbewegung." In: Kerbs and Reulecke, eds. *Handbuch der deutschen Reformbewegungen*. Wuppertal: Peter Hammer, 1998, pp. 77-86.

Lechler, Jörg. *Vom Hakenkreuz: Die Geschichte eines Symbols*. Leipzig: Kabitzsch, 1934.

Linse, Ulrich. "Sexual Reform und Sexualberatung." In: Kerbs and Reulecke, eds. *Handbuch der deutschen Reformbewegungen*. Wuppertal: Peter Hammer, 1998, pp. 211-226.

Miller, E. J. "Teaching Methods, The Herbartian Revolution and Douglas Clay at Illinois State Normal University." *Journal of Geography* 10:3 (2003), 110-120.

Miller, Richard. *Bohemia: The Protoculture Then and Now*. Chicago: Nelson-Hall, 1977.

Rasche, Ulrich Michael. *Reformbewegungen: Kulturpssimismus, Avantgarde, Jugend- und Lebensreformbewegung im späten Kaiserreich*. Norderstedt: GRIN, 2018.

Reinhardt, Kurt F. *Germany—2000 Years*. New York: Unger, 1961, 2nd ed. 2 vols.

Rentsch, Arno, ed. *Fiduswerk: Eine Einführung in das Leben und Werk des Meisters Fidus*. Woltersdorf: Fidus-Verlag, 1933.

Schwarte, Ulrich. "Anthroposophy." In: Kerbs and Reulecke, eds. *Handbuch der deutschen Reformbewegungen*. Wuppertal: Peter Hammer, 1998, pp. 595-609.

Thorsson, Edred [= Stephen E. Flowers]. *Rune Might*. Rochester: Inner Traditions, 2018, 3rd ed.

Toepfer, Karl. *Empire of Ecstasy: Nudity and Movement in German Body Culture, 1910-1935*. Berkeley: University of California Press, 1997.

Tyler, Stephen A. *India: An Anthropological Perspective*. Pacific Palisades: Goodyear, 1973.

Ullrich, Heiner. "Freie Waldorfschulen." In: Kerbs and Reulecke, eds. *Handbuch der deutschen Reformbewegungen*. Wuppertal: Peter Hammer, 1998, pp. 411-424.

Wedemeyer-Kolwe, Bernd. *"Der neue Mensch": Körperkultur im Kaieich und in der Weimarer Republik*. Würzburg: Königshausen & Neumann, Würzburg 2004, pp. 153–164.

———. "Runengymnastik: Von völkischer Körperkultur zu alternativen Selbsterfahrungspraktik." In: eds. G. Ulrich Grossmann and Uwe Puschner. *Völkisch und National: Zur Aktualität alter Denkmuster im 21. Jahrhundert*. Darmstadt: Wissenschaftliche Buchgesellschaft, 2009, pp. 329-340.

———. *Aufbruch!—Die Lebensreform in Deutschland*. Zabern, Darmstadt 2017.

Zerbel, Miriam. "Tierschutz und Antivivisektion." In: Kerbs and Reulecke, eds. *Handbuch der deutschen Reformbewegungen*. Wuppertal: Peter Hammer, 1998, pp. 35-46.

Biographical

The life of the author of this book has been greatly affected by the ideas of the German (and English) Reform Movements. The same can be said of everyone in the "Boomer" generation and all subsequent ones. The greatest area of effect is in the field of "religious reform." Given the basic theory of *holism*, that the individual, and even culture itself, is an indivisible holistic model in which "physical" and "spiritual" aspects are but parts or valences of one holistic structure, we are forever linked to the mythic and "religious" aspects of our ancestors. The body and spirit/soul are not divided, but are one, whole thing in a given individual. The "body/mind unity" is a major premise of the Reform ideology, even if it is often not fully understood or expressed. This body/mind unity, expressed over time, and through ancestral descent, provides the theoretical link between the individual and the great mythic matrix to which the individual psychosomatic complex is connected. The individual is but a momentarily visible and tangible expression of an ocean of being. The symbols and signs belonging to that particular stream form the bridge between individual consciousness and this great mythic matrix. From early in his life he had a fascination with the arts, philosophies and experiences surrounding the Divine Marquis and Sacher-Masoch. He was involved with the social organization of alternative sexualities from the mid-1980s forward, originally on an "underground basis," and later more openly. He, led by the generous and compassionate spirit of his wife, Crystal, has for many years been active (as a follower) in the cause of being kind toward animals. He and Crystal have rescued many dogs, thirty potbelly pigs (and two feral hogs, including the mighty Russian boar, Burglar*) but most especially cats (TNTC). Crystal was for decades an activist in the trap-neuter-return movement and we have a continuing haven for those dogs and cats who could no longer remain safe where they were.

(*) Given recent events, Burglar later preferred to claim that he was a *Ukranian* boar.

www.ingramcontent.com/pod-product-compliance
Lightning Source LLC
Chambersburg PA
CBHW051040160426
43193CB00010B/1008